An Oxford Childhood

Carola Oman

AN OXFORD CHILDHOOD

HODDER AND STOUGHTON
LONDON SYDNEY AUCKLAND TORONTO

Contents

Illustrations

OMAN

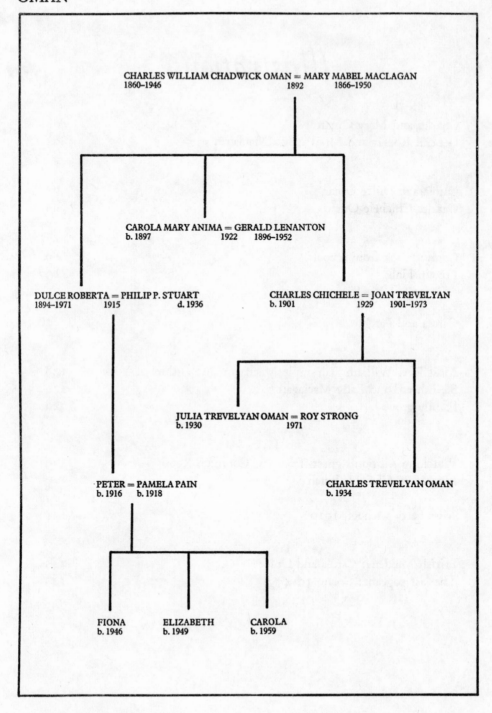

CHARLES WILLIAM CHADWICK OMAN = MARY MABEL MACLAGAN
1860–1946   1892   1866–1950

CAROLA MARY ANIMA = GERALD LENANTON
b. 1897   1922   1896–1952

DULCE ROBERTA = PHILIP P. STUART
1894–1971   1915   d. 1936

CHARLES CHICHELE = JOAN TREVELYAN
b. 1901   1929   1901–1973

JULIA TREVELYAN OMAN = ROY STRONG
b. 1930   1971

PETER = PAMELA PAIN
b. 1916   b. 1918

CHARLES TREVELYAN OMAN
b. 1934

FIONA   ELIZABETH   CAROLA
b. 1946   b. 1949   b. 1959

CHADWICK

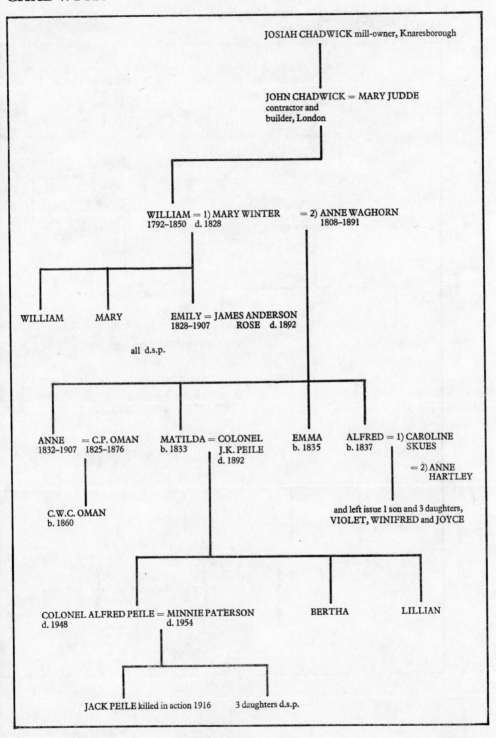

JOSIAH CHADWICK mill-owner, Knaresborough

JOHN CHADWICK = MARY JUDDE
contractor and
builder, London

WILLIAM = 1) MARY WINTER = 2) ANNE WAGHORN
1792–1850   d. 1828   1808–1891

WILLIAM   MARY   EMILY = JAMES ANDERSON
                       1828–1907   ROSE   d. 1892

all d.s.p.

ANNE   = C.P. OMAN   MATILDA = COLONEL   EMMA   ALFRED = 1) CAROLINE
1832–1907   1825–1876   b. 1833   J.K. PEILE   b. 1835   b. 1837   SKUES
                                          d. 1892
                                                                  = 2) ANNE
                                                                       HARTLEY

C.W.C. OMAN
b. 1860

and left issue 1 son and 3 daughters,
VIOLET, WINIFRED and JOYCE

COLONEL ALFRED PEILE = MINNIE PATERSON   BERTHA   LILLIAN
d. 1948   d. 1954

JACK PEILE killed in action 1916   3 daughters d.s.p.

MACLAGAN

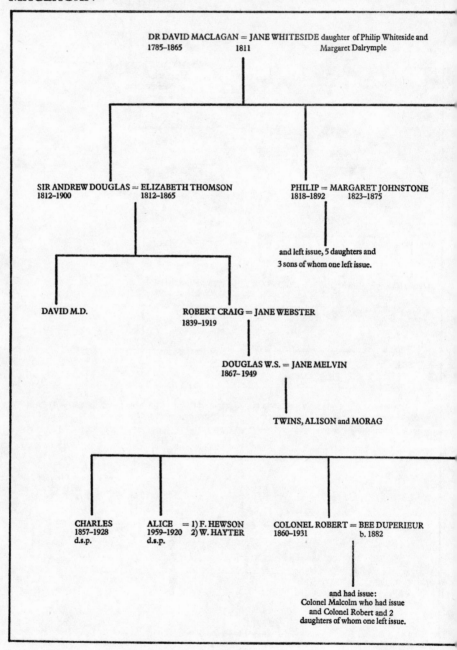

DR DAVID MACLAGAN = JANE WHITESIDE daughter of Philip Whiteside and
1785–1865   1811   Margaret Dalrymple

SIR ANDREW DOUGLAS = ELIZABETH THOMSON
1812–1900   1812–1865

PHILIP = MARGARET JOHNSTONE
1818–1892   1823–1875

and left issue, 5 daughters and
3 sons of whom one left issue.

DAVID M.D.

ROBERT CRAIG = JANE WEBSTER
1839–1919

DOUGLAS W.S. = JANE MELVIN
1867–1949

TWINS, ALISON and MORAG

CHARLES
1857–1928
d.s.p.

ALICE   = 1) F. HEWSON
1959–1920   2) W. HAYTER
d.s.p.

COLONEL ROBERT = BEE DUPERIEUR
1860–1931   b. 1882

and had issue:
Colonel Malcolm who had issue
and Colonel Robert and 2
daughters of whom one left issue.

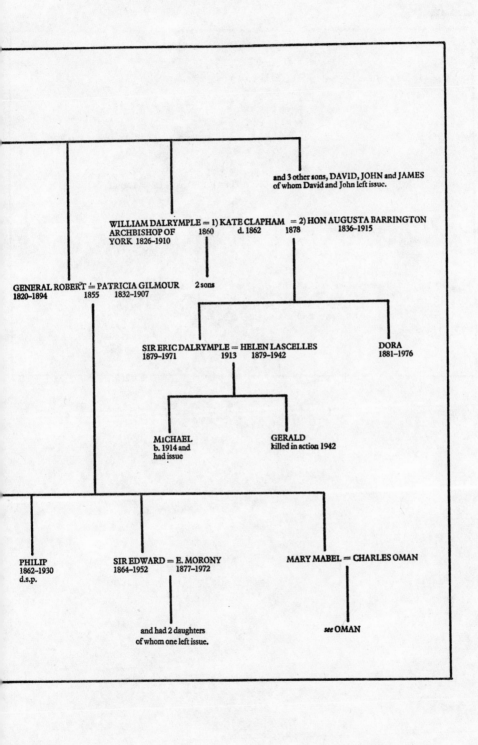

and 3 other sons, DAVID, JOHN and JAMES
of whom David and John left issue.

WILLIAM DALRYMPLE = 1) KATE CLAPHAM = 2) HON AUGUSTA BARRINGTON
ARCHBISHOP OF   1860   d. 1862   1878   1836–1915
YORK 1826–1910

GENERAL ROBERT = PATRICIA GILMOUR   2 sons
1820–1894   1855   1832–1907

SIR ERIC DALRYMPLE = HELEN LASCELLES   DORA
1879–1971   1913   1879–1942   1881–1976

MICHAEL   GERALD
b. 1914 and   killed in action 1942
had issue

PHILIP   SIR EDWARD = E. MORONY   MARY MABEL = CHARLES OMAN
1862–1930   1864–1952   1877–1972
d.s.p.

and had 2 daughters   see OMAN
of whom one left issue.

GILMOUR

JAMES GILMOUR of Londonderry ═ ELIZABETH ROBERTSON
        d. 1815

PATRICK ═ CHRISTIAN HAMILTON DALRYMPLE

9 daughters of whom JANE DOUGLAS m. R. SAVI, PATRICIA,
GENERAL ROBERT MACLAGAN, MARGARET, CAPTAIN J. MAXWELL,
JESSIE, C. LANGTON, JULIA, CAPTAIN HAMILTON DUNLOP, R.N.
Patrick also left 3 sons of whom one, JAMES, left issue.

The Wedding:

The Maclagans

I

ON THE MORNING OF MARCH 1ST, 1892, A DREADFUL MESSAGE REACHED 44 West Cromwell Road from Norfolk Mansions Hotel, Harrington Road. Mrs Oman might not be well enough to come to the wedding. This was to take place at two thirty at St Mary Abbot's, Kensington. Luckily for Mary Mabel Maclagan, a very nervous bride, she had sage advisers—'M.W. & J.F. with me.' As these little figures reappear throughout this story, they had better be explained at once.

M.W. was Margaret Wilson, 'Ming', and I conclude by origin Lancashire, as she was passed on by Aunt Jessie Langton to be nurse to the expected sixth Maclagan. I can perfectly picture her standing foursquare on the platform at Preston, early on the morning of June 5th, 1866, to go on board the express from Scotland. General Maclagan disembarked, handed over Phil and Eddie, and caught the first train back to Scotland. Ming took the little boys to stay with the Langtons at Barkhill, near Liverpool. Here, after an unexpectedly long wait, they heard of the arrival at 129 George Street, Edinburgh, of Mary Mabel on June 20th. Mary's nurse went with the family twice to the Punjab. I remember my mother's nurse well. She was a dumpy little woman in spectacles and seemed to me immortal. I was always fascinated by her needles, made for those with failing sight. You simply pulled the thread in at the top—no moistening of an end and repeated shooting at an eye. I do not know whether she was an orphan, or had simply lost touch with all her relatives. She could write a clear hand and had no discernible local accent.

J.F. was Jane Frame, 'Jeanie', and if we had all been animals, she would have been a Border terrier. She was active and sandy. She had plenty of

relations, domiciled at Berwick-on-Tweed and Dunbar. Great-Aunt
Miss Margaret Dalrymple employed her at Cheltenham. Both these tiny
retainers had enormous courage, moral as well as physical. When Aunt
Al, the beauty of the family, wrote to say that she could not be left alone
when her husband went into camp for the winter, a brave little message
was soon winging its way to Abú, Rajputana: 'Jane will come.' Her
passage was actually booked when another telegram arrived—'Delay
departure.' Frank Hewson, Assistant Political Agent, had received new
orders. In the January following, Al had a stillborn son, 'her second
disappointment'. The Hewsons were coming home on leave. On the
whole, the General was inclined to regret that Jane had not gone. Jeanie
Frame was a tranquilliser.

Her two comforters told the trembling Mary Mabel, at some hour
during the seemingly endless morning of March 1st, that Mrs Oman's
maid had displayed to them the headgear her mistress had ordered for the
great occasion. This was a hat, no bonnet, though she was a widow. 'Set
your mind at rest. She means to come.'

Amongst the many virtues of my Chadwick grandmother, Mrs
Charles Philip Austen Oman, was that, except for a breakdown, mysterious
and alarming, to her sixteen-year-old son, when she was about forty-six,
she never ailed. She lived at Cheltenham, where she had a large acquaintance. She travelled on the Continent in search of antiques. For the last
ten years she had been imploring her brilliant only son to provide her
with a daughter-in-law. In vain she had pressed on his notice the leading
Cheltenham belles. Many years later he could only remember the
names of Amaryllis Blazes and Cydelise Flathers. He avoided mixed
tennis and bathing parties, croquet, picnics; he did not dance. But when,
at the age of thirty-two, he had followed his mother's instructions at
last, she had not been enthusiastic. 'But, dear Mrs Oman,' said her
neighbours, 'you yourself asked the young lady to stay and said you had
known her family for many years.' This was indisputable.

Her son's first memory of his future bride had been when she was a
skinny little girl of five, with many Indian silver bracelets running up and
down her arms. She had been sent down to entertain him in the drawing-
room and show him the illustrated edition of *Lallah Rookh*. He had been
eleven and at the Misses Hills' day-school at the same time as her second
brother, Robert. When her youngest brother, Edward, had to present
himself at Winchester to sit for a scholarship (which he got), Mrs Oman
asked him to stay. Two years later she had gone out of her way to attend

the funeral of Miss Margaret Dalrymple, the great-aunt who had looked after the bulk of the Maclagan young while their parents were in India. The General noted that she had sent a wreath, as well as attending personally, and had brought 'her son, Charles'.

Despite Jeanie Frame's assurances, Mary Mabel grew more and more unhappy as her old nurse began to dress her for the church. She was realising that, like most girls of her age, she really knew very little of her bridegroom. This was not quite fair, as he had been a regular correspondent since their engagement, and after that she had been to Oxford twice, chaperoned by Bob. Her fiancé had been asked to West Cromwell Road and to Al's house, 27 Argyll Road. He had been 'Mr Oman' up to October, and since then she had not yet decided how to address him. She had started with 'Charlie', but there were disadvantages: it was her elder brother's name and Mrs Oman's name for her son. He became C.C.O., C.W.O. He still signed himself C.W.C. Oman, but prefaced by 'Yours now and for ever', which was promising. He began always 'My own dear Mary'. She had asked him what was his daily routine as a Fellow of All Souls. It sounded very bleak—pupils for an hour each at regular intervals, even after supper: a walk after lunch. He had reviewed a book on Hannibal for the *Athenaeum* and spoken to the Royal Historical on Aristotle. He had read two Ibsen plays about Julian the Apostate. The only time when she had really seemed to be getting closer to him had been on his call before All Souls' Day, when he had lost the last train to Oxford. This was owing to his having come back for one last kiss before plunging out into the freezing fog. 'It was worth it. . . . How can I ever forget those happy moments when your hand was in mine and your head on my shoulder.'

When she arrived with her father at St Mary Abbots, it was all part of this nightmare that she had never seen such crowds gathered there. With becoming modesty, she always told her children that this had nothing to do with her. The fact was that this was the first public appearance there of her uncle, William Dalrymple Maclagan as Archbishop of York. In the days when he had been vicar at this popular Kensington church, he had had eight curates.

Mary Mabel discerned her third brother, Philip—'Pelz'. If Mrs Oman had had a heart attack, or was even now lying dead, of course the bridegroom could not have let her know. She asked him in a terrible whisper, '*Is he there?*'

Mary had been so weakly in January that the problem of a wedding on March 1st seemed better avoided, though with presents pouring in, two hundred visiting cards engraved, a double passport ordered, and banns called at the University church in Oxford, she was fairly committed. C.O. had bought a new London top-hat. She had to ask her mother to write to put him off from calling: she feared he might think her playing fast and loose. An epidemic, no respecter of persons, had swept away the Duke of Clarence, twenty-eight, heir presumptive to the throne and engaged to be married to his cousin Princess May of Teck.

On the day of his funeral, mourning was widely worn in London, and shops and theatres were closed. Oxford was enduring the worst experience since the influenza and cholera outbreak of 1859. The opening of term had to be put off by ten days. In the General's house it was evident that he, Charlie, Al and Phil, had all been stricken, but to the last possible moment he would not admit the fact that Mary's very severe cold turned out to be 'something worse'. An over-worked doctor called daily while she experienced headaches such as she had never known, which left her weeping, and even fainting-fits. Al and she went to Eastbourne. C.O. was a little franker. He wrote that the influenza had felled both him and his mother, but she had been to London to meet the Maclagans 'satisfactorily'. Mrs Oman 'always good and kind' had begun by 'crying a good deal' when her son had told her of his engagement. He pulled out all the stock phrases about her not losing a son but gaining a daughter. She had never needed a daughter, and could only say she hoped to learn to love his choice. She got much worse with the influenza, weeping all the time and declaring she could not be left alone when he returned to Oxford. She had a full staff, dragooned by Eliza Blackman, C.O.'s old nurse. It was disappointing that after having seemed to be 'in the best of tempers and placable', she had relapsed on arrival in London to stay before 'the fatal first'. But Cheltenham during the epidemic had been enough to make anyone apprehensive—bells tolling repeatedly, and blinds drawn down in house after house.

When he got to Oxford, C.O. had black hours and sleepless nights. He said that when he had gone to church in Cheltenham, the little charity school-girls had looked quite ashamed of their scarlet cloaks, the only vestiges of colour in the congregation. He tried to cheer Mary by re-counting 'a quaint experience. A long talk with a young man whose private hobby is the designing of women's frocks, though his avocation is that of a stockbroker. He showed me several of his choicest imaginings enshrined in *The Lady's Pictorial*. Altogether a type, I wonder if a high one, of our moribund nineteenth century.' For himself, he had taken on as a 'by-job' lecturing to the Cheltenham Working Men's Club. The harangue in the end had shaken itself down into a History of Books— their shapes, prices, bindings and illustrations. He was quite astonished when he made his audience laugh at the trials of the author. Mary told him that Rudyard Kipling was following their example. His father had been curator of the Lahore Museum, and his mother had undoubtedly good connections and was a wit, but they had been seldom asked to parties because they were not Army or I.C.S. Also, Rudyard, who was a journalist, had been seen about in the bazaar making merry with private soldiers. 'What sort of a wife would you advise for the volatile youth, an admiring one who would believe everything perfect, or a critical one to eliminate his not infrequent vulgarities?' His bride was an American with whose brother he had collaborated in a book.

II

The four bridesmaids, all children and cousins, were Dora, daughter of the Archbishop; Louisa, daughter of Canon Trench; Dorothy Gervais from southern Ireland; and Julia, daughter of Captain Hamilton Dunlop, R.N. They provided the only touch of colour in the assemblage, as deep or half-mourning was *de rigueur* in London since the influenza. They wore turquoise-blue corduroy velvet costumes and white felt hats with long, white ostrich feathers. They carried baskets of nameless white and pink flowers. Their mosaic brooches, gifts of the bridegroom, had been the object of one of the happy couple's London shopping expeditions. They had been designed by the famous firm of Giuliano. There did exist fifteen first cousins on the Oman side, but not one bearing the name, and Lily and Bertha Peile were rumoured to be both over thirty, with Roman noses. The Peile girls could not now have come, in any case. Their father had been an influenza victim. It had been necessary to suppress one of the surprisingly small invitation cards engraved in silver and filled in for 'Mrs Peile and the Misses Peile' (all the letters 's' with long tails) and also fill the seats in the front pew on the bridegroom's right-hand side, chosen for them when the bride and bridegroom had paid a call to discuss arrangements at the church, with the Rev. and Hon. Canon Glyn.

The vicar and the choir now proceeded to the west door to the strains of 'O Father all creating', and the fully choral service began. This was one of the few subjects over which the happy couple had seemed likely to come

B

into collision. C.O. had written pleading that there should be no hymns. 'Music killed the solemn words of the rite.' All Souls College Chapel had not even an organ. The Archbishop wrote hymns. C.O. retired hastily.

Three leading sources have always been available from which to picture the wedding of Charles Oman and Mary Maclagan. Press photography did not yet exist, but *The Lady's Pictorial* had a pen-and-ink sketch—'Miss Maclagan's wedding dress'. This was a correct title. The mincing visage and enormous height of the bride bore not the slightest resemblance to fact, but the dress was a very good likeness.*

The all-over design was a reproduction of one of those brought to Spitalfields by the Huguenot weavers of the seventeenth century. The bodice was decorated by a cascade of Brussels lace, of quite another pattern, the gift of the bridegroom's mother. The ruched skirt and train lined with taffetas, had more of the same lace; but the leg-of-mutton sleeves had ruffles and cuffs of yet another variety—the gift of the senior Miss Maclagan from Edinburgh. A plain silk tulle veil and a wreath of mixed natural and artificial orange blossom contained some of the waxen flowers worn by her mother, Patricia Gilmour. The shoes looked pathetic: they were so minute and so narrow, cream satin, thickly embroidered at the pointed toes with ferns and fronds of seed-pearls.

The Queen for March 5th, 1892, an astonishingly large publication for sixpence, was also remarkable for the very large number of advertisements of wasp-waist corsets, hair-pieces and, perhaps inevitably, aids for a disordered complexion. It offered a little more information, including a list of guests at the reception. As usual, those with titles had been selected, and most were not hereditary but the result of honourable service in India, at the Universities, or in medicine. *The Court Journal*, not quite so large as *The Queen*, had an awe-inspiring supplement, "Marriages in High Life'. It said that one of the hymns at the service had been set to music by the Archbishop. *The Cheltenham Looker-On* loyally detailed the outfit of Mrs Oman of St Philips Lodge—a 'grenat' velvet *princesse* robe opening in front over a petticoat covered with antique Milanese lace. The hat displayed to M.W. and J.F. evidently defied description. She carried a bouquet of roses and orchids sent by the bride. (She had been

---

* I have it still, carefully labelled, in a box in my linen-room, and during the Second War when coupons had to be produced for clothes, I lent it to three beloved young friends. Although it defied every canon of modern taste, it was and still is absolutely lovely. It is of cream brocade, now a glorious ivory, and has a delicate fern and frond pattern, exactly right for a bride of small stature.

almost insufferable about this and eventually only condescended if it was 'posy-shaped'.)

The congregation, who had been requested on the face of the rather severe-looking Order of Service, to join in the singing, accomplished the seven verses from Psalm 67, and another hymn. Mary Mabel duly put her hand in that of Charles William Chadwick, and breathed a maidenly, almost inaudible 'I will'. Thereafter, to the best of my belief, she never took a major independent decision in her long life, but in matters of etiquette her ruling was paramount. No source discloses anything about the Archbishop's Address, and Mrs Maclagan, mother of the bride, was noticed only by *The Cheltenham Looker-On*. She wore a dress of silver grey and black lace and carried a bouquet of pink flowers. She was a bewildered hostess to above a hundred and fifty well-wishers at the South Kensington Hotel (Bailey's, Queen's Gate Terrace). Her daughter wrote to her from Dover. Leaving for the honeymoon had been difficult. It would apparently be impossible for them to cross tonight. They drove round and round Hyde Park. It began to snow. When they got to the Lord Warden Hotel, *faute de mieux*, they found that Bob, best-man, brother on leave from India, had zealously wired, and they had been assigned the honeymoon suite. They had a month in Paris and Italy to consider and did not want to be cleared out by the Lord Warden before they ever left England. They had their first good laugh together as husband and wife. As early as possible next morning, despite intimidating seas, they embarked and reached the Hotel du Rhin, Amiens, that night.

It had been a reassurance that C.O. had added a highly-placed cleric to their wedding collection—the Bishop of Southwell, late Headmaster of Winchester. At 4 West Cromwell Road, the General opened his diary, untouched since February 24th, a sign of great mental disturbance. 'Our dear Mary's wedding-day. Everything went off most satisfactorily and the weather although not bright was fair. At night came snow.'

III

The wedding was over. Her maid packed Mrs Oman's 'grenat' velvet and antique Milanese lace for return to Cheltenham. Nobody knew better that she was now demoted to being Mrs Charles Philip Austen Oman, and her son's wife was now Mrs Oman. But she never gave way. She had been the beautiful Miss Chadwick of Haverstock Hill, and at sixty was

still majestic, with curly white hair and blue eyes. Not very many years
later I was caught by my father in front of my mother's full-length
mirror, and he descended to announce that at the age of three Carola had
evidently inherited his mother's fatal love of dress. Why an attempt to
make the best of oneself, especially in old age, should be considered fatal
I cannot see, and a beautiful material kindly distracts the eye of the
beholder from the face. Granny Chadwick, who had to be called 'Bon-
Maman' (soon 'Bamama') was a great dresser to the last, when her wardrobe
disclosed a chinchilla cape and muff, a coat trimmed with sables, and a
crocus brocade evening cloak—my favourite. A fancy-dress costume for
the character of Mary, Queen of Scots, had the keys of Lochleven, outsize, hanging from the girdle.

IV

My mother had sixty-one first cousins. Her father had been one of
seven sons, and his wife, Patricia Gilmour from Londonderry, had a
brother at each end and one in the middle of a procession of nine sisters.
We always heard with awe that only the most beautiful of the Gilmour
girls had failed to marry. She had been engaged but her young man had
died 'of a consumption'. He had given her a fascinating flexible gold
chain, which came to me, and eventually to the burglars who carried off
nearly all my mother left me.

Dr David Maclagan had sailed for the Peninsula in 1811, leaving
behind a hopeful bride. When he had returned, the boy, Andrew
Douglas, had been old enough to be sitting at the dining-table eating a
mutton-chop. Dr David was painted by Geddes in 1817, and an inspiring
bust by Samuel Joseph, dated 1825, confirmed that he had been a very
fine looking man.* I wish I had known him. He was presented at the
first Holyrood House levée when George IV visited Edinburgh, and
appears as 'Dr Maclaggan Physician to the Forces'. He had been Assistant
Surgeon of the 91st Foot since 1807, and became Physician to the Forces
in 1814. He had a grandfather, Robert, variously described in legal
documents as a banker in Perth and a chamberlain, as was his father—
also Robert—who had died in the year he was born. He said he believed

* Dr David's diary is with the Misses Maclagan, Carlops, Penicuik, Midlothian,
together with the Geddes portrait and two busts; also the original of *Maclagan
Families*, privately printed by Sir Edward Maclagan.

his grandfather to have been a Jacobite. He himself had been the only child of a second marriage, and his mother, Margaret Smeiton, had died while he was in the Peninsula, so he was not strong on his family history. On his retirement from military service he had gone on to become President of both the Royal Colleges of Physicians and Surgeons at Edinburgh, posts afterwards held by his eldest son, Andrew Douglas, who was knighted in 1880. I have, in my bookcase, in the study where I type this, five tiny leather-bound volumes—*Histoire de Gil Blas*—published in Paris in 1814 for the armies of Bonaparte. Each is inscribed on the title-page in a very neat hand 'Dr Maclagan', and I was always told that they were intended to be thrust into the cuff of a uniform coat. He kept a diary but as he was overwhelmed by business as soon as the Portuguese corps of which he was in command as medical officer came into action, it is disappointing. On the first occasion that he saw Wellington, on a pouring wet March 23rd, 1812, outside Burgos, he was impressed. 'His countenance, I thought highly indicative of the activity and determination which mark his character.' It will be seen that Dr David's literary style was stately; but he appreciated scenery. His son, my grandfather, Robert Dalrymple Maclagan, began to keep his much more readable diaries in little notebooks with marbled covers, bought on the South Bridge or in George Street, Edinburgh. He wrote on the right-hand page his daily chronicle, and on the left notes of what letters he had sent off and on what dates. His entries began when he sailed in the *Scotia* from Spithead on September 1st, 1841.* His eldest brother went with him from Portsmouth harbour, and *en route* as they were both sightseers, they visited HMS *Victory*. Douglas went ashore at eight thirty p.m. and the *Scotia* weighed an hour later.

Robert saw no land after the Canaries, but shooting stars, dolphins, spouting whales and the albatross furnished him with daily matter. A boy fell overboard hanging out clothes to dry, and was lost. There were birds which the intelligentsia recognised as from the Cape. They crossed the

* I was anxious that the seventeen notebooks containing my grandfather's diaries should be preserved. He had been educated at Edinburgh Academy and Addiscombe and entered the Honourable East India Company's army (Bengal Engineers) in 1839. He served in the Sikh War and got back from leave in time for the Mutiny. He became Principal of the Government Engineering College at Roorkhee, and from 1860 to 1879 Chief Engineer and Secretary to the Punjab Works Department. He visited the United States and Canada. On the advice of Sir Frederick Bourne, K.C.S.I., and Sir George Abell, K.C.I.F., I sent the diaries to the Director of the Centre of South Asian Studies, University of Cambridge, in 1967, and they were microfilmed and returned to me.

Line at noon on October 16th, and stood into the Trades and much better weather. But they knew that they had now passed all chances of meeting ships homeward bound. They overtook *The Duke of Argyll* which had left Portsmouth a fortnight before them. The sunrises and sunsets as they entered the Bay of Bengal were superb. Robert longed for Claude Lorraine.

Robert was quite an artist. Cadets for the Engineers at Addiscombe were trained to sketch, and his diploma piece had been typical of its date.* His teacher had been marine-painter to George IV, William IV and Queen Victoria—John Christian Schetky of Transylvanian origin, traditionally a descendant of a follower of Prince Charlie, settled in Edinburgh. Dr David had made friends with a Schetky surgeon with the Portuguese forces in the Peninsula.

It was now so warm that the principal time for exercise was on deck from ten to midnight, and I fear I detect from internal evidence that amongst the agreeable passengers to whom Robert had become much attached in the past three and a half months, was one 'bright particular star'. Of course it was quite hopeless. He was twenty-one, and if she was one of what was unkindly termed 'the fishing fleet', the annual injection of supernumerary nieces and cousins brought out to India to marry, she would be, most likely, even younger. He would marry when he came home on leave with sufficient rank and income to support a wife and family—which is exactly what he did when he was thirty-five. 'We have had our last promenade on the poop together, and now nothing remains but that the best of friends must part.'

Fortunately, a more rewarding interest now claimed his attention. 'Kedgeree on the larboard! The first sight of the land of my fate and fortune. It is rather hazy and the land is still rather indistinct. The smell of it is strange and pleasant.'

V

I always rejoice that the diaries of my grandfather, Robert Dalrymple Maclagan, from his retirement, record almost unbroken happiness. He had earned it and he got it. Of course, since this life is not Heaven, he had some setbacks, but on the whole he enjoyed what he had planned to enjoy.

* I have General Maclagan's Addiscombe *Loch Awe* which shows a little white sail on the middle waters, beneath gracefully inclining sap-green trees and blue and lilac mountains.

I do not know how soon he realised what he never admitted—that of his six children he had got two sons (the second and the fourth, Bob the soldier and Eddie in the I.C.S.,) who were winners. His beloved first-born and his handsome third son were passengers. It would not be fair to say that his beautiful elder daughter was a disappointment. She was simply star cros't. Her disastrous story is inextricably mixed up with my mother's happy one, so that will unfold.

It had been much the same with the seven sons of Dr David. Only three were outstanding, though a better proportion might have been expected as Dr David had a remarkable wife. Jane Whiteside was said to have been rather fierce. When people commiserated with her as Andrew Douglas was followed by Philip, Robert, David, Willie, John and James, she would blisteringly reply: 'What would I do with a lass?' It seems probable that her avowed contempt of them sprang from a secret longing for a daughter. She had been born a grandchild of Dr William Dalrymple, for sixty-eight years Minister of Ayr, and celebrated by Burns as 'D'rumple mild'—and this surname was religiously passed down as a second Christian name to descendants for many generations. Indeed, I have been told that when I arrived, with everything embroidered 'C' for Charles, I narrowly escaped being Claudia or Clarissa Dalrymple. But my mother had a superstitious belief that it was not a lucky name, since Janet Dalrymple, the Bride of Lammermoor, celebrated by Scott, had tried to murder her bridegroom in the nuptial chamber on the night of August 24th, 1669. However, before and after that *contretemps*, as Scott claimed, the family had produced within the space of two centuries as many men of talent, civil and military, as any in Scotland. The branch of Dalrymple of Langlands died out with Great-Aunt Margaret who looked after the little Robert Maclagans at Cheltenham. Every Sunday afternoon, Miss Dal had folded a newspaper over her sitting-room table and brought forth her treasured Coramandel desk. She put on her glasses and dipped her pen and began her weekly chronicle of every child's prowess. The anguished parents had once departed actually from her house, and Robert remembered the juvenile excitement when the 'growler' had driven up to the doors and the luggage was put on board. 'Aren't you going to leave? Aren't you going to India?'

Of my grandfather's seven brothers, William Dalrymple the fifth, six years junior to him, had always been the closest. His career had been unusual. After Edinburgh High School and law classes, he had changed his mind and sailed for India, aged twenty-one, to join the Madras cavalry. Robert had been very nearly beaten by the climate of Singapore, and after two years of it Willie had to resign his commission in obedience to urgent medical advice. To the end of his life he drew his modest military pension. Rather an attractive half-length oil-painting of him, in uniform, always hung on the dining room wall in my Oxford homes. My brother Chas, when studying Robert's diaries, formed the opinion that he too would have been suitable for the church. He was accustomed, in whatever country, to attend regular worship and write down his opinions of sermons—often annihilating. When I joined the London Library, that redoubtable figure, Mr Cox, told me that he remembered General Maclagan well from his predeliction for books of sermons.

As they were making preparations for packing up their Simla house in view of retirement in 1878, the Robert Maclagans heard that Willie, who had risen steadily in his late-chosen profession as an episcopalian clergy-man, had accepted from Lord Salisbury an offer of the see of Lichfield. Lord Lytton had now arrived in Simla, and at a dinner party at Government House, spoke with great affability to Robert about the marriage of the Bishop of Lichfield to Lady Lytton's cousin, youngest of the five brilliant daughters of Lord Barrington, who had died last year. 'Will Miss Barrington make a good clergyman's wife?' asked Patricia Maclagan timidly of a fellow guest. 'A very good Bishop's wife,' was the reply.

It next transpired that the Vicereine, though in weak health, had expressed a desire to call on the Maclagans by command of Augusta, 'to see us and tell us something about her'. Even if the present Viceroy had not been quite the showiest yet, this situation staggered the Maclagans. Willie had brought an Organiser into the family. They offered at once to go themselves to Government House 'as was more proper'. They were able to give Lady Lytton full and most desirable information about Willie. Their last letter from him had been from Scotland, where he had been staying with Lord Aberdeen, Prime Minister, on his way to preach to Her Majesty at Balmoral. He had infinite fire, but a spirit of moderation and gentle sympathy. He was a tireless worker and not very strong. He needed looking after. He had been married before, shortly and sadly at a very early stage in his career when he had been a pale young curate struggling in the slums of Paddington and Marylebone. Miss Mary Anne Clapham had been one of his adoring parish workers. After the births, in rapid succession, of two sons she had died of scarlet fever.

When the Robert Maclagans got back to the lodgings at 12 Brompton Square on December 4th 1879, in which they were existing in misery from cold until they could move to their first London home, they found a note from Willie. It told them of the birth of a son at the town house of Augusta's sister, 20 Cavendish Square. This little boy, who turned out to be artistic and very unusual, became a great source of enjoyment and anecdote to the Robert Maclagan family and their descendants. He was to be named Eric, after Augusta's Foreign Office brother, and Robert Dalrymple was asked to be the second sponsor and namesake.

Next day the pipes burst at 37 Lexham Gardens, to which they were waiting to move, and Patricia, who had been confined to their lodgings with a most severe chill, bravely got up. There was skating on the Serpentine and in St James's Park. It may seem a little strange that this was the season chosen by Robert to go up to the top of the new spire of St Mary Abbot's. It had been announced at a service that the scaffolding would remain up for a week after the final stone and cross had been installed. He took Charlie, hoping that he could see the developing area of South Kensington displayed. It was a very clear day, but on the whole the effort was unrewarding, as under a cloudless sky, smoke at a low level hid so much. In the direction of the Albert Hall and the new Natural History Museum, nothing could be seen.

The Indian mail was in, and it appeared that Al might arrive at any moment on doctor's orders to stay until her husband on leave fetched her next summer. But the plum in the Mail was an official intimation that the Calcutta Bank had been obliged to suspend payment. Robert had no idea whether the promissory notes which the Calcutta Bank held for him were a total and permanent loss. It was never his habit to expand on large financial affairs in his diaries and he did not allude to this one again. For the moment, he took Eddie from Winchester to the Albert Hall with tickets provided by the Liverpool Langtons for a much advertised concert —Mendelsohn's *Hymn of Praise* and the *Stabat Mater* of Rossini. Eddie was the son who was so tone-deaf that in later life his wife had to poke the Lieutenant-Governor of the Punjab to rise when 'God save the Queen' was played and to disregard 'Heart of Oak', 'Cherry Ripe', and other sudden orchestral noises.

All of the children were arriving for Christmas. Phil had brought a friend to stay and see Mr Irving as Shylock at the Lyceum. Phil had not yet made up his mind as to a profession, neither had the beloved first-born, Charlie, who was thinking of leaving Oxford prematurely, as, if you were to enter on a career in diplomacy, a degree did not really matter. The eventual reason for the anxieties which to some extent clouded the General's last years was probably the fact that Charlie, who had taken up a City career, very briefly, had invested and lost the parental capital guilelessly entrusted to him. After the failure of the Calcutta Bank, the Robert Maclagan family continued, for the next decade, to travel continually and to take a country retreat every summer. When they moved from 37 Lexham Gardens to a smaller house—4 West Cromwell Road—it was largely because the resident family had dwindled. The problem of Al had been increased by the sudden death of her husband from typhoid in Bombay in 1886. There was never any question of widowed Al or Mary, by then nineteen, embarking on any gainful occupation, although Al did not re-marry for six years. When one of the Dunlop cousins, in the next generation, went off to train as what was called 'a hospital nurse', her conduct was considered eccentric. Mary, who had been most unhappy at the carefully-chosen boarding school to which she had been sent as a child of parents absent in India, never left home again except to 'finish' in Germany. She lived with the Siemens family in Hanover, who afterwards became wealthy as an industrial firm. Upstairs, the grandmother, widow of a Hanoverian General, felt the annexation of her country very bitterly. She was unaware that her grand-daughters were entertaining young Prussian officers. One of these turned up presently with a bouquet accompanied by a note expressing sentiments which Mary could not understand. The Siemens girls, much diverted, had to explain that the poor young man must have been trying to propose.

Mary went on visits to the Edinburgh cousins and to balls on board ships of the Royal Navy at Rosyth—a favourite chronicle in our nursery. Frank Younghusband could not possibly be called a stupid soldier, but she would not accept even his photograph. It was true that he had gone off exploring again in such a rush that he had been obliged to tell her to collect it from his sister. He had dined at Cromwell Road four nights before reading his paper, on his journey from Pekin to Kashmir, to the Geographical—but only the General, Al and one of the Langtons had gone. Her mother, at some time as Mary passed from nineteen to twenty-five, pointed out that if she did not marry, the dear father would not have it in his power to leave her adequate provision. This made her much less likely to marry. She was bright. She went to classes at Bedford College. She was fluent in French and German, not much good at needlework, and did not know how to boil an egg. She had never needed to learn such things, as on the death of old Miss Dal the parents had collected Jeanie Frame, and Ming, who had taken a post at Brighton when Mary was sent to boarding school, had gladly returned. Nor were these two sterling assistants expected to cook and clean. Jeanie accompanied her mistress, Al and Mary, on every expedition in the capital if no male escort was available. London was not safe.

In April 1891 the Langtons invited Mary to go with them to Greece. It was a drawback that none of them had really done their homework, and she was not likely to meet what was hopefully called 'someone suitable' in an unintellectual party marshalled by a courier. Nevertheless, they did achieve the desired miracle.

Bob was now expected on leave and Mary had written to 'Mr Oman' twice before he came with his mother to dine. After this, Mrs Oman asked Bob for a little Cheltenham stay with his old school chum and to bring his sister.

Charles Oman had published his first book, a short *History of Greece*. He discovered a girl, in his own words 'both merry and wise' who could talk to him about the Acropolis. She had voluntarily attended a recent meeting of the British School of Archaeology at the Hellenic Society's premises. His mind was made up. He showed her the proofs of the illustrations of *The Byzantine Empire*. When Bob and she came to stay at St Philip's Lodge for five days, he suggested that they should travel back to Oxford with him. They saw Christ Church, and had lunch in his rooms in All Souls. He then took Mary, apparently alone, to the Codrington Library of which he had been Librarian for the past two years. This, to anyone who knew him, would have seemed as good as a declaration, for there his heart was to be found. But he had not got to that yet when he was suddenly seeing her off for London. He wished her a pleasant journey. With his large blue eyes starting out of his head, he then uttered clearly the incredible words: 'I wish we might perhaps some day take a much longer journey together.' She could not answer.

After that she heard nothing for a fortnight, except that his mother sent her a bundle of Cheltenham newspapers, and he sent some promised stamps. But on October 24th the General noted: 'C. Oman from Oxford to stay with us for a couple of days.' Bob took tickets for the Garrick Theatre, to see the younger Irving in *The School for Scandal*. It was a Saturday night: next morning the good brother stuck to them going to church. It rained all day: but next morning Mary wrote in her diary, 'Engaged to Charlie Oman'.

II

The Omans:
32 Beaumont Street:

1892–1895

I

I AM THANKFUL TO SEE THAT MY MOTHER'S HONEYMOON DIARY STATES repeatedly 'took a cab'. She must have noticed very soon that C.O. was a compulsive sightseer with very little idea of time, and an iron constitution. He was six feet tall, and indefatigable. She had hardly a moment left in which to write down their stopping-places—Hotel Normandy, Rue de l'Echelle, Paris; Hotel de l'Europe, Turin; Hotel des Etrangers, Genoa (good); Hotel Minerva, Pisa. 'Arrived at midnight in Rome, Hotel Inghilterra', she woke to a beautiful spring day. 'Capitol in morning, afternoon Palatine. Dined friends of C.O.' My sister, Dulce, once resentfully declared that our father had taken her to thirty religious edifices on a German holiday. The Omans, be assured, missed nothing desirable in any of the places chosen by them for their first foreign trip together. Fortunately, my mother discovered as early as Amiens, that C.O. liked to go off by himself to look for coins. He was a numismatist and did not require company on his visits to various haunts where he could find improvements for his collection. 'Vatican, Capitoline Museum, two Saints Cecilia, Catacombs, *Carmen*, St Peter's, Janiculum.' Did one detect a note of puerile relief when the Pantheon was shut and shopping could be inserted? They drove to the Villa Borghese and back through the Pincio before a tea-party and callers after dinner. On Sunday they went to services in the English church and the Sistine Chapel, and had an illegible diplomat to dine. They moved on to Perugia, Assisi, Florence: in this last place, as in Rome, C.O. had acquaintances, expatriates, natives, even erudite Bostonians. 'Went to cathedral; up Campanile.' Mary's handwriting became more and more over-driven. 'Called on Gigolos.' It cannot have been. Anyway, they were not at home. Botticelli's *Tobit* won her heart for ever. I can remember her asking to be taken, after she was eighty, to see the version in the National Gallery, and telling me how my father had enjoyed it on their famous honeymoon. In Verona, after Bologna and Venice, they found a Bellini—'best of all we have seen'.

Yet, when Mary and C.O. arrived in London on April 7th, her father found them 'both in great health'. The General's relief was now slightly like that of Mrs Bennett in *Pride and Prejudice*. 'Three daughters married. I shall go distracted.' To be sure, he had only two, but he had given away poor Al twice.

II

Mr Wells and Mr Turner, as they always appear in Mary's journal until they became 'Uncle Turney' and 'The Warden of Wadham', were such great friends that they took tea with Mrs Charles Oman at the Randolph Hotel before the newly-weds moved into 32 Beaumont Street.* They were shown over the house with all its new Maples suites, gifts from the Langtons, and furnishings from the Army and Navy Stores. Whatever the state of her father's finances, Mary had been given first-class linen from Northern Ireland by her mother, and a lovely trousseau. We always asked what had been the colour of her dress in the engagement photograph. It had been lilac chiffon, with many tucks and a train. Only half-mourning colours had been in good taste after the influenza winter. Her going-away outfit had been grey and white.

I think that their first years of marriage, before any of us were coaxed into the world, were perhaps the happiest of their lives for the Omans of Oxford. They might attend dinner at All Souls with the Warden, or go to meet the Vice-Chancellor. On such occasions, my mother had been instructed, she would go in a bath-chair tugged by a Shakespearian-looking character, and her husband would walk beside her in full evening dress and cap and gown. She would seldom sit next to a host of less than seventy,

* Cuthbert Turner had been an exact contemporary of C.O. at Winchester, but Joseph Wells was five years senior, from Reading School, and now at Queen's College: son of a parson.

for the first year, and always on his right hand. Katharine Darwin, whose father succeeded the Warden of the Omans' early days, afterwards bore witness that until her father, Frank Pember, came into office in 1914, the Warden of All Souls always had a footman in powder. There was no hope of entertainment by the Warden of New College. James Sewell, born in 1806, stayed in his post till his death in 1903. He was a bachelor and his only guests were at breakfasts—rather occasional—for outstanding scholars. Even so, the Omans were carefree. They had a tall, small house, conveniently next door to the Ashmolean and opposite the Randolph Hotel. Mary got two maids easily, and one of them was the best cook, she always declared, and the cheapest that she ever had. The Omans had a procession of callers and guests: most of the dons and their wives, and many bachelor friends of C.O. Mrs Madan was a connection, *via* Al's second marriage. There were a few distinguished single women: Miss Kate Norgate who had already published *England under the Angerin Kings*, and Miss Wordsworth, head of Lady Margaret Hall. As nearly all of their new acquaintances stuck, I will describe them in detail as I come to our childhood.

The General presented himself for the day on June 4th. 'Dear Mary is most comfortably settled, thoroughly entering into her husband's aims and interests, and taking her part in the congenial life of Oxford.' A bogey that a Fellow must resign on marriage had been banished in November after an interview with the Warden of All Souls. Mary went to hear her husband lecture on 'Twelve Roman Statesmen'. Eights week was chosen for a visit from the dreaded mother-in-law.

Then, in the very gayest season for Oxford, one of the General's elder brothers died at Berwick-on-Tweed where he had been a doctor. He had been past three score years and ten and never close to them, but this is when a strange habit of my mother began to assert itself. All entertainment at Beaumont Street was called off; Mr Fisher of New College was told that the Omans could not come, Mary did not go out. She was busy superintending alterations to her wardrobe. A photograph of Patricia Gilmour in India, showing her in mourning, for perhaps one of her eight sisters, has crepe halfway up the crinoline. But I think my mother must really have inherited her admiration for mourning from her father. His many cousins were now being gathered rather rapidly, and he excelled in dashing up and down to Scotland and Ireland for funerals. I was grown up when my mother, in her turn, lost relatives with such regularity that she was hardly out of black for one before another claimed her attention. My father then struck. He pointed out that neither of them had even liked the man. She patiently went out and made some extraordinary purchases —a parrot-green scarf, most unbecoming but a good match for a long spindly umbrella with a parrot in full colour as finial. Her duty done, she soon returned the scarf to her chest-of-drawers for ever, and gave me the umbrella.

To attend a lecture by one's own husband could, it seems, be reconciled with mourning for an unseen uncle by marriage, and after that Mary accepted a meal with Mr Joseph of New College. A breath of fresh air blew in at Beaumont Street, 'Mr Putnam from America'. He was the first publisher I ever met, and I was hauled up at a tender age to tell him I had written a book. He asked the subject. 'Poetry,' I breathed. He said he was sorry to hear it: there was no market. His costume spoke of a warmer clime than Oxford. He was rather short and had fought in the war of North and South. Later he achieved a famous airwoman as daughter-in-law.

My father loved entertaining. The programme for the General and Mrs Maclagan's stay opened with a tea-party for nine, including the Spooners. Mrs Spooner was large, commanding and gracious; her husband an albino and very small, with a pink face and wondering look. They were impiously known as the Madonna and Child. Dr Spooner, who later became Warden of New College, unintentionally added a word to the Oxford English Dictionary. I never myself heard him utter one of what he humbly called 'my occasional infelicities in verbal diction', but we collected some good ones—'We all know what it is to find a half-warmed fish arising within one's breast'; 'Our Lord is a shoving leopard'.

He was a born organiser, and once seen never forgotten. When presents were raining in at Oxford before my wedding, one was delivered without wrapping or address. But from the parlourmaid's description we all instantly shouted: 'The Warden of New College!' It was a copper tray with a highly raised dianthus design. Mrs Spooner was interested in a local craft in the Lakes. It presides in my hall, and after fifty years has a high polish—'Warden Spooner's Gift'.

There were many Wykehamists, one way or another, for the General's stay. Professor Margoliouth was a venerated Semitic scholar, admittedly the best Winchester had ever known. He seemed to us to have yellow eyes, 'like a tiger,' said our mother, who must know. He married a voluble good-natured lady who gave up the struggle of trying to impress their surname on Oxford tradesmen. 'Just call me Mrs Marge.' She had the best dressing-up box for charades I ever saw. The General's Whit Sunday was just to his taste. Mary took her parents to University sermon and her father wrote down the Bishop of Lancaster's leading points with unqualified approval: 'very clear'. For their luncheon party they had Mr Fisher, whose grandfather had been the leading English physician in Calcutta in John Company days, and the Rev. Arthur Headlam, another of my father's old Wykehamist school-friends: he had already taken orders. The parents enjoyed their second service that day in New College chapel, having met the chaplain and his wife at tea. On Monday, which was perfect weather, they were shown Worcester Gardens, behind that college, with a lake, and St John's, off St Giles's. Two senior couples came to lunch, Professor Montagu Burrows, a retired Librarian of All Souls, and the Rev. Hereford Burke George, who had a large auburn beard and was Dean and History tutor at New College. Mother and father were exercised in Mesopotamia, a romantic walk between waters. Tuesday was their wedding anniversary, but they must be got off after lunch as Tuesday was sacred. My father always dined with the Tutor's Club. They were taken on their most beautiful expedition yet—Magdalen Grove. There was just one guest for lunch, Mr Reichel, an enthusiast on 'Kriegspiel', an intellectual sport which faded in 1914.

The General had appreciated everything. 'A most satisfactory visit to Oxford, weather beautiful. Dear Mary and her husband prospering, busy, and happy.'

The best term of the Oxford year slipped past. On Mary's birthday her two little maids gave her a basket of flowers, and her husband took her to a garden party and on the upper river. They had relatives from both sides for the Encaenia, the last major function. The Gervaises who came just for the day left after the fête in Worcester; Alfred Peile stayed and got two fêtes. Mary sat at the luncheon in Codrington between the President of Trinity and Mr Morrell, M.P. (pronounced MURRELL). Schools began on June 23rd and C.O. was much engaged, examining. Term ended and the Omans went up to London for the Varsity match, and to the Academy. They used to choose a water-colour most years. *The Vale of Gloucester* by George Bartlett, R.A., 1893, is still envied (nicely) by successive occupants of my green spare-bedroom. C.O., as a President of the Gloucestershire Archaeological, could identify the spot.

They decided that, as they had both so much enjoyed boating on the Cherwell, to hire 'our boat' for some early weeks of the Long Vacation, which would last till October. They set off on August 4th on an adventurous cruise, by river and canal, to Warwick, Stratford-on-Avon, Tewkesbury and Cirencester, ending up on the Thames at Lechlade. They stayed at small inns with picturesque names—'The Golden Lamb', 'The Blue Seas'. Another advantage of this inexpensive holiday was that C.O. was able to work off his superfluous energy at the oars, and at locks, while Mary sat with the tiller ropes over her shoulders and steered.

They had their set-backs. The dinghy was run down by a barge in one lock. Mary once steered it onto the shallows. Saturday 13th had a stoic entry: 'Boat sunk', but it 'did not suffer'. They had rain and wind at Bredon and arrived home in a storm. On the whole the water holiday had been a success and became a source of nursery anecdotes. They had dutifully been to stay at Cheltenham, and had Mrs Oman twice to Beaumont Street, and it was still only the end of August. They daringly decided on another very short foreign trip—The Hague, Delft, Leyden, Amsterdam, Utrecht. On the last day of September, home again, they walked up Boar's Hill to call upon the Evanses. This was the walk from which you saw 'the line of festal light in Christ Church hall'.

On November 21st Mary went up to London by train and met her mother who went with her to 63 Brook Street, Grosvenor Square (Dr J. Williams). She took the five p.m. home. She told the diary nothing, but a sofa was delivered at 32 Beaumont Street. They spent Christmas week with Mrs Oman and as the weather was open, walked to Leckhampton. A hard frost set in and 'dearest girl' (never Mary) and C.O. watched the skating on Worcester lake. They were alone to hear the New Year bells ring in 1893. In January Mary paid another visit to 63 Brook Street, and on her return home got in touch with Dr Mallam, whose name was to become a household word with the Omans, and Mr Morgan, presumably his partner, of whom I know nothing. She continued gentle walks, C.O. always with her, in the Parks and to Worcester again to watch her brother Pelz skating. Mrs Driver, wife of Canon Driver of Christ Church, Regius Professor of Hebrew, was said to have skated on the river as far as Islip. Eddie arrived on leave from India for just five weeks. Mary sent for Dr Mallam and had a couple of days in bed. He came nearly every day after that and beloved Ed had to be pushed off to dine in various colleges and eventually departed without having seen her. On the night of February 22nd there came a dismal entry: 'Taken ill in the evening.'

It is necessary at this point to deal briefly with the maternal history of her sister Al. My brother, when I once alluded to her sufferings, said: 'Oh yes! she had a miscarriage and never had any children.' It was much

C

worse than that. As a child I was told the immortal story of a little girl in a red cloak with a hood who called with a basket of dainties and found instead of her Granny, in Granny's bed, a wolf. I got this lurid tale inextricably confused with the story of Aunt Al's first 'disappointment'. It can hardly have been a wolf that she surprised in her bedroom; the choice of wild animals at that date in Rajputana is wide. I should suppose it was a jackal.* I should also guess that this was her second disappointment, not her first which seems to have been a slight affair. She came home in June 1882 and sailed alone to rejoin her husband three months later, but the *Nizam* was very nearly lost at sea. She set out again, overland, and came home again, with her husband, the next year to take a course of waters at Schwalbach. But the pattern of frustration was set. She was a widow at twenty-seven, and Maharajah Sir Pertab Singh of Jodhpur, with his Secretary Captain Hamilton, called at 4 West Cromwell Road. He brought the sincere sympathy of his heir, on whom Al's husband had been in attendance, and he had hoped to deliver a portrait, but this had been lost in the wreck of the *Tasmania*, and even if salvaged must have been spoiled.

In 1891 the General archly told his family that he believed their absence from the house would be tactful on a certain July afternoon. 'On our return to London we heard the not-unexpected news that our dear Allie is engaged to Mr Hayter. There is great disparity of age, but in every other respect it is most satisfactory.' Al was dreadfully nervous before her quiet wedding—only twenty-one close relatives invited. 'What do I do with my handkerchief, Mary?' 'Anyone would think,' said brother Charlie, 'that Mary was the one who had been married before.' But she was not even engaged yet.

I can hardly say that I remember William Hayter, though I did see him always at their house in Argyll Road. I remember clearly being told in a whisper, by a member of their staff, that he had left over eighty pairs of trousers. Brother Chas owns a despatch case from which he deduces that William Hayter had looked after Queen Anne's Bounty. He got his wife and Mary seats at the Reform Club from which to watch the stricken German Emperor proceeding to a reception in the City. Aunt Al came to stay with us in the full panoply of her second widowhood, and I have a vivid picture of her arrival. When she saw the three children of her younger sister tumbling noisily down the stairs of our antique home, she lifted her veil to wipe her eyes. Our mother had appointed her god-mother to the

* My nephew, Peter Stuart, born 1916, says it might have been a Royal Bengal tiger!

first of us, but by the time Dulce had learned to read she was not pleased by the annual gift of a story of how an Indian child found Christianity. Aunt Al had become absorbed in missionary activities. Dulce chanted ungratefully, 'Missionary, Missionary mine, You are not at all in my line.' Aunt Al's second marriage was happy and peaceful, but in spite of the General's mention of the great disparity in age, she had two more frustrated pregnancies.

This preamble is long and sad but must be attempted to show how shattering to Mary was her failure in the spring of 1893. She felt everyone was saying, 'It is going to be her sister's story over again'; and most unfortunately she learned that her mother-in-law was announcing, 'Charlie had got a delicate wife'. Anyone observant might have concluded this from her mere appearance—the profuse soft waist-long hair, the tiny feet, the taper fingers which could never tie a bow or even a knot that held fast. Five years before she had very nearly succumbed to pneumonia after measles staying with the Robert Craig Maclagans at Coates Crescent. Jeanie Frame had nursed her. The parents were summoned to Edinburgh, by wire in snowy weather. Her fragile look was part of her charm.

III

The youth of Charles Oman had been, by his own account, most unhappy.* As to his origins, he had early satisfied himself that his surname, unusual in his own country, was Scandinavian, and the family who had spelled it in half-a-dozen ways since 1500 had been settled in the Orkney mainland since 1469 when the northern isles had been transferred to the Scottish crown as part of the dowry of Queen Margaret. He had gone in the long vacation of 1887, with his friend Joseph Wells, to inspect the cradle of his race and had identified the tombstone of an ancestor in Kirkwall churchyard. They had seemed at one point on this expedition likely to have taken root in the Orkneys as their steamer signalled that it could not get into Wick harbour owing to the rough weather. They boldly accepted a proposal that a stout smack should take them out into the open sea, run under the lee of the vessel and hoist them on board. They were accordingly decanted with their luggage after three boss-shots in total darkness into the alternately appearing and disappearing Aberdeen steamer. We always loved the story, and the names of the Orkney Oman

* *Memories of Victorian Oxford and of Some Early Years*, Sir Charles Oman, Methuen, 1941.

proprietors, Clerdoun, Foulmires and Savedale. We delighted to picture our father as a Viking, drinking blood from an enemy's skull to cries of 'Hey! Sa! Sa!' He quite looked the part.

Three of the sons of David Oman of Clerdoun (1763–1838) went out to India in the service of the East India Company, and Charles Oman I, built up a large indigo-planting concern in Jessore. Even allowing for the fact that the financial world at their dates was unstable, I think I was unlucky that my grandfathers on both sides put nearly all their capital in affairs which failed. Charles Oman II (Charles Philip Austen Oman) had bought a factory 'at Hattowrie, on the borders of the Durbunga and Bettiah districts'. That is how our father was born in Mozufferpore. Charles Oman II was fortunate in that his factory was not destroyed in the mutiny year of 1857, but during the consequent anxiety he had contracted ague. He took leave for the first time in twenty years and got married in Marylebone parish church on November 11th to a second cousin, Anne Chadwick. They sailed for India before the year was out, but their stay was to be short. On his return to Hattowrie grandfather's ague became so agonising that there was nothing for it but to realise all his Indian investments and take his wife and child home. Charles Oman III, born January 12th, 1860, was in charge of an ayah who wept for most of the time after they were installed at 13 St Edmund's Terrace, Regent's Park.

Unlike the Maclagans who had all been Army or Civil Service, my Chadwick grandmother detested life in India as wife of a 'box-wallah'. An English nurse, Eliza Blackman, replaced the ayah, and became a fixture in the family through thick and (mostly) thin for thirty-six years. A collision off Sydney harbour sent 'The Thames and Mersey line of steam packets trading to India and Australia' into liquidation and the Omans left London for Cheltenham to economise. Henceforward, my grandfather was almost entirely dependent on his wife's Chadwick inheritance. There was no Married Women's Property Act and many men did exist complacently in such a situation, but he declined. He published at his own expense a novel of Indian life which no descendant I have ever met has managed to finish. He began another but had not the spirit to complete it. His ague had now been exacerbated by a recurrence of another trouble dating from Indian service—periostitis. A shin bone had splintered, but had not been actually broken, by the kick of a horse.

His principal interest during the years that followed was in the progress of his son at the little day-school kept by the Misses Hill of Douro Villas. They pronounced that the boy ought to try for a scholarship somewhere, after a year at a preparatory school at Malvern. The choice was well advised. Two pupils from this establishment had won scholarships to Winchester last year. The Rev. William Gedge evidently knew the form, given a bright boy.

In July 1872 when the Oman trio arrived at the Royal Hotel, Winchester, there were 120 candidates for the scholarships and a list was put up daily in the shop of Wells, the college bookseller, of those who were still being considered. C.O. was one of thirty interviewed personally by an august board. He answered coherently, but ended by fainting and had to be picked up and carried into the Warden's Lodging. When the 'Roll' was published, mercifully the same afternoon, he was astonished to find his name at the head of the list of fourteen successful entrants.

After this triumph, tragedy, the worst yet in his life, set in speedily. He had pleurisy and was in no state to arrive a month late at a college which was undergoing one of those waves of sadism by prefects which afflict schools at intervals. Eventually, a boy called Macpherson sent a letter to his father who wrote furiously to the headmaster. A Wykehamist friend gave the story to the Press. Macpherson, actually a Commoner, had been thrashed, 'tunded' in Wykehamist parlance, by a prefect who had broken five ground ashes on him. Letters from other parents were given prominence by leading newspapers. The Omans, whose son had written at three weekends, saying he was unhappy, performed the most sensible action. They did not, as many other parents and acquaintances advised them, take their boy away; they took lodgings for themselves near to him. He could come to visit them every Sunday and on Saints' Days. Winchester's Reign of Terror ended, but C.O.'s parents stayed on having secured a lease of an odd but likeable dwelling, the White House, St Peter's Street.

His last two and a half years in college were a happy memory but his ill-luck held. His father had been quite a companion, telling him strange tales of Indian life; giving him, at suitable ages, tin soldiers, a bantam and two hens, trips to Brussels and Paris. But by the time C.O. was fourteen his father could move only from a bath-chair to a carriage. His daily trip to the club for a game of billiards had to be given up. Finally, he became bedridden. It was not possible to ask anyone to stay or even to meals; the house smelt awful, a mixture of ointments, lotions and the suppuration they were supposed to cure. C.O. became what in modern times would be called a 'loner'. He had a hidey-hole at the bottom of the garden. Here he read avidly, made uninstructed and disappointing chemical and electrical experiments, plaster casts and even toffee. His lair was a very small four-roomed cottage once occupied by a gardener.

In February 1876, conscious to the last but many months after the doctors had given him up, his father died. C.O. possibly got his hatred of mourning from the funeral which was the last he experienced with full Victorian ritual—tall hats swathed with weepers of crepe, and a formal distribution of gloves to the seldom-seen relatives from London. The procession moved slowly, in bitter weather, up to the cemetery. From that day it seems the childhood of C.O. ended. He was just turned sixteen.

When his mother recovered from a breakdown, she gladly moved back to Cheltenham. When C.O. got his scholarship to New College, Oxford, he refused her offer of an allowance. It seemed a mistake. She would have liked to help her clever boy. He very fairly acknowledged in later life that he did not think either of them had realised what Oxford was going to cost and his refusal increased the distance between them. Moreover, the Chadwick property of Grove Park had become a building site and was being covered with residential houses paying substantial ground-rents. The widow, at last, was well-to-do.

He found that he could not afford to dine in Hall. He always maintained that he had done pretty well on bread and cheese, cold meat and hard exercise. This was nothing compared to Winchester where he had been half-starved and the meat had been walking with weevils. He had never cared for clothes. He had delightful company and he liked exams. He only once felt anxiety about one, that for 'Greats' at the end of his fourth year. Success in that was essential to his career. Between the papers and the *viva voce* he seized the opportunity of taking another examination, that for the Civil Service. He did not get the clerkship in the Treasury which he had—inexplicably to me—thought might suit him. He absolutely enjoyed his *vivas* with 'a Cambridge man' who scolded him for his bad Greek grammar, and with Samuel Rawson Gardner (Modern History) who looked like an ogre but was most kindly. For some weeks after that he was the recipient of offers of posts in the Inland Revenue, the Admiralty, and finally the War Office—not to be sneezed at. But in the end he read in the train, in a casually-bought *Standard*, the name of Charles Oman as one of the small class of eight to get Firsts in 'Greats'. George Curzon, Balliol's white hope as a future Prime Minister, had got a second. He decided for an Oxford career—another year and then a second 'finals'. There should be a New College fellowship next May. He had an enjoyable twelve months during which he reckoned as his greatest gain that he made the close acquaintance of Dr Stubbs. This beloved teacher was one of those who questioned him in his next *viva*, humorously as was his custom.

C.O. got his second First but not the hoped-for fellowship. He always thought there had been hanky-panky about this. It was given to a Cambridge mathematician. He could hardly believe his eyes when he saw the announcement in the University *Gazette*. He concluded that the governing body disapproved of the rather combative Conservative views that he had been airing at the Union, and of an old-fashioned Low Churchman. Cuthbert Turner had been disappointed of getting a Wykehamical fellowship year after year, although he was unquestionably a leading authority on the Early Church, with a First in Theology. In the end he had accepted a Magdalen fellowship. His trouble seemed to be that he was a High Churchman and a Liberal. The set-back rankled, but C.O. was resilient. He too would just have to try some other college, much against his inclination. There was an annual competition next term for two fellowships at All Souls, but he feared this would be much above his touch. He got the greatest surprise of his academic life when Harry Reichel, the only Fellow of All Souls he had ever met, burst into his 'digs' accompanied by C. R. L. Fletcher, an elfin King's Scholar from Eton, to tell him that George Curzon and he had got the two vacancies. What was more, he must move in that night and dine in Hall: it was his right.

IV

When he went with his mother to dine with the family of General Maclagan at West Cromwell Road in 1891, C.O. had rejected an offer from New College that when his seven years' fellowship at All Souls ran out he should return to the fold. He was doing very nicely, tutoring no less than forty-one of the brightest men from six colleges who needed assurance and polish before their 'Greats' or History finals. He was lecturing twice a week. He had won the Lothian prize essay on 'The Art of War in the Middle Ages', and was reviewing in *Blackwood* and *The Athenaeum*. He could perfectly afford to marry and if he meant to do so had better consider it seriously. But I cannot discern from any source that he was doing what my mother always pityingly described as 'looking for a nice wife'. ('As if anyone looked for a nasty one; but see what they get.') Both my grandparents had married cousins whom they had met for the first time a few months before they sailed again for India. C.O. had no such problem. During his first idyllic summer term at Oxford after his wedding he had come to realise that he had found an ideal partner. When, after her sad disappointment in the following spring, he had to face the possibility of losing her, he became anguished. He could not believe that the cup was to be dashed from his lips so soon. Nurse Huzzy of the St John's establishment in Drayton Gardens took her leave; the summer term passed. Still, Mary felt fit for nothing. Dr Mallam made an appointment for her with a London specialist. Dr Champneys advised an immediate operation. She wired to C.O. who replied, panic-stricken, 'Delay'. He also wrote a letter which an unfortunate house-guest who was just leaving was told to deliver by hand in London that evening. The letter was almost incoherent.

> I will go straight to Cromwell Road from Paddington unless by your orders in any letters you send I am otherwise directed. The name of operation is so bad that it has quite upset me . . . If anything is absolutely necessary and must be done tomorrow, let me at any rate meet you and go with you to the doctor. I should be so horribly anxious if it were to take place before I arrive. My Dear must of course do all that is right and I will consent to anything the Doctor advises. I suppose your mother has heard all and agrees.

She was still 'My dearest Girl' at the opening of this *cri de cœur* but it ended, 'Oh my dear child! do take care of yourself.'

Dr William Playfair (it must have been very good of him) saw them the very next morning, a Saturday (£2). He was Obstetric Physician to King's College Hospital. He had been, throughout the Mutiny, Professor of Surgery at the Calcutta Medical College. Moreover, he had introduced into Great Britain with enthusiasm and success the 'Weir-Mitchell' or Rest-Cure treatment. He was thirteen years older than Champneys.* According to my mother, 'he not only deplored the notion of an operation;

---

* Sir Francis Champneys, first baronet (1848–1930) had been a Winchester scholar, and taken a First in Natural Science at Brasenose where he had been Captain of Boats. He became Physician Accoucheur to Barts a year before the Omans consulted him, after experience in Vienna, Leipzig, Dresden and at St George's, London. Both the specialists to whom they were sent by Mallam had links with the Maclagans: Champneys as the husband of a Dalrymple and a Wykehamist, Playfair as an Edinburgh man with an Indian background.

he absolutely forbade it'. He advised treatment. Dr Playfair who had delivered two difficult royal duchesses had charming but authoritative manners which at once won my mother's confidence. Also, of course, he did not want to operate. The treatment began with a month's holiday in Switzerland. C.O. had been there before on one of the annual spring trips which he had undertaken with his mother after he had become a Fellow and could afford them. He said that she was a rapid and restless traveller. This sounds like Satan reproving sin. However, he had now found a companion nearer his own age who did not expect to dictate. When it rained all day, Mary was given a new occupation—'Made Index'. It was her first job in this line for her husband. He told her she had an unerring eye for misprints and promoted her to proof-reading. Switzerland was beautiful, but they had come a little late and except at Interlaken and Berne there was not much opportunity of finding coin-dealers. C.O. now realised the advantage of having married into a very large family. The General had taken a house for August and September at Lochearnhead. Bob would be on leave and available for a walking tour, and Pelz and Hamilton Dunlop would join up at intervals. There would be fishing. After a deceptively gentle start, events moved rapidly. Mary sent letters to C.O. to await arrival at Dunkeld and Braemar. C.O. in return chronicled the splendours of the Pass of Killiecrankie, and having posted proofs and Index to publishers. Bob never sketched except professionally, but he now had a photographic camera with which he 'snapped at everything'. They climbed on north from Braemar but 'saw nought of royalty except a distant carriage in the Balmoral grounds. It contained a royal ghillie and a pink-turbaned Hindoo.' Her Majesty succeeded in keeping herself secluded, as there were no bridges on the Dee for ten miles except the one commanded by the front gate of her castle.

Mary had constant company. Aunt Bessy came over frequently bringing Gertie Wedderburn from Madderty and her baby, and Aunt Julia brought her young family. For unknown callers they had the English chaplain and his wife and Colonel Stuart of Ardvoirlich who was asked to lunch and took the boys fishing up Glen Ogle; of course, never on Sundays. Up here sermons were prodigious and Lady Helen Macgregor played the harmonium while her daughter sang in the choir.

C.O. returned strongly impressed by the romantic beauties of the Trossachs in the Fall, the Highland air which made one sleep so deep, and the diversion of a little fishing. The Omans went home by easy stages, staying a night at Birmingham and arrived on a Saturday night at Beaumont Street. Dr Mallam was there on the Monday morning. On September 29th a telegram from Lochearnhead told Mary that her father had had a stroke. The picturesque small holiday home was remote. A second wire said that he was better. Only one 'ploy', a day's expedition, had been attempted during Mary's Rest-Cure stay. It had been unfortunate. Her parents had got wet through at Dunblane.

The General lay paralysed and partially conscious until the end of October when the weather became very cold. His soldier son went up to superintend the removal to Edinburgh. But there are no more entries in the General's diary after September 25th when he had written as serenely as ever, 'Bob off for a day's excursion to Callendar, Aberfoyle etc.'

His memories were so happy—the day when the wire had come telling him that the university of his native town was giving him a degree . . . He had sat for a three-quarter oil-portrait, wearing his Doctor of Laws gown over his full-dress uniform, with his plumed hat on an occasional table. But that triumph had been for himself alone. The enthronement of William (now 'W.D. Ebor') as Archbishop of York had been glorious. Augusta had invited every possible member of her husband's family to Bishopsthorpe. She had all the qualities of her defects. She was a compulsive organiser but forgot nobody, however dim. Indeed the prospect of all the Maclagan cousins seemed to be accepted by her as a challenge . . .

But perhaps the proudest hour in the General's memories had been that on which he had gone down to Winchester for 'Domum'. Ed. had won the Gold Medal for Latin Prose and Verse, and the Warden, in his speech in Old School referring to that success, had coupled the name of General Maclagan with his toast of The Army—'Received with universal applause'.

V

There was a regular rota of the colleges which had to provide a proctor every eleven years. All Souls and Magdalen came up in 1894. Warden Anson represented to his senior and almost sole resident fellow that it was his duty to assume the office. Nothing could have been less welcome to Mary who realised that this would mean that for a year her husband must be absent at irregular hours, and possibly suddenly at nights, when she most needed him. But there was no escape. She went with C.O. and Mr

Underhill of Magdalen to a solemn ceremony at which the Warden of All Souls and the President of Magdalen presented their nominees to the Vice-Chancellor from whom they received rusty bunches of keys. The drill was that the in-coming proctors bought new gowns for high occasions, and the last year gowns of their predecessors, half price. White ties and bands must be worn every day and all day during term. Luckily for C.O. Hardie of Balliol was also over six feet, so his velvet-sleeved gown and ermine hood fitted well enough. Mrs Oman had told her daughter-in-law that her Charlie's obstinacy was phenomenal. As a small boy, put to stand in the corner for some misdemeanour, he would stand face to the wall until he dropped to the floor senseless sooner than admit his guilt. Mary, who was beginning to know her man, perceived a golden opportunity for getting him to replenish his wardrobe which had always been in a parlous condition. She pointed out that for the many stately functions at which he would now have to appear, the boots in which he had ascended the Cairngorms were a little worn and heavy. He obediently got a new pair of shoes 'of a summery and respectable sort, not unfit for the higher walks of the proctor'. This was the thin edge of the wedge. He was in Cheltenham, where the shops were good, so while he was shopping a new felt hat was advisable. He was surprised that these were worn very low now. A quite superfluous array of ties, day and night shirts and even underwear, would apparently be needed by a proctor.* In 1894 a bespoke overcoat from a London tailor (Foster of Waterloo Place) cost £5, to which must be added the train fares to London for fitting. But he was going to London quite often these days.

He made the further acquaintance of Mr Arnold, the publisher, who had been to tea at Beaumont Street and taken away the first instalment of a *History of England*. He said in surprise that it was quite lively. He evidently thought a history book must be dull. Whatever objections might be made to Oman's history it was never dull. He had a very sharp eye for dullness. I once complained to him of a biography by a revered Oxford historian. He fell upon the book, read the author's name on the spine and said with great satisfaction before looking inside: 'Ah! the leaden pen of a dear old friend.' After a very few moments he tossed it aside, saying

* My Brother considers that our father's wardrobe remained unchanged with hardly any modification in style after his great proctorial spending spree in 1894. He could never be persuaded to throw away any old hats or coats and these remained in his possession—a collection only surpassed by that of his elder daughter whose effects in 1971 included solar topees worn by her in India in 1916.

with wonder, 'Who would have thought it was possible to make Bonnie Prince Charlie dull?' It was shortly after this that he parted with a genuine little piece of biographical research *Warwick the Kingmaker*. He sold the copyright for £100. It was a success. He warned me, when my time came, never, never to part with a copyright. Both my brother and I did this, each once. Both books ran into many editions. He also warned us never to appear in a series. You were judged by the worst, not the best, of a motley array.

In London in the winter of 1893 he made valuable contacts in the coin department at the British Museum. He bidded for coins for the Bodleian. He wrote to Mary on the elegant paper of the Burlington Fine Arts Club. He attended a dinner given by the Quarterly Review to Prothero of All Souls.* This brilliant Fellow had given up the law, owing to eye-trouble, and become an outstanding contributor. Covers were laid for forty-four at Browns Hotel, and there were seven courses opening with *Potage des Gastronomes*. These were the days! C.O. met his first Murray of Albemarle Street—Hallam.

He stayed with his mother at Cheltenham when the spring blossom was making Gloucestershire a fairyland. Mary had refused to accompany him. She was determined not to lose this second child. It was sad that she and her mother-in-law had scarcely a taste in common. The old lady returned in triumph from the Bath Cat Show where one of her Persian kittens had won a prize. It did look rather winning with a gold medal hanging round its neck from a pink ribbon. But Mary could tell if there was even a cat in the house. They filled her with horror. She said her father's gallant brother-in-arms, Lord Roberts of Kandahar, suffered from a similar allergy.

C.O. sent her memoirs of the wives of Napoleon's marshals. She read these in French. He was told to pass on to his mother, if he thought it adequate, a letter of regrets. Was it because the cuttings were no more? Mrs Oman was an ardent gardener, or rather liked instructing her gardeners, and had noticed with interest that they had a greenhouse at Beaumont Street. From the evidence I gather that the cuttings had died because nobody watered them or gave them protection from frost.

C.O. was very uneasy away from his dearest girl, though he was 'at the end of a wire'. The least hint of a bad turn would bring him back. Doctor Mallam was calling every second day. It was C.O., provided with

* Rowland Edmund Prothero (1851–1937) administrator, author and Minister of Agriculture; Baron Ernle, 1919.

measurements, who ordered at Cheltenham the blue and white wallpaper for 'the little back room' and what he thought a very pretty fawn and blue carpet. The word 'nursery' was never mentioned. It might never be needed. He searched the Promenade for a pink parasol. He noted the costumes in church and in shop windows. Toques were being worn small, coloured fichus very long. Anything that might amuse her went into his daily letters, and he once travelled to Oxford having taken Birmingham in the day, asking no more than coffee and cakes to be left for a late-comer.

He went twice to see her father. The General, who had recovered from congestion of the lungs in January and perfectly knew him, talked about a sergeant of the 93rd regiment in the Peninsular War. But the poor little partner was in a very sad way. She had 'quite a little cry' on the broad breast of her son-in-law as she told him that the General liked to see her whenever he opened his eyes. No one else would do. He would not hear of Aunt Bessie, whom he really liked. He was clearly acting quite out of character. C.O. could only suggest that the good Scotch nurse should be asked to come back. But he was sitting up and talked of getting up. Both the valuable sons were in India. C.O. had to break to Mary that he had been astonished the moment he had entered her father's house. Charlie, the first-born (born in darkness for fear of a shot from the mutineers in the workshops at Roorkhee), had been at work. He had chosen this extra-ordinary moment to order in the painters and decorators. Everything was *Nouveau Art*. There was considerable evidence of expenditure and the whole effect was sumptuous but not to the taste of C.O. He comforted his mother-in-law by the suggestion that she should run down to Beaumont Street one day, just for the day, soon, and alone. There was no question of her bringing Al who had kind intentions of bestowing an infant's robe prepared for one of her stillborn sons. Mary's diary repeated with terrible monotony walks to Worcester Gardens, St John's, St John's, Worcester. It was quite a relief when C.O. took her to the Parks or Wadham. On Palm Sunday they went to the cathedral and after the service sat in the Broad Walk. She was never left alone in the house. The good neighbours called diligently—Mrs Haldane, Miss Wordsworth, Mrs Maxmüller, and two new ones, Mrs Reginald Poole and Mrs Horatio Symonds both of whom were to become important in her life.

At last, on April 3rd, her mother's postponed visit took place. They went together on the little duty walk to St John's. No source discloses whether Mary showed her mother the cot with blue trimmings for the boy—Charles Robert. After the old lady had left, C.O. took his wife to

All Souls and heard her chronicle of a very sad day. But mother's visit had done the trick. Mary was taken ill that night. The babe was born at four p.m., very vociferous. The news spread like wildfire. Mrs Spooner was first in the field with a pot of lilies-of-the-valley. My mother had a sentimental affection for these flowers thereafter, although she was not a flower lover. Roses and sweet-peas she tolerated, but a little silver lily-of-the-valley vase was always on her desk in season. They had to call the Babe the new arrival just 'the Babe' at first. It was a girl.

VI

C.O. had a busy evening on April 4th, 1894, sending off the important letters and wires. The Babe continued to be so-called but by the time the Registrar arrived at Beaumont Street she was 'Dulce' after 'Dulce Dulce Domum' the Winchester song. Later she got her second name, Roberta, for the General and her god-father uncle, Robert Smeiton Maclagan.* Three weeks after the birth the mother went for a country drive with the monthly nurse and child. Bagley Wood was very pretty at this time of year and famous in May for nightingales. After that a carriage called by arrangement every afternoon—Cumnor, Cowley, 'the Five Mile Grind'. She had gone two days after her first drive to be churched at St Mary's in the High Street, later our favourite, but only as far as exterior went. It had a rococo porch, a noble word, above barley-sugar pillars surmounted by the University arms. Inside it was darkish and the sermons were special. You had to keep as quiet as a dead mouse.

On May 8th, escorted by Pelz, and her mother, who had been staying, Mary arrived with her husband and nurse and baby for the christening. The Archbishop officiated but the family gathering was small—just the two godmothers, Bertha Peile and Aunt Al, Alfred Peile, Georgie Gervais and her child-bridesmaid daughter. Ming, of course, was in attendance, and Jeanie Frame. Mrs Oman came from Cheltenham for the day and C.O. returned to Oxford. In his letter from home that night he hoped that 'our poor little Christian' was now happy and silent. The General had slipped

* At this point I must draw attention to an interesting example of the fallibility of deep-rooted family tradition. We always knew that she was Dulce, pronounced Dul-say, because of 'Dulce, Dulce Domum' and we poured scorn upon people who addressed her as 'Dulcie'. But when her son went through her effects after her death in 1971, he found that she had been registered as 'Dulcie'.

away peacefully on April 22nd. Whether he had been brought to realise that he had at last a grandchild, I have never been able to discover.

Mary took the chance while she was in London of seeing Dr Playfair. All appeared to be well but she was languid. Boxes of things left to her by her father began to arrive, and going through them depressed her further. The books included a beautiful series of engravings illustrating some of the works of Sir Walter Scott, published for members of the Royal Association for the Promotion of the Fine Arts in Scotland. The General had always kept up his reading. Several of the volumes were inscribed on the fly-leaf 'Colonel Maclagan, Lahore'. He had been the most faithful attendant at *levées* after his retirement, but kept so quiet about this that even his son-in-law never knew details. At a date when there was complaint about Her Majesty shutting herself up, he had met her twice at Marlborough House garden parties given by her son, with whom he had been able to converse about a private inspection of the jewellery of the Gaekwar of Baroda, and impressions of other potentates. Although the month had been January and he had been seventy, he had walked in the procession from the Tower to St Paul's for the funeral of Lord Napier 'very impressive—coffin let down into the crypt by opening in the floor under the dome'.*

The mourning stationery for Beaumont Street arrived, a quarter of an inch of glossy black border and even the name of the house and the All Souls arms on the envelope, all black as could be. Finally, Nana from Scotland arrived. They had considered a Yorkshire woman but the Scot won. She had been wished upon them, I gather, by Maxwell cousins, and could come now. Her wages were high—£22 a year, but she had the highest qualifications and references. She had graduated in the nursery of the heir to a Scottish peer and her reason for leaving the Ogilvies was simply that the youngest son was now beyond nursery age. My mother guilelessly told this paragon that she knew nothing about children and Nana took charge. In appearance she modelled herself on the Princess of Wales for which she had a flying start as she was extremely neat in figure and coiffure. But there the resemblance ended. Punctuality was an obsession with her. She strongly disliked Roman Catholics, England and

---

* When she was an octogenarian I took my mother on a sightseeing expedition to St Paul's. She was extremely interested in the tomb of Lord Napier and sent me to find out how many steps there were down to it. We arrived just as the verger ended his explanation as to who Lord Napier of Magdala had been. In the silence my mother said, in tones of great clarity, 'He frequently lent me an elephant.'

the English. Soon after her arrival the Spooners' dedicated old-style Nana said, inadvisedly, that the Oxford shops must seem wonderful after Edinburgh. I wonder the poor woman survived. When the Babe was four months old her mother took charge of her alone for a Sunday evening. This became a regular duty. Nana was a Presbyterian and had a reserved seat in her own place of worship. She resented having to pay for it. This was England! I never heard that she made any friends there. She was so superior.

The Babe was successfully vaccinated, taken twice to the photographer in St Giles's, and put into short dresses. This was inconvenient for her father who like carrying her about, tucked under his arm, sometimes topsy-turvey, to which she made no objection. She was perfection: but it could not be denied that she was small. They anticipated criticism by calling her the Babelet. She had the darkest sepia curls all over her head and quick dark eyes. She was a little 'Robinetta'. Where she had got her looks nobody could say, but her Uncle Pelz had fiercely curling hair, equally unexplained. During the first War he was often mistaken for the Archduke Michael: he had a pointed short beard.

The Hayters had taken a house at Grantown on Spey and Mary with Nana and the Babelet travelled with commendable ease to try whether Highland air and peace would banish her lassitude. From Oxford C.O. sent her bundles of proofs of the *History of England*. 'Queen Anne is nearly dead. I am in 1713 and she died the following year. Then tomorrow I go on to the two worthless Georges.' The maids went on holiday and he moved into college; Miss Sanders, the caretaker, moved into Beaumont Street. The only thing about which she had not been frank was the parrot. As the house looked bright after its belated spring-cleaning and it was clearly a case of the parrot or no Miss Sanders, that objection faded from C.O.'s letters. She had dropped all mention of something worse—the Cat; and she watered the greenhouse. The only All Souls news was that the Warden had given an enjoyable sit-down supper party after Lord Salisbury's capital oration in the Sheldonian about how the old Universities were now reconciled to science and the latest discoveries in chemistry. A Salisbury daughter, rather a plain girl, had fallen to the lot of C.O. and in the dining-room with the Charles I portrait, had talked about that and other pictures 'rationally'. The college was shocked by the behaviour of one of their most promising juniors, Thesiger, who had given only three weeks' notice of his forthcoming marriage to Miss Guest. 'The only reason that is given was that they wanted to get it over before her brother's coming of age festivities early in August. It surprised people in London as much as here.'* The Warden might not have been available.

On August 12th, C.O. had a particularly congenial day. He walked up in the heat to see 'Mr Evans's new palace on Boar's Hill. Evans has built a log-hut, a house in a tree, a lake-dwelling and all sorts of vagaries'. At the moment his father, Sir John, archaeologist and numismatist was staying, and Sir Henry Howarth and other experts had been invited. The Conybeares had a carriage, so C.O. got home dry when the storm broke.

He followed his family north and had another of the fishing holidays which were to become an annual relaxation. This was the first time that I can trace the family luggage, labelled OMAN getting to Oban, another regular habit. After the Highlands, and a duty visit to Cheltenham, they landed Nana and the Babelet on 4 West Cromwell Road and set off for three weeks in Italy. As usual golden sunshine and exorbitant sightseeing banished Mary's lethargy. In Bologna they saw seven churches in two days. When they got back for the autumn term their new interest pushed even All Souls out of a young mother's diary. Babelet went to a children's party at the Spooners and to tea in Beaumont Street just a few doors down the road, to make the acquaintance of Ralph Symonds born August 17th. She was so bright she knew her Maclagan grandmother. She had written a letter to her father. He had bought her a doll.† All Souls did enter in C.O.'s correspondence. A new window was being put up in the library. He had seen the plan for the Codrington window.‡ 'I think the old colonel stands out grandly in his scarlet and the general effect ought to be very brilliant. We have now to puzzle out an inscription in Latin to go below.'

The important year passed out peacefully. 'Dined with the Provost of Oriel—sat next the Vice-Chancellor.' And for the first time the infant was mentioned by name. 'Christmas Day. Tree for Dulce in the afternoon.' She was eight months old.

* After being Viceroy of India, Thesiger returned to All Souls as Warden and 1st Viscount Chelmsford in 1933.

† 'Dussie' was taken to the studio of Mr Henry Charles Heath, 22 Pall Mall East (1829–1898) in April 1896. He was miniaturist to Queen Victoria, and the result was a gift to her mother on June 20th.

‡ The Codrington window was up for Whit Sunday, 1895, in ample time for All Souls luncheon.

III

'The First Man I Ever Saw': 39 St Giles's:

1897–1902

I

THE CURTAIN NOW RISES AFTER TWO AND A HALF YEARS ON A FESTIVE scene. 1897 was Golden Jubilee Year and the Prince of Wales was coming to Oxford. He could not as yet be regarded as an heroic figure, but his figure was the worst thing about him. He was fifty-five and had the reputation of exuding irresistible charm. Oxford put out more flags, and families vied with one another in booking windows overlooking his route. He was going to review the Queen's Own Oxfordshire Hussars on Port Meadow, and after a luncheon at the Randolph Hotel, open the new municipal buildings and the Sarah Acland Home. Nana Oman was taking Dussie to Cousins-and-Thomas, our chemist in St Giles's. As the Thomases had children of their own, I think this was good of them, but I cannot help feeling that 32 Beaumont Street must have been amongst their best customers. If Dussie had the least chill or cold Dr Mallam was called upon to prescribe. He once sent Dr Morgan, whose pronouncement that the cough was of no importance was received huffily. It might have been the influenza, so much dreaded that C.O. was the only person in his house to give it that name. Two winters ago it had struck Beaumont Street and certainly Mary and one of the maids, and probably the Babe, had been amongst those laid low. From All Souls had come the tidings that George Curzon, who had just announced his engagement, was amongst the sufferers.

It was quite maddening for my mother, but the Prince's procession must pass directly under the windows of our home and Nurse Huzzey, summoned for a date in April, had now been in the house for over a fortnight. There was a comforting theory that a late baby meant a boy. On Monday, May 10th, my mother walked with Mrs Poole in the Parks in the morning, and with my father in the afternoon. This pregnancy had been attended by no anxieties. The summer holiday of 1896 had been spent at Burford vicarage, an agreeable roomy house in a romantic little town. The invaluable William Hutton had acquired the seventeenth-century Great House and sent interesting residents to call. The Omans had been at Burford from the last day of July until August 28th and made excursions to Minister Lovell, Bourton-on-the-Water, Lechlade, Brize Norton . . . The Bourton expedition had added an expression to Oman language. 'And then,' announced my father, 'we shall take the Bourton bus home.' My mother, who was beginning to know him, asked where they caught that. 'Oh! outside the station.' But at the end of a long August day it became apparent that no such vehicle had ever been expected at the station. In fact the Bourton bus was the mere figment of wishful thinking. Thereafter, when something quite hallucinatory was proposed in the way of transport, my mother would say 'Ah! the Bourton bus, I suppose.'

The Omans heard the New Year's bells ring. 'Dulce brought marguerites.' Nana took her annual Edinburgh holiday in January in case the baby came early. But there was no fear of that. At last at two thirty a.m. on May 11th Nurse Huzzey performed alone. The latecomer had simply rushed into the gaily-decorated expectant world. Doctor Mallam was forestalled. He called twice during the day, so I cannot really support Nurse Huzzey's reputed claim, 'The First Man baby ever saw was a Prince.' At any rate I was held up at the window while many bells pealed and His Royal Highness in the highly-coloured full-dress of a Lieutenant-Colonel, attended by a clattering guard of honour, passed below to the sound of loud cheers and clappings. He had come by the ordinary nine fifty a.m. from Paddington to which a special saloon had been attached. He had to begin with inspecting the 1st Oxford Volunteer Battalion drawn up opposite the platform in the station. He was to stay with the Dean and Mrs Liddell at Christ Church, dine in Hall, and admire Tom Quad in moonlight. After that there was to be a reception for upwards of two thousand in the newly-opened Town Hall. Many guests at the luncheon in the Randolph came from the surrounding landscape and bore names which were to become familiar in our nursery—Dashwood, Markby, Abingdon, Dillon, Saye and Sele. Lord Valentia was the host.

He commanded the Hussars. I always see him with a buttonhole of violets. He was Conservative M.P. for Oxford City and had got a majority of 5,648 last year.

My mother lay in bed and heard the roar of the crowd rise and swell and the sound of horses' hooves. Across the ceiling of the birth-chamber passed a miniature reflection of the procession in shadow. She was told that baby had seen the prince. Mother had been very good. 'Little daughter born!' said her diary. C.O. had dined in college as I had tact-fully arranged my arrival for a Tuesday and I think must have seen me, as he wired to Cheltenham on his way out to dine, 'The Little Impostor has arrived'. The blue cot had been re-furbished. My mother often told me that in the silence succeeding my appearance she had eagerly asked, 'Is it the boy?' and then, 'Or a girlie?' 'I said girlie so that they should not guess what a dreadful disappointment it was.' They had, once more, to find a name. Everything was marked C. They finally dismissed Clarissa and Claudia Dalrymple and settled on Carola Mary. There were two Carolas on a tablet in Westminster Abbey, named after the ruling sovereign, Charles I. There was no question of London or the Archbishop this time.

My Maclagan grandmother was much too ill and would not even recognise my mother. The invaluable Dr Playfair had found a nurse for her, and presently a home at Chiswick for cases like hers. The poor little widow had never really looked up since the death of the General. Six children and forty years of India had been too much for her. She had never been as close to Mary as the General; she had been unintellectual but very sweet-natured and her children had loved her. Nothing could have been more admirable than the way that my mother, for the next ten years, toiled up to London to visit her, and be assured that she was as happy as someone who has lost their memory can be. Her husband gave her every support though it had to be acknowledged that telegrams summoning her had an uncanny predeliction for choosing leading University occasions.

It was settled that Carola Mary should be baptised by Hensley Henson, Vicar of Barking, in All Souls chapel. This produced problems. As Fellows had been celibate the chapel had no font. A makeshift was contrived and I was christened in the largest punch-bowl the college could muster. A fortnight after the birth my mother was moved to a sofa in her bedroom. By May 30th my father had carried her down to the dining-room, and they had an early meal there on several evenings. The Registrar called on the morning of June 5th and on Whit-Monday my mother recorded an expedition which I think marks me for ever as born into the Victorian world. She was again churched in beautiful St Mary's in the High Street, but this time she went in a bath-chair. My father walked beside in cap and gown, and after the service they went on, bath-chair and all, for a turn in the Parks to meet neighbours and receive congratulations.

Jubilee Day, May 22nd passed off without any disturbance needing the proctor. Dulce was taken to see a school-children's procession to a feast. The illuminations used for the prince's visit, much augmented, were again lit. Two Jubilee Conversaziones were announced, one by the Bodleian, one in the new Ashmolean. On the morning of June 23rd my parents called at All Souls and saw Bates about the decoration of the font— white roses—and Mr Henson about the service. It was Midsummer Day. Mrs Oman had come from Cheltenham, with Ming, and Douglas and Jane Maclagan (married last June) from Heriot Row, Edinburgh. William Hayter acted as proxy god-father for Edward Maclagan, absent in India, and Mrs Leigh, wife of a don, for Lily Peile. I am astonished to see that about forty people turned up. It was always the kindly boast of Frank Pember, a junior Fellow since 1884, that he was the last survivor of those present at my christening. There was no music because the chapel had no organ. As the congregation filed out to enjoy a christening cake, to be cut by Dulce, the Regius Professor of Civil Law joined us. He said, 'I have been thinking that as this is the first time that a child has been baptised in the chapel, you might have named her Anima.' The parents almost shouted at him, 'Oh! Professor Goudy, why on earth did you not mention this before? We should have loved to have called her Anima for All Souls.' He looked very furtive. 'I did once make a suggestion for the baptism of an infant. It was not at all cordially received.' Well, it was too late, but the parents looked into the possibilities and in 1914 I was duly confirmed as Carola Mary Anima.

Before Mrs Oman left she was taken to see 39 St Giles's. This had been kept approximately private, but the Omans were moving. A perambulator and Dussie's mail-cart, and Dussie's dolls' mail-cart all in the little hall at 32 Beaumont Street were too much. The Omans had been looking at new homes before I was born. They had not wasted much time on 37 Holywell, very attractive, but really a first home for a newly-married couple. It was conveniently near All Souls but in a narrow and noisy street. St Giles's offered three possibilities. By the time they took Mrs Oman to see it, they had been several times to Number 39. It was the garden which turned the scale. My father would be able to keep hens.

II

They were due to move in on Friday, October 8th, 1897. On Tuesday came a telegram from brother Charlie asking Mary to come up on Friday. C.O. was unexpectedly under the weather. He had cut his hand in the process of packing cases. Messrs Archer duly arrived on Friday betimes and my mother caught the two p.m. for London. The news that awaited her was that her mother was now pronounced well enough to come home but would need constant unalarming companionship until she settled. Ming would come daily to help, but not Al, who was beginning to get worried about William Hayter. C.O., left to do the move alone, said that the men had got everything shifted by two p.m. on the Saturday afternoon and seemed to consider fifteen shillings magnificent backsheesh. Gradually the study and the parents' bedroom and nurseries became habitable, but he experienced all the horrors of a move. The old ladies from whom he had taken the lease of 39 were making ridiculous sudden claims, and he was asked to come to see for himself the state of the house he had evacuated. Its condition would explain why it was not yet let. He went and was made quite melancholy. It had been nobody's business to tidy up after the exodus. It made him feel guilty to see the little house in which they had been so happy left so neglected. He got it cleared up, and the agent reported a client in record time.

After a week of taking the pathetic little old lady for gentle walks in Kensington Gardens, our mother returned to Oxford, but only for the weekend. By All Saints' Day when the Archbishop was expected for All Souls festivities, she was at home, but only for four days. The heavenly old man was shown Carola Mary and announced that she was the prettiest baby he had seen for a long time. Our mother took to going to London for the day. A visit of Dussy to Cheltenham escorted only by Nana had been a success. She and Bamama's superb cook were superior together, and the attractive little girl instructed the staff at St Philip's Lodge, 'Bamama is my grandmother and Fava is her son, and I am Mama's pet.' Nobody seemed to notice that the elder grandchild resembled her Bamama strongly, perhaps in features, certainly in disposition. She was naturally peremptory and had a great sense of occasion. When they met Ralph Symonds in his pram in the Parks, raising roars of rage, Dulce said, 'He should cry in his nursery.'

In the end it was Dulce who brought her mother home. A little note dictated to her father, with one page entirely covered with kisses, said, 'Do come back soon to your dear children.' This coincided with opinions that the invalid was now serene and could be left in the permanent care of Ming. Mary came home, exhausted, and a stay at the sea with Nana and the two children was prescribed. It seemed a strange choice in March and they had snowstorms to watch from the windows of 3 Southsea Terrace, lodgings kept by some spinster sisters, the Misses Harrington. At Oxford, the new housemaid got housemaid's knee, and the bath-water was still stone-cold, but the hens were beginning to lay, and the garden was bright with unexpected crocuses, purple and white.

I think my mother was never in better health in her life than during the summer that followed my birth. She had a week in Paris, and during the months of June and July her walks with C.O. were prodigious—the Five Mile Grind, Yarnton, Headington . . . An undemanding old single lady, Miss Hunt, had taken Beaumont Street off their hands, and Bob, a tower of strength, was expected from India. Dulce was old enough to be taken to the Warden of All Souls' Garden Party and enjoy Punch and Judy in the Hall. Bob arrived and was a guest at All Souls lunch. It was all too good to believe. With the first month of the Long Vacation came a telegram from Brother Charlie which meant that Mary must take an early train from Chipperfield, where her mother had been on a holiday, and stay with her until a nurse came from Chiswick.

The Omans had taken Burford vicarage again and it was as peaceful and delightful as ever. A fortnight after they had returned from their longest Italian holiday yet, the ominous words 'Not Out' began to appear in Mary's diary, and on October 28th Dr Mallam's son came. Dr Mallam himself called twice the next day, and told my father our mother had typhoid fever. It was Sunday evening, and there was no such thing as a telephone in the house; but a letter should be in London next morning. Father wrote to Aunt Al and to the Superior of the St John's nurses. There were now three maids in his employ and a Nana, but typhoid called for special trained experience. A St John's nurse arrived the next afternoon. C.O. seems to have dined out only once during the dark period which followed, for All Souls Gaudé. George Curzon was coming. He was announced to follow Lord Elgin to India as Viceroy, and had accepted an Irish peerage so that he could still perform in the Commons. I think this must have been the date when it fell to my father's lot to read the lesson in chapel. His wife's temperature was still rising and she was far beyond his recall. He read with horror—'Lord, all my desire is before Thee and my groaning is not hid from Thee. My heart panteth, my strength faileth; as for the light of mine eyes, it also is gone from me.'*

Mary's fever increased until November 10th, three weeks, then it dropped to normal and remained so. After another week she sat up in a chair. She always attributed her recovery to her excellent trained nurse, but there is a twist in this story. Nurse told mother that her case reminded her so much of that of another lady she had attended—'Just like you, madam. There was such a nice-looking gentleman, and two little ones in the nursery, just like you. Well, after the poor lady died, you should have seen the husband's mourning! His top-hat had such a wide band of crepe, there were only about two inches left plain above it.' She settled my mother for a nice little sleep and said as she stole out, 'Of course, he married within the year.' Mother decided to live.

III

I have found that if a party is going stickily, one solution is to ask your neighbour what was his first memory. This generally works and everyone can join in. My own earliest memory is rather paltry. It is Mrs Burns's pet lamb at Callender eating Uncle Phil's *Strand Magazine*. Uncle had brought it up from London and it was popular with the family, so a universal loss. He had imprudently left it on an outside ground-floor window-ledge at the farmhouse. The date must have been August 1899. We had stayed at Bishopsthorpe on our way up, something much more memorable, but I have not the least recollection of that. I am told that I fixed my fancy on the butler who was probably majestic. The Archbishop and Augusta entertained on a large scale and thought nothing of welcoming C.O. and Mary, Dussy, Carola and Nana. I was now generally known as Wuz as I had fuzzy-wuzzy hair. Uncle Ed joined us, and there were seven other disconnected guests. Once there was Mr Balfour. I have been told that in cold weather Bishopsthorpe burned a ton of coal a day. We stayed at Callendar until mid-September and all three bachelor brothers-in-law walked and fished with C.O. I have the clearest picture of the whole family being called out to look at the demolished *Magazine*. The Scottish summer holiday had become an established pattern for the family.

At Oxford on our return Lady Ottoline Bentinck had arrived on the

* Psalm 38, 9–10

scene. She was to marry Philip Morrell of the firm of Morrell, Peel and Gamlen, solicitors, and also of the local brewing family. She wore a white beaver top-hat two-feet high.

In December, Uncle Bob was ordered to the Cape. My mother went down to see him off and said it was most dramatic as the ship turned and then went out broadside on. We were told to remember Uncle Bob in our prayers. The Boer War was not going well.

In January 1901 a tremendous celebration took place at All Souls. This was the Mallard Centenary. The site of the college to commemorate the souls of all those who had perished in the Hundred Years' War had been, according to tradition, determined by a wild drake which had arisen from its nest at a strategic moment.* A medal was being produced larger and more handsome than that issued a hundred years before. C.O. came into the nursery before he set out, to explain it to us. There would not be such another torchlight procession along the roof, accompanied by song, for a hundred years. A hundred years hence we should all be dead. 'ALL?' 'ALL.' We wept to hear. In the same month we passed from the Victorian to the Edwardian age. C.O. went up to London to watch the funeral cortège of the old queen pass from Victoria to Paddington for burial at Frogmore.

On their ninth wedding anniversary mother gave her husband a clock for his study, a necessary gift. Her presents were always realistic. Next year it was incandescent gas for the study. Her diary was not kept for a week in mid-April, then it took up with the arrival of the St John's nurse on May 23rd. But not until June 4th came the entry, 'Ill all day.' This must have been a day of horror, but I took no notice when Nana said at bedtime that next morning she might have something to tell us. She rather specialised in lurid forecasts. Dulce poked me awake whispering, 'She says we have got a baby brother.' I knew we had not, so I turned over. Still, there evidently was something in this. Where was he? We would be taken to see him when he was ready for us. He was in mother's bedroom. I might have guessed he was coming, for I had been hustled out

* *The Oxford Sausage* (Cambridge, 1822, new edition) prints pp. 57–58. 'The celebrated song of the All Souls' Mallard.' It consists of four verses, and chorus, but is almost impossible to understand. It may be of Tudor date which would explain the reference to King Edward, murderer of King Henry VI, Founder of All Souls. It ends—'Therefore let us sing and dance a galliard, To the remembrance of the MALLARD. And as the MALLARD dives in pool, Let us dabble, dive and duck in bowl. Oh! by the blood of King Edward! Oh! by the blood of King Edward! It was a swapping, swapping MALLARD.' January 14th, 1632, is the first recorded date of a Mallard Festival.

of the little slip of a room on the first floor landing, the Kippy Room (Christmas room) when I had just had time to admire a brand new cot with lace and muslin curtains and wide pink satin ribbons. Dulce, as the eldest had the first look at 'Sonny, born at 12.15 after midnight.' Then came my turn. I was still not quite sure that this was not a hoax. I lifted one of his tiny hands. It had fingers, and nails with moons on them. This was no doll. I had a brother. He was to be Charles Chichele and was the fourth Charles running in the direct line. There was a wonderful feeling in the house that bright Derby Day. Dr Mallam suggested that the child ought to be called Flying Fox after the winner. The flowers began to arrive and continued all day. Sweet-peas were at their best. In the afternoon Nana took us to St John's gardens and later C.O. took Dussy to the Warden of All Souls' garden party. That night, Professor York-Powell, a colleague about whom my father's comments were apt to be denigrating, rose at the History dinner to propose Sonny's health.

We heard with awe that the St John's nurse this time was something very special. She was a lady-nurse. What that was supposed to mean we knew not but she was certainly no nurse. She left my poor mother on a hot June night lying on a rubber sheet. 'Let me see, where is that kitchen?' It was too much trouble to go down two flights to collect a clean draw-sheet. Sonny was to be fed, as it would interest her to have a patent-food bottle baby, on a vaunted brand of dried milk out of a tin. I heard piercing yells coming from the spare-room. The lady-nurse was changing baby. I asked, 'Why does he make that awful noise?' 'Because he's a naughty boy,' said the lady-nurse, looking up with the face of a fiend. She took her leave, but not until July and Nana then obeyed instructions to stuff the infant with a patent food rich in carbohydrates to which he took readily. It was still fashionable to have a fat baby. When Queen Victoria had been shown her future son-in-law, born the Marquess of Lorne, she had commented approvingly that though pale, he was a lovely fat red-haired baby. It sounded horrible. Sonny was christened in All Souls Chapel and Hensley Henson, now Canon Henson, who was a god-father, officiated. 'Dussy held the book.' The Warden was the other god-father and Mrs Oman came from Cheltenham to be god-mother. Perversely, she now displayed no interest in the triumphant grandson but much in me. I regret one of our conversations as reported to me later.

'Shall I live longer than you, Bamama?'

'Most probably. Why do you ask?'

'When you are dead, may I have that picture?' (It was a reputed

Honthorst of a child of Charles I which now hangs above my dining-room fireplace.)

About half a century later I had the same enquiry from my great-niece, Libby Stuart, with the same result.

If I had not found this in the diaries, I could not have believed that Bamama took me to the London Zoo when I was five. I cannot imagine that she accompanied me on the elephant or any other outsize quadruped as she was three-score-years-and-ten, of an increasingly heavy build, elaborately dressed. As for me, I would never willingly go to see animals in cages. The only time at which I was a fairly regular visitor to the Zoo was while it housed some Archangel bear-cubs which arrived in the London docks, addressed to my husband's office in Bishopsgate, under the mistaken impression that his senior partner owned a country estate something resembling in extent those then known in Russia. The cubs were taken down to his house at Dartford, Kent, and chained to the sundial in the garden. They brought this in with them to a tea-party. The Zoo was summoned. I believe they flourished and multiplied. We used to take them tins of honey on Sundays when we had a London flat.

For our summer holiday of glorious 1901 we had taken the ferryman's cottage at Portnacraig, on the Tummel, near Pitlochry. I do not think we were ever very clever in getting there. 'Left Oxford 7.30-a.m. arrived Perth 6.30-p.m. Had to stay till nine as the Highland train gone.' We arrived at our destination for a midday meal. But the terrors of getting to Portnacraig rather increased its fascination. Next year we tried a four-wheeler to Oxford station at an even earlier hour and caught a workers' train to Bletchley Junction. Here we joined an express to Crewe. This was a fire-spitting impatient dragon, and we had to find the reserved coach. We had a tin bath as well as several varieties of wheeled vehicles for infants. The great excitement at Perth was not to lose at least your luggage for the night. I remember once we arrived having lost well-nigh everything. Nana plumed herself that she had at least the children's night-bag. But alas, this piece, when it burst open, disgorged nothing but stuffed animals. The obedient nurse-maid had perfectly known that it was 'The animal bag, Nana. You told me never to lose hold of it.' We had to go to bed in our vests, well pleased, each with a favourite bear. My brother also had always known it was the animal bag.

After Perth the journey became thrilling, darkness fell and the fragrance of coniferous country was unmistakable. The very names of the stations were music—Stanley, Dunkeld and Birnam, Ballinluig . . . When we disembarked at Pitlochry the best was yet to come. Mrs Duncan Forbes, and Sandy Forbes the boatman (no relations) were there with the wheelbarrow and our manageable belongings were piled in and manœuvred down a precipitous side path from the little station towards a very pretty little glen with a babbling brook. The last stage was heaven. We clambered into the ferry boat and Sandy rowed with practised skill across the wide and powerful Tummel, under the shade of the Craig itself until we drifted on the tide to the jumping-off stage on the opposite bank. Whatever the hour, there was a meal of trout baked in oatmeal and drop and soda scones and home-made jams.

Portnacraig was really a collection of cottages—in the centre came a terrace, inhabited by several families, all with the same surname but not all relations. They were only alike in that they mostly pursued occupations in Pitlochry and after hours practised the bagpipes in preparation for the Highland games. The terrace was guarded at one end by the Forbes's beloved hideous house and at the other by the Thompsons'. These had flower and vegetable gardens in front of them much bigger than themselves. While we rented their premises the Forbeses lived in a large and a small room across the yard. I adored Mrs Forbes, who let me help with the washing, and the preparation of lucid blue water filled with starch, and peeling green peas and beans, and scraping potatoes. Mrs Forbes was eternally making, in her spare time, a thick white satin tea-cosy with a design of peacocks, adorned with sequins. It was for the bazaar at Christmas, and was kept in a press done up in a sheet. Her other outstanding possession was a straw basket embroidered with life-size wool carrots, and labelled mysteriously CANNES. It had been the gift of a lady summer visitor.

Having found a place which had something for everyone, we stuck to it. The premises were rather restricted. Guests had to be asked to stay at Fisher's Hotel in Pitlochry. But my father had a first-floor study in which to begin *The History of the Peninsular War*. In March 1902 he wrote to our mother, 'I have bought a complete copy, clean, in half calf, of the Wellington Despatches—twelve volumes. I shall be so constantly at work on them all the next two years, that I thought £1 was not too dear. But it will take up an amount of shelf room.' One of his oldest Wykehamist friends calculated much more accurately what would be the eventual scope of this undertaking. 'I am so sorry, dear Lady, to hear that Oman has decided on this *magnum opus*. For it can only be a torso, dear Lady. It can only be a torso.' *The History of the Peninsular War* ran into seven volumes, the last published in 1930. My father was by then huge but hale. As my mother laid out his cap and gown for him to attend a funeral at the University church for which a deep-voiced bell was sounding solemnly, she said softly, 'Torso, indeed!' The contemporary who had prophesied so authoritatively had himself died, in spite of having taken the minutest care of his health. He had been seven months junior to my father.

The New Year of 1902 was crowded with events. The Spooners gave a fancy-dress dance for children. Dulce was to go as a rose. I was struck with emulation when I heard her announced as 'The Queen of the Roses'. I had to think fast. When my turn came, I replied 'Princess Forget-me-not'. This caused a ripple. 'It was marvellous.' reported Dulce, 'to hear the little creature.' As well as her annual diaries mother kept accounts of the prowess of her children in marbled note-books. All too soon it was reported of Carola:

A great love for dress and ornament was displayed by her. Any gay coloured ribbon or stuff was instantly put round her own neck, and with her head on one side she would say 'pretty baby', so that her sister said, 'She's a Vanikin thing'. However, she did not need entertainment as Dulce had done at a similar age, and so long as she got her meals regularly she did not complain, though she was of an imperious temperament and not at all abashed by the presence of any strangers, or impressed by the sense of propriety which was always so present in Dulce.

Nor, it seems, was she so quick to realise when her mother was anxious. Dulce would ask again and again, 'Do you think he's all right?' if our father was late, as he most often was.

We were now promoted to scrap books and made an unholy mess with paste made from flour, sent up from the kitchen. From this source, too, came the basin full of hot soapy water with which we blew bubbles out of clay pipes. We were taken to the pantomime. I cannot think why our parents went on wasting money sending me to a form of entertainment I despised. The pantos had titles meant to attract children, *Puss in Boots*, *Jack and the Beanstalk*, *Mother Goose*. But the plots were hardly recognisable as the stories we knew and loved. My worst disappointment was *Alice in Wonderland*. When Alice came on, she was not even dressed in the traditional blue. I objected loudly. Meek Miss Horsely, daughter of the Manciple of All Souls who gave primary instruction to us and the two youngest Trevelyans, whispered kindly when the limelight threw a brilliant beam all over Alice, 'Now she's blue.'

On June 2nd we were allowed to stay up until darkness fell to see the bonfires in honour of the Peace. I remember my father exclaiming in alarm that a little girl had jumped right into one of them. But she must have been fished out, and there was no recurrence of the violent scenes that had disgraced London on May 17th 1899, when the news of the relief of Mafeking had added a word to the English language. Uncle Bob brought us a flag, captured, according to family legend, from outside Mafeking station. A third of it was a plain bright green. It eventually escheated to my brother who tells me that he thinks he still has it somewhere wrapped up in an upstairs loft together with other period pieces.

Our father was going to the coronation of Edward VII on June 26th. I had always understood that he owed this invitation to a canon of Westminster, the handsomest man you ever saw, a friend on my mother's side of the family: my Grandmother, Patricia, had nursed him when he was at death's door in India He was much valued by the royal family, as one of the spinster princesses had wanted to marry him. Neither of them ever married. This was thought very beautiful. But I do not find this donor suggested either in my mother's diaries or my father's two letters describing his experience. He dressed up for us to come and see him in the dining-room one evening in his black velvet knee-breeches and *jabot* and all, and let us draw his sword. The news that the King was ill was the leading topic at the All Souls lunch on June 24th. He was going to have an operation. The coronation was indefinitely postponed. Most of the foreign royalties went home. Sir John and Lady Evans heard the bad news at King's Langley station from the stationmaster who was a great friend. The had engaged rooms for themselves, Joan, aged nine, and Joan's Nana, at the Euston Hotel and would never have got them had not the hotel authorities known the famous archaeologist for what he was. They decided to go. A Rose-du-Barry brocade dress for Lady Evans would have been delivered. Joan's Nana had sewn all her employer's best diamonds into odd parts of Sir John's clothing.

We all left for Scotland as originally arranged, but on August 8th C.O. went south again. It was generally believed that the postponed service, much cut down to suit the king's weak state of health, would be rather a poor affair. But there is no evidence of this from my father. To be sure, his progress did not seem to have unmixed bliss. He had a violent cold in the head, which when the historic show was all over, he was inclined

to think must have been influenza—'such dreadful headaches, sleepless-
ness, cramp and hot and cold shivering fits'. The Gervaises with whom he
had hired a carriage had been told that they had better order it for six thirty
a.m. So he rose at five fifteen, swallowed a cup of tea which he could not
taste and got into his court dress. Frank Gervais looked 'most glorious in
his Deputy-Lieutenant's scarlet'. Georgie, a very handsome woman,
wearing all her best jewellery was regrettably not described. What my
father always blightingly termed 'articles of female dress' made small
impression on him. Their carriage came round to Al's house in Argyll
Road, very smart and with a very smart horse. But this animal disapproved
of the whole expedition. He proved 'a jibber'. He utterly refused to
advance for the Abbey. The passengers, tightly packed in their uncomfortable panoply, heard the coachman crack his whip. They were moving, but
sideways, and then backwards. The carriage mounted the pavement and a
crowd of loafers began to gather. 'The beast then stood on his hind-legs
and pawed the air. This was too much. So we walked down Earls Court
Road to the stables and got another steed of less dignified appearance but
more tractable.' It was disappointing on reaching the Abbey at seven
fifteen to find there was hardly anybody there. C.O. parted from the
Gervaises whom he never saw again, and before he went off to 'a proper
breakfast' with the Hensons in Dean's Yard, took the precaution of
identifying his seat. It was quite excellent, in the transept and commanding a perfect view of the coronation chair. 'Just over the peers and
alongside half the House of Commons.' He returned at eight forty-five
and as his cold had now caused him to begin on his third handkerchief, he
noticed that he was a cause of polite commiseration to his neighbours, the
Dean's daughter, Mrs Woods, and Mrs Henson, He never before remembered his eyes running like this. 'But I saw it all nevertheless, very well,
including the archbishop's vagaries.' The Dean of Westminster had been
appointed in 1881 and the Archbishop of Canterbury was an octogenarian.
Both were to die within the year. There was considerable nervousness as
to how they might perform their duties. But there had not been a
coronation for sixty-five years and nobody had been able to persuade them
to depute much. C.O.'s first letter, nevertheless, was enthusiastic.

It was true that the Archbishop made a loud adjuration to the king
to protect the widower and the orphan and had a giddy fit while doing
homage; but some of the younger bishops got him on his feet and
helped him away. He was better than the Dean, who actually rolled right
over, luckily while he was still reaching for the chalice. The Queen's

four duchesses looked charming, three dark and one fair. C.O. appreciated the heraldic cat-a-mountain embroidered on the train of the Duchess of Sutherland. Queen Alexandra had resolutely refused, it was whispered, to let Archbishop Temple crown her. He might wreck her *coiffure*. She thereafter always called the Archbishop of York 'My Archbishop' as he had put the crown on her head. She wore the most extensive diamond collar that C.O. had ever seen. 'Her long neck was swathed with it from chin to shoulder. Her hair,' he added thoughtfully, 'was rather red-brown today.'

Old Lord Rolle had stumbled and rolled when paying homage to Queen Victoria, an incident which had been the subject of many illustrations, but the behaviour of the senior clergy in 1902 did not reach the Press. They gave prominence to a story that the king, in true Sir Philip Sidney vein, had refused a cup of soup prepared for him and insisted on it being transferred to the Archbishop of Canterbury. C.O. thought the king walked with a firm step and took his oath to the nation in a clear ringing voice. 'He looked like a man thoroughly relieved to get the business over.'

IV

There was one more major social event in the Omans' coronation year. It was the agreeable habit of my parents, after family prayers, to open and comment on their letters. My mother employed the time when there were none for her, in rolling cigarettes in a machine, for my father's daily consumption. Sometimes we were allowed to help in this but it was important to get firm results. Prayers consisted in the maids trooping in and sitting in a row in the dining-room. I cannot recollect that Nana ever so condescended. She was, of course, not Church of England. Dulce and I and Brother as soon as he was able, were always expected. My mother opened the outsize Bible at the Lesson, and indicated unsuitable passages better omitted. This warning was sometimes fatal. After the lesson we all turned round and knelt for prayer.

In the middle of September an exciting letter came for mother. It was from Eddy Earle, who requires explanation going back to the Maclagan grandparents in India.* He was a grandson of a very old Mr

* The author wishes to thank Mrs Mildred Archer and Mrs Judith Chibbett of the India Office Library of Records for information about the Savi family. Robert Maclagan's

Charles and Mary Oman.

General Robert and
Mrs Patricia Maclagan.

Carola and Dulce Oman.

'I was a Fauntleroy Boy.'
Charles Chichele Oman.

Savi whom the General had been assiduous in visiting in London on his retirement. Julien Robert Savi, of Nohatta, Jessore, one of a large family, mostly indigo planters, had been the husband of Patricia's much older sister, Jane Douglas Hamilton Gilmour. After the birth of four children, the last in 1848, she had died. This child, Marian MacKenzie Savi, had been a bridesmaid, aged eight, at the wedding of Robert and Patricia. At this point I am confused between the plot of the first act of *The Second Mrs Tanqueray* and what actually happened. Whether Marian Savi suddenly arrived in Calcutta from Ireland to devote herself to looking after her widower father, or whether she was already there in 1869 and had realised that he had what was delicately termed 'formed another attachment', she was certainly wished upon my grandmother for a long visit. She was quite useful with their younger children as Patricia was very unwell. When she had been a member of their family for fourteen months Captain Edward Earle, an engineer officer, proposed and was refused. She liked him very much but feared he was not sufficiently religious to support her throughout life. She said he did not seem to read much. Patricia said to her husband, 'When did Marian ever open a book?' However, they could not point out how very desirable this marriage would be. The romantic legend is that when they had returned from a walk they had found Marian, whom they had left sitting on the verandah, had called to Earle, who happened to be passing, and dissolved in tears on his breast. She had made a mistake and was miserable. They were married three months later from the General's house and he, not her father, gave away the bride. Mr Savi stayed in Calcutta but he sent a splendid wedding dress, the cake and two diamond rings. One was for Patricia. Marian wept again and said how glad he must have been to be rid of her. She refused her ring. Patricia, I gather, kept both. She had earned them.

diaries, volume VII, tells his side of the story. There had been a much earlier family connection with India. In 1773 John Fullarton, who retired as a Major-General, married Janies or Janice Khainam of Sandella in Oudh, aged fourteen. A mausoleum erected to her in Berhampore, Bengal, declares in various tongues that she had died in childbed with her tenth infant aged thirty-two. 'Her poor solitary associate mourns separation from so precious a spark of sacred purity and excellence.' He never remarried and died in 1804. A son, William Fullerton of Skeldon, of whom a fine Raeburn portrait recently came into the market and was reproduced in *Country Life*, married Susanna Whiteside, sister of Jane Whiteside, wife of Dr David Maclagan. A prized Fullerton table-cloth was taken up to London in 1922 to be used at my wedding; my mother's hasty note, pinned on, says, 'Used again for dear Carola's funeral'. All the daughters of Janies were reputedly of outstanding beauty. *Dalrymples of Langlands*, J. Shaw: 134–135.

E

The Eddy Earle from whom my mother got a letter in September 1902 was one of the sons of this match. The extraordinary bridesmaid pattern was to repeat itself. Mary had been a bridesmaid at the wedding in Lahore of Eddy's mother. Now he was asking that Dulce Oman would be his bridesmaid at St Peter's, Cranley Gardens, on Saturday, September 20th. She would be the only one from his side; the other three came from the evidently lavish supply of his bride. He said he was sure Dulce would 'cut them all out', a phrase unknown to me.

The outfit for Dulce had to be ordered from London. Taking her up to fit presented no problem, but when the result arrived Nana was loud in her contempt. She could have made the whole show for half the sinful price demanded. She proceeded to make a replica for me. I thought the dress quite lovely. It was severely simple, cream Roman satin, and the large floppy Leghorn hat had ribbons to match. Our journey up to London by train on the longed-for Saturday was remarkable for our number of bandboxes, and for good measure we had taken Baby Brother. When we arrived at the church he was fractious so Nana was not there when the bridesmaids were called for to collect their bouquets in the porch. Now the unfortunate result of Nana having made me exactly the same dress was evident. 'Won't you take your bouquet, Miss?' asked the flower-lady pushing one at me. I put both my hands behind my back and closed my eyes. I knew I was not a bridesmaid, much though I longed to be. This trouble was solved by the arrival of a leading relative on the bride's side. She asked my mother, 'Could your little girl step forward to take the bride's gloves before they go into the vestry? My little girl has hurt her hand.' I did not see any sign of any bridesmaid with a hurt hand but my mother accepted the tactful offer of prominence for Dulce. All the females present seemed to be wearing a quantity of ostrich feathers, in hats and as boas, and there was a great deal of bowing and smiling and whispering. The heat, the tension, grew almost unbearable. At last came a hush. A fairy-tale carriage with a pair of greys drove up, and Brother had to be carried outside again to stop him clucking at the horses. I cannot recall anything further of Eddy Earle's wedding except that we were told that some of the other bridesmaids were 'the little Millais—the famous artist. "Bubbles", you know.'

V

I cannot imagine why most guide books, and even the City of Oxford volume of the *Royal Commission on Historical Monuments* insist on calling St Giles's, St Giles *Street*. It is a wide thoroughfare containing two colleges (Balliol, very plain, St John's, very beautiful) on the east side, and good little shops and houses on the west. It stretched from the Martyr's Memorial, in front of Balliol, almost to St Giles's church, just before which it subdivided into the roads leading to Banbury and Woodstock. Trams ran up the Banbury road. C.O. before his marriage bought five ten pound shares in the Oxford District Tramways. These vehicles exhibited a notice asking you not to ring the bell unnecessarily, so as to spare the horses. There was a line of planes in front of our house which faced east, but they did not prevent us seeing incessant objects of interest. Cabs plied from a rank outside St John's. An important figure in our youth, Mr Rhodes the riding master, had his stables at the Lamb and Flag (St John's property). Undergraduates, finely mounted, trotted north from his premises. There were weddings and funerals at the church. We went there most Sunday mornings. Although it was of commendable antiquity, I never liked it. That was largely because I always saw Satan there. He was up in a window, wrapped in a scarlet cloak, staring at me. Actually, the window represented the raising of the daughter of Jairus and he was Jairus; but judging from descriptions I knew he was Satan. I began to make excuses not to go to church. Saturday was spoilt for me, although usually a party day, because Sunday came next. In the end I told my mother about Satan and she said she would look out for him. She put up her lorgnettes. She was short-sighted. I whispered 'There! There!' She could not see him. This was worse than I had ever imagined. Only I could see him. That scare died out gradually, but I never liked St Giles's church.

Number 40 St Giles's, as it was then called, was the home of Mrs Bywater Ward who had two girls much older than us and a son, Jack in the Navy. Their house stood further back from the throughfare than ours and had a core dating from 1600, part of a large house owning many acres. But in 1821 an heir had decided to part with some of his property. Our home, 39, and 38 were built about nine years later, and advertised as 'residences for persons of the first distinction'. There was a garden wall between us and the Wards (which looked old but was probably made of fragments from Beaumont Palace) and a small Gothic house. Thirty-nine was in the doll's house style, thin but tall. On the ground floor came a row of windows with round tops of the variety generally known as Venetian. They represented the dining-room. We did lessons there, after prayers and the parents' breakfast. The study came behind and to the side, and looked out on to the garden, but we never went in there except by special invitation. The staircase was difficult. It had a hand-rail and climbed up three steep stories. I used to tremble when I was sent up alone after dark. The parents' bedroom and dressing room came over the study, and a spare-room. The only bathroom was at the bend, halfway up the stairs. Uncle Bob used to develop his photographic plates in it with clanking noises. I still think he was not very clever about teaching me how to make exposures.

I got my first camera, a number One Brownie, for learning my multiplication tables up to twelve times. I used to put a piece of tracing paper over a piece of mirror and try to trace the outlines of trees and lochs. The camera was bought and at intervals brought forth from mother's wardrobe to show to me. It had a hideous little square box with a portrait of a Brownie of repellent aspect. It cost five shillings. I was told that Uncle Bob would show me how to use it, in Scotland. I won it, and he allowed me to take the whole of my first film of the heavily shadowed Black Spout waterfall. None was worth printing. The films had to be developed in Pitlochry at the chemist's shop where Henry Gordon from Portnacraig cottages worked. I used to wait for him coming home from the ferry and call, 'Are my photographs done yet?' I had been told they would take a fortnight. I thought of them all working like mad in what they called 'the dark room'. Then at last they were done, but not exactly. There were no pictures. My next film too was not good enough to warrant printing. The chemist held it up to the light and announced at last, 'It appears to be a sheep.' That was right. I was getting there.

Our nurseries at 39 were on the second floor. The day-nursery had a pretty Kate Greenaway paper and housed old Dobbin, the rocking horse. We pulled his tail out fairly soon but that was a good thing because he had a hollow inside, poor old boy. We fed him surreptitiously on all our stodge puddings and slammed the tail back and cried 'Gee up'. We also had hideous clay models of pigs and old men's heads on which we sowed grass in furrows, and we looked at eclipses through smoked glass. Outside the windows we put saucers of strawberry jam in hard weather but we never got strawberry ice. Dulce was faithful to only one doll but I had a large family. I can still hear the early-morning noises of Nana scratching a match in the night-nursery and the plop as the gas came on with a smell. The maids' quarters and a box-room in which we delighted were on the floor above us. It had a large cupboard fixed to the wall and we used to climb into the shelves and lie full-length and be people going out to India in a liner.

Both the parents' bedroom and the study had speaking tubes to the kitchen. We were sometimes allowed to give an order. You blew hard and heard a whistle sound below. Once Dulce blew with such zest that she sent the receiver into the ice-bucket. I do not know how we contrived to put a greenhouse, a hen house and a rockery in the strip of garden. The Ursuline convent, for refugees from the anti-French government, which occupied number 38, had a similar strip and fitted in a tin-roofed chapel. We were fascinated to watch pupils in veils and blue and white garments going in procession chanting hymns on holy days. After we left 39 in 1908 the convent bought our house and turned the pair into a single building. They added a storey. But in 1922 they went back to France and the whole was numbered 38 and became St Benet's Hall, a permanent private hall of the University. The foundation dated from 1897 when the Benedictine Abbey of Ampleforth opened a house of studies in Oxford.*

There was only one really sad thing about 1902. 'Nov. 20th. Eric took his degree.' This was Eric Maclagan, son of W. D. Ebor, and while he had been up at Oxford he had been a constant visitor to our nursery. His appearance was rather odd. Everything about him was long—face, teeth, particularly hair. Once he got back to his rooms in Christ Church to find a row of little men with little bags awaiting him 'To cut Mr Maclagan's hair'. His friends had decided that the time had come. But I fear he sent all away.

To watch him draw was a revelation, 'Now, would you like to see how the Founder of the two colleges of St Mary, Winton, is really, NEARLY, a *Rabbit*?' He was tracing an outline which we at once recognised as the statue of William of Wykeham, kneeling, in a mitre above the entry to New College Gatehouse. Eric was lovely with children.

* In August 1975 I visited what had been my home for eleven years and I would like to express my gratitude to Father James Forbes, O.S.B. for allowing me to see all I needed and for telling me much that I had not known.

Brother Chas:
39 St Giles's:

1902–1907

I

WE GOT THE BAGATELLE BOARD FOR CHRISTMAS 1902. IT WAS A GIFT for everyone. We were enchanted by the click of the white and red balls. The only drawback was that it was too big for anything except the dining-room table so games had to be carefully planned. C.O. had given eleven shillings for it, second-hand. We had the magic-lantern for his birthday, January 12th, 1903.

A rather pathetic figure appeared with this New Year—Mlle Cuchard, to teach us French. She was the first of a procession of failures. There was delight when she failed to turn up one morning and it was because our adored perfectly-mannered fox-terrier had bared the teeth at her. She could not continue to present herself at an establishment where there was *un chien féroce*. He had kept her at bay for half an hour.

Warden Sewell died in March and mother had to write from Southsea to congratulate dear Mrs Spooner on her husband's election. There had been some doubt about it, as to look at he really was not at all like other heads of colleges. C.O. wrote enthusiastically from All Souls:

I have seen Mr Spooner safely installed in the custodial chair. They sang a Te Deum and had some special prayers, but they did not read the long Latin prayer that was usual in old days, nor did he make the Latin declaration. I went up and made my personal congratulations in the quadrangle together with some others. He was smiling broadly, quite

happy. All his daughters were ranged in antechapel to watch the ceremony of giving over the keys and seals to him, which takes place there.

He had four daughters, Kathie, Rosie, Nellie and poor little Aggie who
never developed. The only son, Willie, was, I suppose, at school.
Unfortunately, Aggie was the one nearest to us in age and I was rather
frightened of her being brought to tea with us, which she was regularly.
All the others were very clever and considerably older. We were asked to
go over their new home. Nellie said, 'And these are the stables,' and I got
into trouble for saying, 'But you have not got any horses.' They were
getting some, and a carriage. We rejoiced with awe. At almost their first
dinner party a guest fell down the beautiful main stairs and did what was
then known as 'broke her leg'. There were no modern skills to pin the
neck of a femur and the poor lady had to lie between sandbags in bed in
the Warden's Lodging for three months.

While we were down at Southsea, Jack Ward, whose mother lived at
St Giles's, met us at Portsmouth dockyard and took us over T.P.D.
Medusa. I owe him an eternal debt of gratitude. He was very clever with his
hands and my mother records on an incredible date, 'Christmas Day,
1899. Doll's theatre for Carola from Mr J. Ward'. It was an abiding joy,
for he made improvements as the years passed, including real footlights
which could be attached to the nursery gas, and several changes of
scenery. There was a glade, and a lake, and best of all, a cave, made of the
thick soft smelly silver paper off our tea-bags. My ambition was to become
'a theatre lady'. Jack went on to make our brother a fitment for a toy
engine shed. But it had an electric battery. That might be dangerous; it
was never used. Alas! I remember as if it was yesterday, Jack rolling up his
sleeve one morning in the bright garden and showing me his arm. It had a
blue snake crawling all the way up and round it. He had been tattooed. I
fled and never willingly went near him again.

'Children began French again,' noted mother patiently. 'Carola began
lessons with Miss Horsley.' I was five and a half and I could not see the
point of a book called *Reading Without Tears*. It had three letter words,
such as MUD very large with an explanatory picture evidently designed
for the feeble-minded, of a dressed-up lady under an umbrella holding
up her long skirts in the midst of a puddle. I had been able to read for some
time though not as early as Dulce. 'Some small lessons' with my mother
had not lasted long. 'Effort of any kind was not her strong point.' But
suddenly I needed to be able to read. I looked forward beyond belief to

the children's hour (though it was never called that), when we were dressed and sent down to the drawing-room after tea and before supper. The drawing-room was a perfect Aladdin's cave. There came a night when, almost at once, I was told to take a note and run upstairs with it to Nana in the nursery. I was not very brave about the dark staircase, but I hurried off, all importance, and delivered to Nana the note scribbled by my mother. Nana's face hardened. She took off my sash and dress and put me to bed. I could hardly believe it. I had been naughty again. The note had said: 'TO BE KEPT'.

I realised in a flash that I could read one afternoon when I was sitting on the sofa in the night-nursery with *Grimm's Fairy Tales* in a large edition with coloured pictures. It was open at the horrible one of the horse's head over the door. I was stringing the words together and they made a sentence. I could read! I could read! I had entered into a kingdom. About the same time I was beginning to sew. I think they might have shown me what kind of a needle and thread were best for what material. My mother kept my first effort, labelled with what was evidently a quotation. 'Needle worked into a ball.' She was not a needle-woman. The only thing upon which I can ever see her at work was scalloping the hems of our flannel petticoats with thick white twisted Mallard floss. We wore a goodly number of undergarments—vests, thick or thin, according to the season, liberty bodices, white embroidered muslin petticoats over the flannel ones, knickers, wollen and embroidered cotton, stockings, thick and thin, buttoned boots and gaiters. Our winter clothes were not comfortable. We had cartwheel beaver hats that year with white feather pompoms, fawn full-length coats trimmed with 'ermine' and 'ermine' barrel muffs. Dulce had a real black velvet dress, collected by Nana from Cheltenham, and I had a sapphire velveteen and a loathed white satin for parties, trimmed with swansdown. I had a violent aversion from feathers of all sorts, and after I was married and had sometimes to go out with the guns, I always took a large bandana hand-kerchief in case I was asked to pick up a bird. I still close my eyes while I ruthlessly hack at a fruit cage to release a screaming captive who has caught a wing. The dress with the swansdown collar made me feel quite sick, but I was photographed in it, and smiling. I suppose that horror ceased simply because I outgrew it. It made me hold my head up.*

* I fancy this aversion is fairly widespread and not a matter of genes, but I have dis-covered by accident that my niece Julia Oman (Strong) and my great niece Fiona Stuart, share it with me.

Our summer party frocks were pretty—openwork muslins from India worn over silk slips. Dulce always had pink and I had blue. We were brought or sent Italian sashes, the palest imaginable rose and turquoise with sometimes unusual thinner stripes of moss-green. We never went bareheaded. Even in the Highlands we wore peaked cherry-coloured caps with thin elastic under our chins. We never went out in Oxford without gloves, and for the dancing class we wore silk mittens. Our best stockings, black or white, had openwork over the foot and half way up the leg. I longed for long golden plaits like the youngest Cannan. Dulce tried to help in my efforts to join the Navy by cutting off my hair and calling me Jack, but there were still difficulties.

Being read aloud to by our mother was one of the delights of our hour downstairs. She read us Lamb's *Tales from Shakespeare*, the poems of Sir Walter Scott, *Lays of the Scottish Cavaliers*, and *The Fairchild Family*. We were warned that this one was a little out of date. Mr Fairchild took his family to see a man who had murdered his brother, hanging in chains from the gallows. This was to show one the point of Brotherly Love. Every story had its message. We pitied Miss Augusta Noble whose gown caught fire when she was turning round in front of the glass to admire herself with a lighted candle in her hand. She was burnt to death. It seemed rather an excessive punishment for Vanity. We revelled in the children's books of Miss Charlotte Yonge. The Little Duke was rescued from captivity by the wicked King of France by a faithful squire, Osmond, who rolled up Richard, Duke of Normandy, in a truss of hay, and said he was going to feed his horse. There was an unforgettable moment when they reached the border and Osmond called out, 'The Epte! The Epte! This is Normandy, sir. Sit up and see your own country.' The King of France had a bad son, Lothair, who ordered his hawk's eyes to be put out and his pony flogged, and a good son, Carloman who wasted away. 'Oh! Carloman, Carloman! I cannot spare you. I love you like my own brother.' But with the words 'I think the Saints and Angels are waiting for me', Carloman fell asleep for ever. We used to emerge with tears running down our faces. 'Your mother will make you ill,' muttered Nana.

A.L.O.E. masked the identity of A Lady Of England who was too refined to descend into the arena and admit herself Miss Charlotte Maria Tucker. She was not nearly so good as Charlotte M. Yonge but could tell a story. Her characters also were black and white. Emily Sarah Holt was marred by being a dedicated militant Protestant, but I never could resist a new book by her as soon as I had enough pocket money. My mother preserved my first literary effort. This was called 'Coral and the Bear'. It was brief but not very coherent. My mother fondly detected that it showed discernment of character.

> One day Coral went out alone and found a bear. Coral said don't eat me and the bear went into a cave and Coral went too and they made friends. Soon they made foes. I must leave a bit of the tale out. Coral had to run unless he would have eaten her. Think of the tale and never go into a wood. THE END.

I followed up Coral with 'The Good Child' and 'The Princess and the Witch' and 'The Nimps and the Witch' by the Author of 'Princess and the Witch' (I was beginning to know the correct form), 'The Treasure in the Well' was illustrated, and in book form secured by paper clips.

Mother noted of me that in my lessons with Miss Horsley I showed great quickness and interest but 'lacked the steady working powers of Dulce'. Nana had a machine and could make clothes for us but she never attempted to teach us to sew. All the same, somehow, Dulce learnt to make hems with fairy-like stitches. She could also write a perfectly clear interesting hand.

There was a fine early spring in 1903 and C.O. was on the top of his form, leading the College Walk on Sundays by devious routes to Bessels-leigh, Garsington, Stanton Harcourt . . . They had bread and cheese and veal and ham pie for fare, with ale, and homemade jams, and all got pretty dirty, but under a heavenly blue sky. His pupils were winning their Firsts, and his son was becoming articulate. The first volume of *The History of the Peninsular War* would be out on March 21st. Of course he had seen it already. His voluble ten-page Preface thanked the anonymous compiler of the Index. Another chief assistant was Mr C.T. Atkinson of Exeter College, expert on British regimental history. 'Uncle Kestor' was to become a friend of all of us, though he was generally averse from females, and an unsparing critic.

During the spring vacation the parents went for a month of research in the Peninsula. They saw the battlefields of Vittoria, Burgos, Talavera, Bussaco by moonlight and Salamanca. They saw some riots in both Spain and Portugal. In Madrid, as they were choosing mantillas, a boy ran into the shop, 'Look out! There is a revolution on.' The proprietor uttered an exasperated exclamation and went out to let down his heavy iron shutters. The Omans returned resignedly to their hotel where they found an old New College man, Sir William Worsley, in the same plight. There was trouble going on outside the British Embassy, but they dined, as planned, with the Durands, and they called upon a native historian who first appears in my mother's script as Artichoke, pardonably as he really was General Arteche y More, author of the only important history of the Peninsular War yet produced. As it was in Spanish and eleven volumes, it was practically unknown in England though it had (said the Preface) been almost as valuable as Toreño's *Guerra de la Independencia* for the purely Spanish side of the war. While C.O. was engaged at the War Office, mother, provided with French-speaking ladies as guides, had many happy hours in the Prado. I fear she must have had many unpleasant ones in the lesser inns they used, but she nobly only mentioned the good ones—'excellent Lenten fare at Talavera'. All the long-distance trains in the Peninsula seemed to go in the middle of the night. The Omans had a very bad crossing from Boulogne, but it had been worth it.* Dulce was awake to hear the cab driving up.

A week before, mother took me to order my birthday cake for May 11th. It was generally accepted now that Dulce had bagged the Army and I got the Navy. She had been allowed soldiers on her cake. There was no such thing available as blue sugar for sailors. This grieved me. We had a stirring octagonal biscuit box, 'Deeds that Won the Empire'. Much the best was Able-Seaman Clark V.C. casting a bomb overboard. There he was, fearless fellow, just like the sailors on the cigarette advertisements, with an auburn beard. He was in the act of casting from a deck a terrible looking ball-shaped missile from which flames and smoke were ascending.

Some regular foreign visitors arrived in June. These were the Rivoiras from Rome. Teresio, who was a peppery archaeologist, was a Commenda-tore. He would bang his fist on the table crying, 'Once he was my friend! Now he is my friend no longer!' The quarrel had been something about the excavation of the Circus Maximus by one Boni. Mrs Rivoira had been a Cheltenham girl, and I think one of Bamama's boss-shots as a wife for C.O.

This year the bestowal of honorary degrees in the Sheldonian was to be attended by royalty, rather minor, but perfectly genuine. The Duchess of Albany, widow since 1884 of Queen Victoria's youngest son, had a marriageable daughter, Princess Alice. They were coming on to the All Souls lunch in Codrington, and Dulce and I were to present bouquets on

* For a full account of their experiences see *Things I Have Seen*, Chapter VII, 'An abortive Spanish insurrection', C. Oman, Methuen, 1933.

the lawn. Dulce got the princess, who took her aback by kissing her. I curtsied three times to the duchess but did not relinquish my bouquet. Nana had made us both complete new outfits, and said that if only I had behaved I might have been kissed by the duchess. Nana's superiority was rather dreadfully increased by our prominence. Now we rivalled Ralph who had the photograph of the daughter of a local peer, 'little Lady Betty Bertie' in his nursery. Mr Symonds attended the family. That afternoon, Nana made me call out to a pupil from the convent, who was standing at a window overlooking our garden, 'Have you seen the princess?' Of course she had not, and I had to shout it again and again, and really I could hardly say that I had seen either royal lady. Our instructions had been so confusing. We must not stare at them, or speak first. We must walk backwards. Above all, we must be perfectly natural.

Before we left for Scotland Bamama alarmed the family by having a slight operation and C.O. had to go off to Cheltenham in the middle of examining. But she made a quick recovery, and in any case he never travelled with us. We left Oxford at nine a.m., changed at Leicester, York, Edinburgh and Perth and were at Pitlochry by ten thirty, but without luggage. We were now old enough to undertake favourite expeditions. The Black Spout did not sound much but was thrilling. Loch Tummel was placid as satin. The Falls of Tummel, much grander, was dismissed by Brother in a single composite word—'soda-water'. Cluny Bridge was rather eerie and so was Killiecrankie. At one of them there was a rock overhanging the river where we were told an old woman had sat after the battle hooking in soldiers' bodies to take the buttons and lace off their uniforms. Killiecrankie had a wishing-stone. Queen Victoria had patronised it and you could see Marie Corelli's cottage nestling in the woods above it. This authoress, now famous, had been invited by Mr Robertson to the Encaenia lunch, and seeing a pair of gilt chairs on a sort of daïs on the lawn she had immediately decided it was hers and installed herself. I saw her. She had golden curls, and a great many frilled petticoats and high heels, and sat under a becoming pink parasol. Someone brave had to be sent to say that the chairs were for the duchess and the princess.

At the wishing-stone Dulce wished for three more wishes. I wished to write a book. Brother began to look rather unhappy in the train going home. He had wished he might be a hippopotamus. The Scottish holiday was the one time in the year when we were taken for walks by our father. On Sunday evenings at home he would sometimes come to sing hymns with us in the drawing-room, while mother played the piano, but the

Sunday evenings at Pitlochry were much better. The drill was unvarying.
Wet or fine we set out and he told us stories and let us choose. 'Well,
which is it to be, a murder or a ghost story?' One of his best murders was
the poisoning of a lover from her rich father's works, by Madeleine Smith.
He was called l'Angelier and had no money and she was thought to be
spotless and was engaged to a middle-aged suitor. 'Of course,' said my
father, warming to his theme, 'nobody in Glasgow dreamt that she had
been for months the mistress of l'Angelier.' We nodded sagely. We knew
from school stories that not all mistresses were paragons, though arsenic
sounded a little strong.

And so one more Scottish holiday had ended and we had walked up for
the last time at sunset to Carrabeg. I picked up a pebble and slipped it in
my pocket, a real Scottish pebble. We had early gone through the
disillusionment of picking pebbles out of the river which looked like semi-
precious stones and became just dull when dry. Katie and Jeanie at the
farm were great friends; but we were going home to St Giles's now. It
had its charms on misty autumn evenings when the Blue Hungarian band
played the Skater's Waltz 'Les Patineurs' by Waldteufel—the very
names the essence of romance.

We always stayed at the Rutland Hotel in Edinburgh on our return
journey from Portnacraig, and my mother always asked for rooms 16 and
17. At first I loved looking out at the splendid view, but then someone
told me that if I was naughty a man with a green bag would come and take
me away. By ill-luck I saw a man with a green baize bag over his shoulder
coming towards our hotel. It was quite big enough to take away a little
girl of five. I shrank from the window and waited for him, more terrified
than I had ever been in my life. Gradually I realised that I had been spared
this time. But it was so difficult, never knowing when one had been good
and when naughty.

We called in at Heriot Row most years on our journey south. We were
rather strangely supplied with sponsors. Dulce did the worst, with Aunt
Al shelling out missionary tales for birthday and Christmas. Lily Peile
sent me an amethyst necklace for my christening and after that once a
pound box of chocolates from the Army and Navy stores, but it was
addressed 'Miss Oman'. Brother was sent for to the drawing-room one
December evening. Sir William Anson had brought his godson a present.
He was a little old gentleman with a ruby tie-pin and had brought the
largest teddy bear we had ever seen. It quite eclipsed him. Mother was
flattered by the personal attention but Brother was principally

embarrassed. 'Baloo' was so very big. Long after his eyes had fallen out, and one of his ears had been lost. he was the *doyen* of our nursery.

But my godmother Jane Maclagan was a queen amongst gift-choosers. She sent me a brooch with a ladybird on it and a doll so well dressed (all the clothes to take on and off) that she was instantly confiscated. I was told I might perhaps have her in bed some day when I was not feeling well. Rest assured that I had symptoms in record time. It was wonderful watching Lady being fetched from the cupboard in the darkened room. We heard with interest next year that my gentle lady-bird godmother had got a baby of her own—two, Alison and Morag, the twins.

'Oct. 1st,' said the diary. 'Dulce and Carola began French again.' 'Oct. 21st. Mrs Trevelyan's funeral.' This took place at St Giles's church and we saw it from the windows. We had been to a children's party at the Trevelyans' recently and played charades and their mother had scolded Hilda, her eldest, for being so slow.

II

'January 26th, 1904. D. and C. began music.' It may as well be admitted at once that Dulce's name soon vanished from these entries, because she never pretended to take an interest in anything she knew she disliked. Hopes were pinned on me. My mother explained to my teacher that she expected nothing remarkable. I was just to play to my father in the evenings. This was dreadful. The teacher kept on asking if I had played to my father yet and that meant asking mother to ask him to come to listen. At last I was considered sufficiently advanced. A shower of questions followed. Had I made any mistakes? What had my father said? I could not divulge that. My piece, played as fast as I could, to get over had lasted a very short time. I had not the *nous* to play it over again at once. 'Well,' was the comment, 'some day you shall play me a real piece.' I continued lessons but there were disadvantages. The early morning hour for practising was so bitterly cold in the drawing-room and my hands did not seem to grow any larger. I could not stretch an octave. The keys were stiff.

In February there was a war between the Russians and the Japanese. I had to be the Japanese because I had some Japanese dolls. Dulce was almost too old for dolls. She was nearly ten. In that same month an important interview took place. Mother walked up to 77 Banbury Road on the corner of North Parade. She had an appointment with Miss Batty, co-headmistress with Miss Margaret Lee. Miss Batty's school had been founded in the year that I was born, and she stayed in office for a quarter of a century. Miss Lee was a daughter of the Vicar of Leafield, near Charlbury. I did not know until years later that Miss Batty had been one of the enormous brood of a curate and had stayed on as a pupil-teacher at 'Miss Clarke's' where she and Miss Lee had been educated. It was always their dream that they should start a school somewhere. When this became possible Miss Lee published in the school magazine a poem opening 'Yea! it has come'. It must not be thought, however, from this specimen that she was anything but a first-class teacher. I have been told that if you get one first-class teacher in your life you are lucky; if you get two you have been very lucky. We got just Miss Lee, but Wednesday has always been my favourite day of the week.

Literature class came on at eleven a.m. Miss Lyon from Australia was a cousin of Miss Lee and took the Junior Class at 77. She went home to become headmistress of the New England School for girls in New South Wales. Miss Plumer, daughter of the Field-Marshal succeeded her. Miss Batty, with a growing number of assistants as the affair prospered, did the hack-work, in spite of her headaches. Dulce was entered to go at Easter. As yet it was a small venture. It had Ruth and Rachel Daniel, daughters of the Provost of Worcester, Margaret Gay, Cecily Marriott, Rosamond Harris, Hilda Napier . . . All came strictly from University backgrounds.

Before Dulce set off we had a party with a conjurer, also by appointment. He was very quiet. He might do anything. The number of acceptances swelled beyond the forty which was all we could accommodate. Our courage was vindicated. 'Went off quite successfully.' Chairs did not suffice but littlest boys sat cross-legged on the floor.

We went to Southsea again. Attending the parade outside the Garrison church was the highlight of these wind-swept sea-side holidays. The parents went to Italy. It was a late spring and my father had his first experience of lumbago. He was comfortable in Paris where he went with the best French Peninsular expert to the War Office. He saw that he would need another week or two there as soon as possible.

Ethel Stangoe had slipped into our family on September 30th, 1903, so quietly that even the diary did not notice her. Perhaps this was until we saw whether she had come to stay. Nana with three children growing fast, and the eldest to be taken to day-school every morning and fetched, had enough work for a nursery maid. Ethel was about fourteen, I calculate, and her mother had told her when she came from Cheltenham that she must try to stay for a year in her first situation. So Ethel stood silent while Nana raged at her for Brother's bath-water not being at exactly the required temperature. Previous nursemaids had wept and left. It was miserable standing watching little home-sick girls, straight from happy busy Oxfordshire farms, making our nursery a place of horror with their sobs. I once asked Ethel, years later, why she had never cried and she said, 'Oh! but I did, up in the bedroom, every night.' Ethel stuck it. Her mother had been the wife of a sanitary inspector attached to the police. ('No, Miss Dulce, not an Insanitary Spectre'.) He had died, leaving her with four children and a step-daughter, and she had confided all the savings left to her to what I fear must have been a bent policeman. He had been a friend of her husband. She signed everything he arranged for her and when Christmas came he asked the whole family to a Christmas Tree party. It was the most expensive party to which they had ever been, with presents for everyone. When it was over the policeman said, 'I have spent your money, Mrs Stangoe.' Ethel's mother had a feeling like a kettle boiling on the top of her head and Ethel always supposed that was her first stroke. So all the children had to be sent to a police orphanage and go out to earn their livings from there as soon as possible. We loved hearing about them—Win, the half-sister, who later developed Religious Doubt but married a widower whom she met in the Bath 'bus taking a wreath to his wife's grave. ('I am sure,' said Ethel, 'that I have been on the Bath bus often enough.') There were two brothers, one of whom had set his heart on going into the police. But he walked about the town where he had been told to report for hours after getting there by a too-early train, and when they saw him they said he had varicose veins. He was killed in the 1914–1918 War. He had just begun to help his family. The younger brother was 'the stump of the family', very short. 'Eveling' the much younger sister was a problem child.

Ethel's mother sounded interesting. She saw ghosts. I did not know whether I believed in them but I knew that Ethel did. They were much in the 'Room for One More' style, and I was particularly struck by 'The Plume of Feathers' (from a hearse) and 'Mr Tucker in his nightcap'.

Dulce was pronounced the best worker in the school at the end of her first term. She was an ideal pupil. Our circle of friends expanded as Miss Batty's expanded, and I think that we all improved in health now that someone had to take Dulce up to 77 and fetch her, every morning. I much enjoyed going, for one passed Gee, the florist. After some time I collected as much as I knew Gee asked for a bunch of violets. I walked in—the

Coming back from school.

Frewin Hall.

Carola and Patch.

atmosphere was wonderful, and I said barely audibly, 'Can I have a bunch of violets?' But the answer was 'No'. Violets were over.

I got the most splendid and utterly surprising seventh birthday present. It was a doll's house, like but not so tall as 39, and inside there was every resident. All the maids had dressed dolls as themselves. Mary from Ireland, the head housemaid, who had the reddest hair I ever saw had made a wig of wool for the doll representing her. She was proud of the colour. She said it was the sign of a temper.

C.O. must have lost hope of buying 39, for he wrote after one of his many visits to his mother, that he had seen three beautiful Elizabethan manors near East Leach Turville, one of which, with 100 acres had just been sold for £3,000 'far less than Miss Greswell asks for No. 39; and it is only one and a half miles from a station so not really remote'.

Lord Curzon turned up for Commemoration and he had brought C.O. a Roman coin from the Indian frontier. Old Lord Goschen was in a disgruntled mood. In a long burst of somewhat unhappy confidences after dinner in Hall, he said that Queen Victoria had always kept in touch with him, largely over how to deal with Gladstone. He knew nothing of the new monarch except that he displayed 'a radical inability to distinguish a gentleman from a bounder'.

We began to fish in the Tummel this summer and fell in repeatedly but never fatally. Mrs Forbes was wonderful drying me. When Ethel scalded her hand and had the largest yellow balloon of a blister I ever saw, Mrs Forbes, not Nana, was the person to do her dressings. Perhaps she had learnt in the grand hospital in Edinburgh where they had given her her 'falsies' when she left after her operation. She allowed me to see her putting them on for best. But they were not called 'falsies' then.

Dulce was growing up fast. She had discovered 'Compers', that is, Competitions in magazines. Her first success, from *Woman's Life*, was nothing less than a racquet. She had also, for almost the last time in her life, need to visit the dentist. When you were seated in the chair in his house in Broad Street, the view was of all the mouldering old heads of Roman Emperors outside the Sheldonian. To add to these terrors, there was a large reproduction of a football match picture on the walls of his waiting-room, 'Play up, Guys!' He was a burly man and we were told that he had probably taken a leading part in such affrays.

The dancing class at the Girls' High School was another new experience. Dulce had begun to have lessons at the Randolph Hotel from a mistress who came down from London and was thought very superior. Perhaps

F

Dulce had been sent too young. She could not distinguish her left foot from her right. Nana had imagined that she detected sarcastic titters. Now we were both to go to the High School class on Wednesday afternoons. Here we met a much wider circle including the daughters of leading tradesmen. Connie Acott, whose father had the music shop in the High Street always led the fancy dance. She had a turquoise blue frock, accordion pleated from yoke to hem. We were taught the waltz, the polka, the Schottische, and the Lancers, the barn dance, the one step, the two step, the gallop, and fancy dances with castanets and scarves.

As Christmas drew near my mother made an entry which heralded my longest friendship, 'Beatrice Madan came to tea.' She was three years younger and at seven and a half that was a big difference; but she was very quick. She was the daughter of Bodley's Librarian and I was the daughter of Codrington's. The parents returned from Ablington, Landsown Road, two days before Christmas. This was Bamama's new house. The saga of her move demands separate treatment. It covered several years.

III

The parents were secretive about Bamama's change of residence. My father's letters record in detail the many sudden summonses to Cheltenham, but never the reason. My mother only tells the dates of his inconvenient absences. Once, towards the end, she went with him and did a round of registry offices with Bamama's personal maid, Elizabeth Clinker. The whole story, however, was written down by my father on a half sheet of writing paper and came to me together with other fragments dealing with memorable occurrences. It is undated.

The nearest appearance to a critical investigation that ever fell to my own lot was, oddly enough, in my own mother's Cheltenham house, a few years after my marriage. As I have mentioned before, my mother had with her all through her life, my old nurse Eliza Blackman, who in her declining years served as a sort of honorary housekeeper, keeping a strict eye on all the other maids and not much liked by them. One of Eliza's hobbies was a fear of burglars. She took to going round the rather spacious house every night when all the rest of the household were in bed, inspecting every bolt and bar, upstairs and down, robed in a grey dressing-gown and carrying a flat candlestick. I often heard her soft footsteps on the stairs when I was reading late in my bedroom. She died in 1897 and we buried her in Leckhampton churchyard, much sorrowing; it was a sad break with the past.

Some days after the funeral my mother was woken just before midnight by a crash and screams. One of her maids, lodged in the upper storey, was in a hysterical fit. She declared that, hearing footsteps, she had gone to the top of the stairs and seen 'Old Eliza' in her grey robe and with her candle, passing along the half-flight below and trying the window fastening. Whereupon, she screamed and fainted. My mother tried to soothe her down and argue that she had merely had a nightmare. The improvement only lasted for a few days, for in the week following, two other maids alleged that they had heard footsteps and seen lights below: one said that she had also seen the figure. All three gave notice and wanted to depart at once. They were prevailed upon to stop for the moment and I came over from Oxford to help my mother in the crisis. Unfortunately, though, neither she nor I heard or saw anything; the panic went on and the maids declared that they heard footsteps almost every night. They went off, and my mother replaced them, taking care to engage servants from outside Cheltenham who had never known 'Old Eliza' and (as it was hoped) would not have heard the story of her 'walking'. Alas! this did not end the matter and after a year of tribulation, my mother gave up the house.

I can trace the date of his last summons, to help her to get out in a hurry, and it was the most inconvenient imaginable. He had arrived at Oxford from research in Paris at six p.m. all ready for the October term. The move had been sadly decided upon and he had been down recently and spent a whole morning 'going over old family papers, wills and marriage settlements many of which I had never set eyes on before.' The 'cream of the collection', the Chelsea and Worcester, had taken him another whole day. His only relaxation was a drive in the evening to the new house. 'It is really a very good house with a far better staircase than this, and rooms slightly larger.' Bamama did not, in view of her advancing years and servantless state, need a bigger house. The garden was four times as large and there were two greenhouses. It looked to him, from the state that the papering and painting had reached, as if the 'flitting' would be rather after than before All Souls' Day, 'but one never knows how things can be "rushed" at the last moment'. It was indeed after, for on November 6th he had been unpacking at all hours for two days, breaking off only for picture hanging. This meant reaching up, and the unpacking meant stooping, 'really fatiguing'. When he had emptied six crates of the most valuable china it was at any rate a relief to find that not one in four hundred or so had been damaged and he had arranged them with his mother in a demonstrably vulnerable Chippendale-style cabinet surmounted by a pagoda with a probably irreplaceable top storey of curved glass. Chaos still reigned in all but the drawing-room and principal bedrooms. Although there must have been expenditure in moving to a larger house and a loss in getting rid of the old one in a hurry, he eventually pronounced that Ablington was quite an improvement.

This is the house that I remember as Bamama's home, and what were hardly known as this date as 'servant troubles' never vexed her again. I do not know whether it was now that she installed two maids charmingly called Eliza Greengrass and Eliza Greygoose. (There are in the London Telephone Directory today no less than ten Greengrasses, though only one Greygoose.) But the loss of face at having, at the age of seventy-two, to invoke a daughter-in-law, not much loved, to get some maids, must have been humiliating. In her married life up to date—twelve years now—my mother records only one dismissal, of a parlourmaid, on a Friday, replaced on the following Tuesday. Maids left for only three reasons, illness, invalid parents, or marriage. My mother lost two from this cause in this year. The one whose wedding took place in St Giles's church had a tea-party for thirty-nine in the dining-room. We all attended, but at the church only. Nana's demolition of nursery maids fell into a different category and lasted two years only. At the end of that time she made an ill-judged effort to unseat Ethel by coming to mother with dark hints that Ethel was 'not a good girl'. But whatever her drawbacks, Ethel was unquestionably good as gold, and in her sheer immobility Nana had met her match.

IV

The New Year of 1905 was a period piece. C.O. wrote from the Charing Cross Hotel of driving sleet and trains half an hour late. He was up for the Royal Historical.

Put on your very warmest things, two of everything, one over the other, and you will not be too warm. And don't loiter on the platform, but go to the waiting room and sit as NEAR the fire as you can. I dread to think of you and my mother both travelling in such weather. The horses are slipping down all along the Strand, the sleet lying deep in the road.

Something strange was appearing in the view from our nursery windows —motor cars. Mr Steel-Maitland who was a Fellow of All Souls and a politician, took Dulce and me out in a beauty we called 'The Grey Lady'. We went as far as the Rollright Stones which were exciting in themselves. They stood on a hillside outside Chipping Norton, two groups of enormous boulders—the King and the Courtiers. The Courtiers had their heads inclining towards one another, but the King stood alone looking down into the Valley. This is where the witch had said to him—

> If Long Compton thou canst see
> King of England thou shalt be.

Mr Steel-Maitland who was also a double Blue and First, drove his own motor, but the Oxford Cycle Co. St Giles's, had headed its paper by 1902 'The Oxford Cycle and Motor Car Co.', and Zacharias, the waterproof shop in Cornmarket, advertised 'Chauffeur's clothing'. Leather overcoats lined with serge, full-length, ran from 49s. 6d.; leather jackets and leggings were 28s. and 16s. 6d respectively. Orders were taken for motor cycling suits. The windscreen was not yet here and Mr Steel-Maitland wrapped us up in long-haired grey fur rugs for our adventure in the Grey Lady, and carried us downstairs one by one.

The parents set off for Paris and it was at Nîmes on April 13th that they got, I suppose, in a letter from Nana, 'News of Carola's Fall'. They telegraphed and got the reply, 'Quite well', but wired again from Avignon two days later—'All well'. I remember this incident with startling clarity. We were at Southsea. Nana was in the next room putting Brother to bed for his afternoon nap and Dulce and I, under-exercised, had begun to play 'Dares'. I jumped for the difficult one of landing on the lawn, over the area, but most have jumped short. I woke up to find myself in bed with a strange kind big doctor looking down at me. Nana was terrified, avowedly because the only doctor who the Misses Harrington had been able to get was a Roman Catholic. I had struck my head and had con-cussion. A legend sprang up that Dulce had pushed me. I cannot see how this had originated as there had been nobody else in the room, and even if she had, I would never have 'peached'. At any rate, the parents returned on April 22nd and I was mustered for Easter Day service the next day at St Giles's church.

My mother's reports on my infancy ceased with this affair after mentioning that I was 'beginning to show creative powers'. I longed to go to school, but 'her excitable temperament made it good for her to stay at home and pursue her studies.'

V

We were taken to *The Mikado* for my birthday treat and Brother was brought to meet us afterwards at Buols, for ices. This establishment flourished throughout my life at Oxford. It announced itself as Swiss and French pastry-cooks and confectioners and had a Brussels branch. 'Caterers for balls, parties etc; milk rolls for breakfast every morning at 8 o'clock sent to any address; all kinds of creams, ices and jellies. An early call and patronage solicited; trade supplied.' Our other leading confectioner, Boffin, although he called himself 'The Oxford Restaurant', did not specialise in ices. Boffin was popular in undergraduate circles. 'After one term's credit, 5% interest charged.')

My mother took me to the Bodleian ('C.O. took Dulce bird-nesting'). It was very old. It had Shakespeare first folios and his signature, not legible, and the very book that Shelley had been reading when his boat capsized. I had seen the memorial to him in University College from which he had been sent down for an atheistical pamphlet. My parents said he looked like a fish lying on a slab, but I worshipped his poems. My father disapproved of Shelley and all his works because of his poor record as a husband and father. My great-uncle, James Anderson Rose, part of whose library I have, carried his disapproval of Shelley so far as to make long pencilled corrections in the biographical volume in his library. They are extremely intemperate but I never could get my father to share my enjoyment in them. I brought home from my first expedition to the Bodleian, reproductions of portraits of Flora Macdonald and those then accepted as Mary, Queen of Scots and Amy Robsart. I was much impressed by the statement that Duke Humphrey's famous foundation, together with six other libraries, had a right to a copy of every book published in Great Britain. For my next birthday I asked my father for a bookcase.

In July came a death which was to make a great difference to us. It was that of Montagu Burrows, born in 1819. He was Chichele Professor of

Modern History and my father had been deputising for him for five years. Last year, when it had seemed quite possible that the old gentleman might go on for another decade, my father had refused an offer of the Regius Professorship of Modern History. It was, he realised, taking a chance. The offer might never recur. (In fact it did, twenty years later.) But he could not bear the thought of resigning his All Souls Fellowship. It was not certain that he would follow Burrows, and other candidates put forward their names. During the interregnum Uncle Ed came on leave in time for the Encaenia. Mother was horrified by the looks of Slatin Pasha who received an honorary degree.

The anxiety during our Scottish holiday must have been considerable but there were distracting new interests. At last one of our mother's four bachelor brothers had married. This was Robert, now a colonel. His bride was Aunt Bee, a daughter of General Dupérieur. A photograph of her in full evening dress but wearing a large hat with ostrich feathers arrived. She was twenty-three and had refused six proposals of marriage. She had kept a diary since she was twelve and her daily entries had a limpid clarity. She appreciated everything when she came to stay with us. 'Went to *Charley's Aunt* and the children said I was going to see myself.' 'Spent such a delightful evening on the river, and had tea at the Trout with Mary and C.O. It was such a pretty evening.' 'Went to see an old church [Yarnton] with curious tombs and stained glass with birds on it.' 'Mary had a big dinner party of 16.' She had unusual accomplishments. She played the violin and even took it on a walking tour in Scotland and on her honeymoon. The first time she brought it to us, Brother came into the dining-room round-eyed. 'There is a wild beast in the spare-room.' She also painted in water-colours, mostly landscape. This was not uncommon, but she had a distinctly individual touch. She headed her letters from picturesque places with a miniature sketch of professional quality. There was only one drawback to this match. She was twenty-three so Uncle Bob could have been her father. He had been born in the same year as C.O., so was forty-five.

The valuable bachelor uncles from India had already given Dulce and me our bicycles. Mother was very nervous about us going out on them and would have been much more so if she could have witnessed some of our lucky escapes. Dulce's first bike was a Raleigh and mine was a Rudge-Whitworth; not quite so dear, still £7 was much more than I could ever expect to earn. We got sixpence a week pocket-money until we were twelve and after that one shilling. I once complained that Dulce had a habit of asking, after we were in bed, 'Kinny, if you had ninepence what would you do with it?' By the time I had considered the dazzling possibilities she had always fallen asleep.

Ethel Stangoe helped us to learn to ride the bikes in the garden. She never shirked a painful duty. We took them to Southsea and went to Portchester Castle, from which Henry V set out for Agincourt. Two of the Misses Harrington went with us. At Pitlochry there were now signs of alternative transport. The puddles up by the turning to Cluny Bridge, where travellers often halted, were now veiled by a liquid that smelt odd and resembled the colours of the rainbow. There was a new sign, '10. MPH.' We read it as 'Eeomph' and could not think what it meant.

The highlight of my year, before Uncle Ed went back to India, was a visit to the New Theatre at Oxford to see *The Merchant of Venice* performed by the Frank Benson Company. To me, after nothing but the silly pantos, it was a revelation. Mother noticed my rapt attention. 'Her love for anything dramatic was very marked, and this treat gave her a more intense delight than could have been expected in so young a child.' The fancy dress dance season opened. The four Drivers had been photographed in their costumes, the boys as gondoliers, Sylvia and Cynthia as fairies. They had wings and wands with stars on the top. There was a huge enlargement of the group in the place of honour in the photographer's in St Giles's. I longed for a wand. I got one, though not quite as good as the Drivers'. I had been invited to perform in Dulce's school play. I was to be one of the pease-blossom fairies in *The Princess and the Pea*. The twin Dowsons (children of Rosina Filippi, a real actress) were green peas. They had what must have been most uncomfortable costumes, with large pods enclosing peas as big as tennis balls, extending quite a foot above their heads. We met at 77 Banbury Road and had to sing while a mistress hammered out the tune on an upright piano.

> When all the palace gates are shut
> And turned is every key,
> Then all we goblin elves come out
> For sprites of the night are we.

Nana said that if I asked again when she was going to make my fairy dress she would never make it. That quietened me. But I thought she would, really, as it was to be used again for the Alingtons' ball at Summerfields.

Dulce was going as 'Winter', a pretty dress with bunches of holly, and cotton-wool snowballs powdered with glitter. Mr Fletcher's charming little boy Reggie went as a Chinaman.* He took off his hat and showed me how his pigtail was fastened inside. But suddenly all my pleasure was turned to horror. There was a Mephisto twirling his moustachios and looking at me. I knew he was not really the one and only Satan, but he might be a lesser one.

The great night of the school play came and I was much dashed that I got no praise for my singing. My parents had not heard me. They had wanted to hear my voice above all the rest. So I simply bawled when we came to performance next year and got scolded for this from the school staff. You could not do right.

At last, on December 16th, 1905, my father was elected to the Chichele chair. It had been founded by the Royal Commission of 1852 so had not the antiquity or prestige of the Regius Professorship of Modern History held in succession by Stubbs, Freeman and Froude. But he had served as long as Jacob for Rachel. Montagu Burrows had been elected two years after my father had been born, and had already, when they first met, been almost past work owing to deafness, but not at all past interest in the affairs of the University, college and city. There were much more out-standing cases of leading University officials who ought to have retired. Even when one of them chased a student round the Radcliffe Camera with an open razor, there was no machinery by which he could be declared redundant.

I think this the moment to begin to allude to my father as 'Prof' which we soon did for ever. Also, Brother, after passing through several other *petits noms*, became Chas. It was most inconvenient that we had an Uncle Charlie in the family, and then three C. Omans. Presently, my father was beginning to get slips from the editors of magazines regretting that they could not publish his sonnets. I had signed myself just C. Oman, when sending them in. There was not much Women's Lib. in my early days. Before the publication of her first book by our beloved Charlotte M. Yonge, a family conclave had decided that it was unthinkable that she should accept remuneration unless her earnings were devoted to the support of some good object. The problem did not really arise until she had an unexpected success with *The Heir of Redcliffe*. She then gladly agreed that her profits should equip a missionary ship.

---

* C. R. L. Fletcher lost two of his three sons, including Reggie, in the 1914–18 War.

Mother went to her first Anti-Woman's Suffrage meeting in 1905. She had been 'Mama' for us always—but pronounced as if it were spelt 'Marmar'. Chas says that he does not remember when we began to call him so, but is quite clear that it was after the Napiers' dog.

Prof:

1906–1908

I

THERE WAS NO QUESTION OF US MISSING ARTHUR EVANS'S TWELFTH Night party in 1906. This year he gave us a conjuror, and what was called a Cotillon. Moreover, it was a Ragusan Cotillon. All the clever little favours came from Ragusa where he had once been in prison and written notes in his blood. His parties were generally considered the most original, and except for the Alingtons', who had the premises of Summer-fields preparatory school at their disposal in the holidays, the largest. I only once had to watch from the nursery window (with a very sore throat) while the wagonette which had picked up the Trevelyans, halted to collect Dulce, for Boar's Hill.

Elections were in progress this New Year. Prof nominated Sir William Anson for one of the two University seats. In the city, Lord Valentia was returned again. A change had come over our nursery scene. Dr Mallam had died. He had been a leading figure under the famous Acland in the typhoid and influenza epidemic of 1854. His successor had to be sent for quite soon. Dr Proudfoot was much younger though he seemed to us quite old too. He had an invigorating manner and a wife who had been a hospital nurse. When my mother congratulated her on the birth of a son, she replied, 'A great responsibility.' But mother thoroughly approved of Dr Proudfoot who was a medical officer to our local Yeomanry and a fine figure of a man in uniform.

The parents did their longest Peninsular tour this spring. In Madrid they found that General Arteche had died. Captain Figueras received Professor Oman at the War Office. They visited Madrid, Badajos, Albuera, Lisbon, Cintra, Bussaco, Almeida. A very slow mule-carriage deposited them at Fuentes d'Oñoro, too late on a wet evening to see the battlefield. They went on to Salamanca. Their travelling after this became slightly exasperating. They were unable to get out at Valladolid as their train simply thundered through. On their last lap, from San Sebastian, they endured a bitter cold wait, and dared not dine before the Paris train came in, very late in the end, and very full, at ten twenty. They had to get breakfast in Paris while they waited for a room to be vacated at the Hotel Normandy.

I was now nearly nine and going to Miss Batty's at the opening of the summer term. My mother, noticing my interest in portraits, took me to a Historical Portraits Exhibition on my last morning at home. This was handsome, for I had caused disappointment on my first visit to the National Gallery. My favourite picture had been the Cherub Choir by Sir Joshua Reynolds. This was simply because I had it in silver on the cover of my best hymn book; but I could not explain.

Almost at once, at Miss Batty's, I had shaming experiences. One of the junior mistresses asked me to go out into the hall and get the right time. Now, as I was no good at figures, I had reached school age without having learnt to read the clock. I tugged up a hall chair and removed the large clock standing on a high bracket. When I got back into the school-room I held it up in front of me for the mistress to see for herself. I do not know what was her expression as I could not see over the clock. I was much in awe of Ethel Madan, our head girl. I was sent upstairs to ask for some more exercise books. I could see a stack of them in an open cupboard. 'Carola! Would it not be better for you to ask the head girl to give them to you?'

I already knew some of the pupils, from having sung in the chorus in the school play. The Dowsons wore bonnets. They had emerged from scarlet fever with hair cropped like boys. They were very charming and did as little work as possible. They were not identical twins. Fanny was the eldest but smaller than Rosie. The odd thing was that, although their mother was a famous actress, they could not act at all. Later Rosie appeared on the stage with success. They had two brothers who went to Lynams, later the Dragon School, nearby, and used to walk past our school on stilts making ugly faces at the windows. Miss Batty's had moved to 12 Park Crescent. It meant a slightly longer walk, but now that we had the bikes a solution was found. Francis, the Dean's verger, from the cathedral, accompanied the Driver girls on bicycles. It was quite easy for them to halt in St Giles's and take us on. Someone who had not got it quite right said it was so touching to see the dear old Canon bicycling every morning to their school with his four little daughters.*

Miss Batty's was taking distinguished outsiders now. We had a Siamese princess. She was asked if she would like to know the boys who looked like her who were at Lynams. She said, 'They are my cousins.' We understood, with interst, that she would marry one of them. She was generally dressed in a sailor suit, which was not becoming, and when she came to tea, liked chocolate biscuits and sardines. The three Cannans qualified as University as their father was Secretary to the Delegates of the Clarendon Press. Like our father, he was a friend of Rudyard Kipling and Quiller Couch. The Cannans' mother was Scottish and tiny, and rather fierce. I think it was Uncle Turney who commented, 'At that table the clash of the foils is seldom absent.' But I liked Mr Cannan very much because he knew about books, and the girls told me he had asked when was I coming to lunch again. They were very bossy, because they had holidays at the very spot where Prince Charlie had landed, and knew Lochiel.

We had a White Russian, very handsome and dashing and much bigger than us, though about our age. Her father was an expert on villeinage. He looked like a Russian bear and had fled his native land because he was too liberal. Later his native land became too liberal for him. With so many new companions perhaps it was not surprising that I had twenty-six for my birthday party. Or were we launching out a little because now we had a Professor in the study? Certainly, for June 20th this year he gave mother a diamond pendant.

'To Miss Smith's wedding', she wrote down, after recording the decorous delight of the Madans' hay party. There were seven Misses Smith, all the daughters of A. L. Smith of Balliol and one of them married happily nearly every year. They had a very high standard of placid blonde good looks and intelligence.

The Millais, one of whom had been a co-bridesmaid with Dulce at Eddy Earle's wedding, had, I suppose, taken a lease of what we called Fonab Castle. This was a large mid-Victorian building belonging to 'Laird Sandeman' couched on a wooded hill above the river. He owned all Portnacraig. We admired the castle hugely which was just the right

---

* Francis had started as a footman at Dean Liddell's and the Liddell girls taught him Latin. He also worked as Assistant Librarian in Christ Church Library. He survived to the age of ninety-seven, and Sylvia Driver took her son Bernard to see him after 1930. She had married Ralph Symonds.

word. The parents went to lunch there and we went to tea and fished with the little Millais and went in the Fonab boat across the river to the Highland Games. These were a cause of great interest as we knew so many of the competitors; but you really got too much for your money. The Games went on for hours and hours, wet or fine, and the hillside seats were hard. Tossing the caber was worth watching but pipers strutting up and down making screeching noises were only surpassed in similarity by groups dancing the sword dance and reels, and flings and Strathspeys. And though I tried to live this down, from the first moment I heard them, the sound of the bagpipes made me tremble.

Mother evidently shared our feeling of wanting to take something from Perthshire back to Oxford. In preparation for making a collection of ferns, this year, she brought a trowel and a pair of pearl-grey gauntlet gloves. Ferns seemed reluctant to co-operate. Their roots seemed to go right down to Australia. I never saw a fern at 39.

We must have been launching out. We were getting a pony and a puppy. The story of the Shetland pony was unsatisfactory. Chas, mounted, looked so like a Little Lord Fauntleroy that mother arranged to buy 'Moosie'. He was to be sent down to 39 and Chas would ride him and mother would take all of us out in a pony cart. He would live at the Lamb and Flag with Mr Rhodes. But we were not to be allowed even this little bit of splendour.

Dulce was now considered old enough to be given what our parents believed the greatest treat in the world—foreign travel. In preparation for a week's absence from Great Britain, she was taken to the dentist, and I was taken along and had an extraction. I suppose the gag, slipped in at the last moment must have been too large. 'Open! Open!' I always reckon ovaries, eye-balls and nipples as highest-ranking agonizers but never have I known such pain as that jaw being forced open too wide. I could not cry out; firm hands restrained my struggles. All I could do was to gulp in as much as possible of the gas and pass out. When I came to, the Roman Emperors were flashing past outside the Sheldonian: tears were running down my face and my limbs felt as if I had walked a hundred miles. I did not complain, but after this experience I would endure a swollen face sooner than ask to go to the dentist. It was only at the end of this nightmare that I realised Dr Proudfoot was going to take us all home in his motor. Mother had never been in one before.

She set out for France under a disadvantage. A midge bite on her cheek had caused wide infection. Dr Proudfoot came daily for a week. This was the moment when it was announced that the Shetland pony was on his way from Scotland.

The parents gave Dulce the full treatment. They took her to the Tuileries gardens, to the English church on Sunday morning and Versailles in the afternoon, to the Invalides, Nôtre Dame, the Louvre, Les Halles, the Carnavalet and St Eustache. They only went into a shop twice and really on the second occasion because it was so wet. It was boring for the parents not to be able to go out to dine, and it was worse for Dulce who had to write down every night what she had seen. ('Napoleon's tomb is made of palfreys.') She had not been told anything about what she was going to see, I cannot imagine why. She returned home gladly as she was feeling so bad. Nana competitively claimed that both Chas and I were also feeling bad. It was a Saturday night; Dr Proudfoot came on Monday. While he was giving instructions to Nana, who looked furious, Dulce whispered, 'He says we've both got small-pox.' I knew about small-pox from my favourite reading—Miss Strickland's *Lives of the Queens of England*. It was a killer in their nurseries. I was most interested. 'Shall we die?' I cannot remember that I felt the least fear.

We had not got small-pox, but we had both got chicken-pox. I was soon rid of it but Dulce was much worse. Mother took to her bed. Chas took to his bed. A message came from the Lamb and Flag that the pony was there. He was brought round to the door so that we could see him, and presently I was allowed to go out on him. Chas got as far as Port Meadow on him twice before he developed chicken-pox and was 'very ill'. Gradually Dulce went out on Moosie and mother did drive Dulce and me in the dog-cart. We were all pronounced out of quarantine the day before Uncle Bob and Aunt Bee arrived for their farewell visit before returning to India. Aunt Bee was expecting a baby in May but that was kept a dead secret.

The weather was now full cold and Prof, tired and rather disgruntled, was grateful when he arrived at Oxford station after dark, to find old Bargus and his cab waiting. His first experiences of lecturing as a professor had been depressing. There was a tiresome old slogan 'Professor's lectures are no good for schools'. He was continuing to give discourses of the same type and scope as those which he had delivered as a tutor but his audiences had thinned. He was at the same time offering some specialist ones which could only attract enthusiasts. They were as well attended as ever. He found it heartbreaking, when he knew he was giving of his best and on topics on which he was a recognised authority, that he now had so few listeners.

Fortunately a new interest in history was stirring in Oxford. There had been a Pageant at Warwick this summer; now there was to be an Oxford Pageant, after the University went down for the Long Vacation. The name of 'Mr Lascelles' began to be heard. His real surname was Stevens and he was the son of a clergyman, but he was Frank Lascelles professionally and Pageant Master of the forthcoming great experiment. Almost everyone we knew at school was taking part. The three Cannans had themselves photographed with their Nana all dressed as attendants on St Frideswide. Mr Ffoulkes, a protégé of Lord Dillon, Curator of the Tower Armouries, was to be War in a real suit of armour, and the Gotches and Dorothy Warren were Bacchus and his crew. Prof was writing an episode very humorous—Friar Bacon. Evelyn Hitchens and Sylvia Driver had Georgian dresses with panniers, in which to drive in on a coach to St Giles's Fair. There was a handsome retired regular army colonel who so closely resembled Charles I that he had to grow his hair shoulder-long and travel all over England to oblige while the pageant craze lasted. By a happy chance, Mrs Driver, who was cast for Henrietta Maria, although too tall, was strikingly like the queen's statue facing that of Charles I which we admired every time we passed through the echoing tunnel from Canterbury quadrangle into St John's gardens. Chas was invited to be Richard Cœur de Lion, born at Beaumont Palace, and I was to be Princess Elizabeth, daughter of Charles I. I was a size larger than Cynthia Driver whose glowing dark complexion and long dark curls made her a little Charles II to the life. I do not know why we were forbidden to perform, and although later we did act in several pageants, the disappointment rankled. Prof, and Beatrice's father, were on committees. Mr Lascelles haunted 39. Dulce had a theory that mother could not allow us to act because she had a weak heart. Chas puts it down to Nana.

The only thoroughly good thing that entered our life that winter was the dog Patch. I must say I think Mr Doyle did us proud. He was a man of divers and unusual attainments, even for a Fellow of All Souls. He had published volumes on the early history of the American colonies, had been annually appointed Librarian of Codrington under the old rules, and had long been a leader of the college Sunday country walks. But what he liked to talk about was horses and dogs. He had won the Derby; he had bred countless pedigree fox-terriers. He lived a very long way from us at a house called Pendarron, Crickhowell. Prof had stayed with him several times and sent letters describing an absolutely ideal domicile. The views over the Grinary above its junction with the Usk were majestic and beyond came the mountains of Glamorganshire. The very sound of Patch's birth-place sounded beautiful beyond compare. Mr Doyle had twenty fox terriers in kennels at his house and many more puppies, boarded in farms, who knew his step. The excitement when we heard that Patch was on his way defied orders for bed. At last we heard the cab from the station draw up, and old Bargus staggering in with something heavy which he set down in the hall. We came tumbling downstairs in our nightgear shouting his name. The little dog put his nose out of the black hole which had been his fate since he left the wide valleys of Brecon. He decided that there were worse things to come and went back again. But we had seen enough to know that he was a little prince. He was a black and white smooth-coated fox-terrier, the breed shown in advertisements of His Master's Voice. But that dog, although he had his head cocked on one side in typical fox-terrier style, was a scrubby affair compared with ours, short-legged and badly marked. Patch was persuaded to emerge and be admired, and was soon offered a meal and notably a long drink after his long journey, and put in his new basket to dream. He must have been house-trained and lead-trained and he could walk to heel and obey orders such as 'Sit' and 'Away ye go'. He had never been fed at table so never asked for bits. He was always cheerful, ready for anything, and never bit any of his young tormentors. If he did not exactly understand what we wanted he put his head on one side. He soon became quite accustomed to photographers, amateur and professional.

I think Patch had, upon the whole, a happy life. He was put out into St Giles's regularly, not our small garden. 'Dog Green' St Giles's had a large and varied dogs' club at which he sometimes met his cousin Sam Trevelyan from as far as Marston Ferry Road. That was quite country, and Sam used to swim across to a neighbouring farm and accomplish havoc for which the Trevelyans' father got bills including the eggs which hens would have laid if Sam had not demolished them. Sam was, naturally, also a Doyle dog, but in our opinion inferior. I suppose they had asked for a liver and white. He was much heavier. It must not be shirked that fox-terriers fought. We heard that the cabbies on the rank outside laid bets on matches between Patch and Sam. But I think these must have been rather jousts than fights for we never had to summon a vet. There was not much development behind Wellington Square as yet and I have no doubt that Patch had a full and interesting life, though not in the class of society to which he had been accustomed. There was little traffic as yet in front of our windows, but St Giles's must not be mistaken for the

G

mountains of Glamorgan. Patch got run over only once, within a few weeks of his coming to us. Jack Ward, on leave at 40 St Giles's, went over him and said he would do. Anyway, at this anxious moment, our poor mother was in bed with influenza.

Agnes Burrows and I had both been wasps in the chorus at the school play this year. Nana, who always wanted us to be different said I should get pneumonia when she saw the low square-cut bodice and short sleeves of the pattern for the wasp's costume. So I was the only wasp with a gold tinsel yoke and long sleeves, and got into trouble with the Queen Wasp. 'Who said you might do that?' 'Impudent little monkey, don't answer her,' said Nana, so I did not answer though I knew that was rude. Nana's comments on our school-mates were always embarrassing. 'Who's the mad child?' she audibly enquired on another occasion. I knew that this child was a descendant of Queen Elizabeth's favourite, the Earl of Leicester. This produced an instant *volte face*. The aristocracy were allowed to be mad.

The Eales family consisted of four girls and one boy. The two youngest girls looked Burmese. There was no mystery about this. Their grandfather had married a Burmese. Gracie had a voice 'like milk chocolate', said observant Beatrice.

Someone said to Agnes, who was a very substantial but sensitive child, that he would not care for a sting from her. She was one of the cases of an outstandingly plain child who turns out a beautiful girl. Her father said she reminded him of the duchess in *Alice in Wonderland* so Duchess was her nick-name. The Burrows' parents arrived from Ceylon this spring. When the old Professor had died, they had inherited 9 Norham Gardens, in the Parks. Nana Pugh who had been looking after Brocas and Agnes, stayed on, but inevitably Mr Burrows had to complain that Brocas had been given all the wrong instructions about his riding, and a château near Compiègne was leased so that Agnes might learn to speak French properly. The Trevelyans were asked to stay. I wished that it had been us. After their first summer there her father reported that Agnes was chattering French like a monkey. Those of us who knew her knew that she always spoke very slowly. Still, she had obviously gained confidence. Our French lessons at Miss Batty's were tacitly recognised to be undistinguished and needing outside augmentation. It was the only class at which we were inattentive and rather unruly. The girls amongst us who spoke French well were those of mixed blood, or those who had lived in France, or those whose mother had a French maid. But we had a German mistress who was an Alsatian, in every sense. She was a devoted daughter of Imperial Germany. She disliked the French, and the English; but she was a disciplinarian and could teach. At Miss Batty's you could take Latin or German. I needed Latin all the rest of my life, but I was told to take German, and we went to war with that country in 1914 and 1939. I longed to know what was the meaning of the large Gothic script texts in white ink on sage-green paper exhibited on the walls of our class-rooms. *'Est Modus In Rebus'*. *'Festina Lente'*.

II

In January 1907 we heard that Great-Aunt Emily had died. She was only a half sister of Bamama, but this death was to make a difference to us. To begin with, the Omans had to fail for a dinner party in London with the Pembers. The black-edged paper was brought forth and this time was to stay for the rest of our lives at 39. Fortunately one of the amenities of the Athenaeum Club was that Prof could get mourning paper for every stage of bereavement. Our St Giles's writing paper had the Oman crest upon it, *'Homo Sum'* above a warrior in a helmet, seeing stars.

For my birthday I got riding lessons with Mr Rhodes. Mother was in bed again most of Lent but set off bravely for Easter in Italy. Chas, on attaining the age of six, got a tricycle and silkworms. He was now to be painted life-size in water-colours by an artist in Park Town called Mr Carline. I was allowed a preview and thought this one of the most beautiful works of art I had ever seen. Chas was represented in a black velvet suit and point lace, surely an inappropriate costume for a woodland glade. He had golden curls and carried an ancestral walking stick of 1860 date. He was given a wistful heart-shaped face, but rosy cheeks; he was almost unrecognisable. I was soon at work on a full-length portrait of Cynthia Driver. When our father died, Chas took his Fauntleroy unlikeness out into the garden and burnt it. But he had reckoned without me. I sent him as Christmas card that year a photograph of a very good time-exposure, taken by me when the picture hung, as it always had, over our mother's desk in the drawing-room. Most of the little boys of our acquaintance wore fancy suits. Ralph was photographed looking very winning in one. Geoffrey Madan had one with an oyster brocade waistcoat in which he had been a page at a wedding. He had long auburn curls and a rose-leaf complexion, and to see him gravely doing up the many buttons of the gaiters worn by his little sister Beatrice was a generally admired finish to a winter party. There was jubilation when his mother called in July to say that he had won the first King's scholarship at Eton.

The Pageant loomed heavily over Oxford and as the end of term drew near, we were taken repeatedly to rehearsals. Mr Lascelles had chosen as his site a water-girt meadow between the two branches of the Cherwell. Glimpses could be seen of two colleges, Christ Church and Merton, but nothing of Magdalen, the owners whose college school afterwards adapted the pageant ground for cricket. The approaches by boat and barge down the river could be used in several episodes. Curiously, as it seemed to our family, academic circles could not be persuaded to take an active interest in the Pageant. Only three well-known authors undertook to write and supervise a scene—Arthur Godley of Magdalen who concealed skill as the greatest University comic poet of his generation beneath a most melancholy visage, Walter Raleigh, and Miss Wordsworth first Principal of Lady Margaret Hall. We already knew her and she was celebrated for her annual *revues* at her college always attended by our parents. She had been once to Miss Batty's to speak to us in Literature hour. She was a little lady who gave an immense impression of age, but rather naïve, though enterprising. She once earnestly enquired from one of our mother's friends whether the cushion offered to her was truly comfortable. It was not. 'Oh dear!' she sighed, 'and I had put three of my old muffs in it." The thought of three undigested muffs in a single cushion surprised Mrs Reginald Poole.

Lascelles, with the aid of Charles Cannan, had collected valuable outside collaborators. Robert Bridges wrote the Prologue, Laurence Binyon, Laurence Housman, Stanley Weyman, all devised typical contributions. There was a noisy popular representation of the Town and Gown riot on Saint Scholastica's Day, February 20th, 1353. Actually, the Town was the most enthusiastic supporter of the Pageant. As rehearsals increased it was nothing strange to find familiar assistants in well-known shops performing their duties attired as Ancient Britons, Cavaliers, and even as one of the Seven Deadly Sins. (They came in the 'Masque of the Mediaeval Curriculum'.) There was a Druid who always bicycled, smoking an anachronistic pipe. An elderly clergyman was so taken with his robes as the Anglo-Saxon archbishop who crowned King Harold Harefoot that he sometimes wore these long after the Pageant was over.

We had rather a wet week for the Pageant. We were taken to four rehearsals and two performances. The heavens generally opened with the

Civil Wars. People said it was all the guns firing. Now at last everyone knew why the Parks at Oxford were so called. They had been the Gun Parks in the Civil War. There were some accidents at the Pageant. Friar Bacon, on his motor-cycle, skidded into the river. He had told his scout to come down as soon as the Examination Results were pinned up outside the Schools. He afterwards said that as he arose from what might have been a watery grave, dashing his hair out of his eyes, he heard his loyal henchman announcing, 'YOU'VE GOT A THIRD, SIR.' Later this excellent humorist became a best-selling novelist under the pseudonym of Dornford Yates.

There was a daring episode of King Henry II, a married man, wooing Fair Rosamond before she retired stricken with remorse to take the veil in Godstow Priory. 'Cuckoo' York-Powell was Fair Rosamond and she had the most beautiful long red hair. But it was decreed that she must wear a rose-pink robe which swore most horribly with her greatest asset. There was a handsome young baronet playing Henry II, mounted on a fiery steed, but this animal, a stern moralist, always shied at the sight of poor Rosamond who had to walk along the river-banks shedding rose-petals. 'Oh dear! Missed her again.'

'Mr Mark Twain, from America' had combined attendance to receive an honorary degree with an appearance at the Pageant. He came to lunch the same day as Rudyard Kipling and gave me a copy of one of his books, *The Prince and the Pauper*. Mr Kipling, on a later visit, gave us a copy of *Puck of Pook's Hill* with a poem in his own script on the front page. He dipped his thumb in the ink-bottle and made a firm impression under his printed name as author which he labelled 'R.K. His Mark'. It might have been imagined that when we had taken all our nearest and dearest to the Pageant, and sent all our staff, and the week was over, that we had seen the last of it. But another new invention awaited us—a Cinematograph. Uncle Charlie had scented that there was prestige in our father's connection with Oxford's latest entertainment. He came for the day. Bamama came to stay. It was hoped she would be edified by the news that both her grand-daughters had been top of their forms in the school examinations. Chas was now being taken to a little day-school, but his education was impeded by Nana's determination that he should never catch anything. She returned pretty often tugging him home. 'Measles at the School!' was sometimes quite a false alarm. She dosed us regularly, but I never saw a clinical thermometer in our nursery, or indeed in any hands but those of Dr Proudfoot, until I went as a part-time war-time probationer to the

Radcliffe Infirmary. She put ammonia in the piping hot water when she washed our hair. We all got red eyes and howled. Mother did discover and stop that.

With the *Grand Finale* of the Great Oxford Pageant, Frank Lascelles did not vanish from our world. He had discovered his *métier*. We went at his invitation to pageants at St Albans, Bath and Cheltenham. We always got the royal box. His greatest venture was the London Pageant in 1911. For that Prof contributed two episodes—Wat Tyler's revolt (with a romantic child-Richard II), and a much earlier piece of London's history, the naval triumph of the Emperor Carausius. For some unexplained reason efforts to bring Rome into the Home in Great Britain are always inordinately popular.

III

Bamama had been for two years peacefully settled in her new larger Cheltenham home. We were sent to stay with her in relays. I was almost due on July 22nd when a telegram came saying that she had been taken ill. Mother got to Ablington by tea-time; Prof, from London, followed at six p.m. Bamama was still conscious, and asked if Carola had come. She was told that term was not quite over, but I would be coming. She never spoke again. Mother went back to Oxford, but her son stayed with the old lady. She became moaning and restless, waving away food. He sat with her hand in his all one afternoon.

Thinking of old far-off happy things of forty years ago that I thought I had quite forgotten. A little song she wrote for me when I was five came back to me particularly. I had not thought of it for these thirty years, I am sure. And the treat that I got for my first prize at Miss Hills', and how I was taken round Paris when I was seven. I do wish she could give me a coherent word or two. We have said things to each other sometimes that we had better not have said, and now we can say nothing at all.

She grew quieter but Dr Blakeney said it was the quiet of exhaustion tending towards coma. Dr Kirkland, a Scottish second opinion, confirmed that there had been a seizure and said he did not like the state of her heart. A night nurse came in. Bamama died peacefully on Saturday 27th and

mother went over to Cheltenham again and to Winchester to make
arrangements for Bamama's burial beside her husband at the cemetery on
the hill at Leckhampton. It was the Long Vacation now but Professor
Margoliouth attended, Alfred Peile, Henry Hardy, the Rivoiras and many
Cheltenham friends. We were sent ahead to Scotland. Portnacraig was
exciting this year. This was due to a breach in the Blair Athole reservoir.
The very Craig itself nearly disappeared when the Tummel rose eleven feet
in one night. Down on the flood came victims—sheep, saplings, pens and
kennels. A fisherman caught on the island below Fonab had an uncomfortable night up a tree. Prof and Dulce watched while a local Hercules
threw him food-parcels from the bank.

On the wishing-stone overlooking the Queen's View in Killiecrankie
this year Chas wished for a hundred fox-terriers. Mr Doyle had died
while we were in Scotland.

'Saw house in South Parks Road,' wrote mother. Now the significance
of the death of Great-Aunt Emily became apparent. She had been the
childless widow of a collector on a much wider scale than Bamama, and
our parents had to prepare to house or dismiss the contents of two
establishments. No less than five vans left Ablington before October.
Some of the contents must have gone to warehouses for storage. We were
all brought down to Cheltenham and had rather a good time of it in
golden autumn weather. There were greenhouses from which luscious fruit,
particularly white grapes, were sent up to the house. We went out every
day in Bamama's open carriage, and at the shops tradesmen came to their
doors with notebooks in hand to take orders. I had a good deal of experience
of that Victoria from drives with Bamama. It had the narrowest imaginable seat back to the horses and when we went round corners smartly I
had to hold on with both hands in the position for a backward somersault
on Agnes Burrows's trapeze. The old lady, having her nap under a fringed
parasol, had no idea whether I was still there or not. Bamama had kept
at least one outsize dog. I fear this must have been as a status symbol as she
was far past walks. Her Persian cattery had to be disposed of. Father
insisted on Katinka, a prize winning kitten, coming to Oxford, 'but
either by mischance or blame' as Milton puts it, she did not long survive.

It was a triumph that all the two loads of antique porcelain arrived
intact; but there was a disappointment in connection with these. In
Perth, in 1902, between trains, Prof had gone to a sale and bought two
gold-anchor Chelsea plates with figures in their centres, for £5. Bamama
and her experts had congratulated him on a real bargain. 'Watteau subjects

were rare.' He had never doubted that her collection, which was one of
the subjects on which they could converse amicably, would now come to
him. But her Will, executed on New Year's Day 1902 left all (which now
included the Anderson Rose windfall) to her three grandchildren. Her
son got only a life-interest. He wrote to his wife that this was the end of
his interest in antique porcelain. There were other surprises. There was a
brother, Uncle Alfred Chadwick, whom we had never seen. Bamama and
he had not been on speaking terms for some years though they sent one
another birthday gifts having ascertained the value of the last received. The
parents soon set off for Hastings and we duly made the acquaintance of our
new relatives. Uncle Alfred had sparkling blue eyes and looked rather
frighteningly like his late sister. I think there was a son and daughter
abroad: there were two daughters at home. He was a widower. Winnie was
a coloratura mezzo-soprano and a poetess. Joyce Chadwyck Chadwick
('so that she need never lose the name') worshipped at the shrine of
Rudyard Kipling. They did not know any young men as there were none
in Hastings and they had no mother to give dances for them.

We were all being sent to a new dancing-class. The Girls High School
one could not take boys. Chas was now old enough to dance (but did
not want to). The new class was not nearly as well housed or lively as
the one at the High School. It was held in Taphouse's Rooms and
Madame Micheu and her daughter, Mademoiselle Pelissier came down
from London. The sessions started with an intimidating grand march in
which your deportment was mercilessly studied. Then came Being
Presented at Court—to soft music. This entailed mincing up, one by one,
to curtsey and kiss the hand of Madame, who did look remarkably like
Queen Victoria. There were also high-falutin exercises to make you
graceful: 'I smell a little flower!' Madame Micheu was rather rude and
poked one with a fan in a part of our anatomy as yet undeveloped, crying
'Out! Out!' and lower down, 'In! In!' I was rather pleased when Dulce's
flannel petticoat fell off one day. It was entirely her own fault as she should
have stepped out of it when Ethel had unfastened it in the nursery at
home; but Dulce did not get the blame. The Cannans had a photograph
of their mother in feathers and a train looking very cold in a low dress,
being presented at Court on her marriage. Joan Evans was just old enough
to go as a débutante in 1913 with a train that had three and a half yards on
the floor, but Madame Micheu's alarming instructions were unnecessary
for most uf us. There were no more evening Courts after the war for some
years. Anyway, very few daughters of Oxford Professors had gone to

them. They had their own society in University circles and in Edwardian days fashionable high-life had been 'fast'.

Somehow the story reached the parents that we were borrowing from Ethel. There was nothing under-hand about it. Even Chas now had his comics, depicting the antics of Sailor Sam and his penguins and Buster Brown. But we went to the newsagent having forgotten our pennies. There was a major show-down on the utter iniquity of debt and Prof was brought from the study to thunder it forth. It made a great impression on me. I never owed again.

The parents paid their household books weekly, mostly in the covered market. It was a favourite expedition for our mother, who had many friends amongst the tradesmen, but Chas whom she had begun to take with her regularly found it dull, except for the butchers which was horrible.

On October 20th, Mother came out boldly with 'went to look at Frewin Hall'. A month later two more visits were paid. But with the beginning of November tragedy intervened. A telegram came from Aunt Al saying that Grandmother Maclagan was taken ill. Father came up to the night-nursery as we were being prepared for bed to tell us that we had lost another grandmother. We had hardly seen her. She had been childish for ten years. A most uncomfortable interview ended with Prof saying, 'Well, your Aunt Al is with her. They will be able to have a good cry together.' That did frighten us. We had never seen our mother cry. Poor mother travelled up by night for the funeral in Edinburgh. On her return Uncle Phil came with her and was taken to see Frewin Hall.

VI

Frewin:

1908–1910

I

THERE WAS NEVER ANY CHANCE OF US BUYING FREWIN HALL. IT HAD belonged to Brasenose College since 1580. By New Year 1908 it had stood empty for seven years. Dr Heberdon, who had taken a lease from Dr Shadwell, who had gone off to become Provost of Oriel, had at last decided against retiring there. Shadwell had been an Oxford eccentric. He had rebuilt the west wing and added a sundial with what was called a chronogram to his façade. This read—

FREVVINI CAROLUS LAETAT
SHADVVELLIVS AVLAM

People who knew said that he had not got it quite right. Instead of saying that Frewin Hall delighted Charles Shadwell, it was saying that he delighted Frewin Hall. There was no doubt that he had loved the house, and particularly his spacious lawn. If he detected a weed he would drop a massive bunch of keys as an order that it be instantly removed.

There were other families going over the house. By an odd chance, Mr George Boyce Allen from New South Wales, with six children, had been recommended to look at it. He had a large enough family, but said it would require as many housemaids. He took 145 Woodstock Road, a large modern villa in which I spent some of the happiest hours of my youthful life. His third daughter, Janet Dundas, was coming to Miss Batty's.

Frewin Hall was said to have five staircases, five halls and seven front doors. This was an exaggeration, but there was an imposing entrance by which you could drive in, from the east side of New Inn Hall Street, and after that two large doors into the garden, as well as what we used as the front door, which came at the end of a passage straight off Cornmarket Street. This finished at an attractive little wooden door with a central wicket surmounted by the date 1666—the year in which London had been burnt like a bundle of sticks. You dived through it and found yourself in a little quadrangle, with a massive front door straight ahead, another lesser door (servants' entrance) on the right, and opposite that a smaller door, beside a window, from which Miss Felicia Skene had been used to distribute potions to the needy. Old Miss Annie Symonds, Ralph's aunt, heard with relief that we had a second entrance from New Inn Hall Street. The one off the Cornmarket led to nothing else except the premises of the Oxford Union Society. If we used that we might meet under-graduates. These she evidently looked upon as being, one and all, ravening wolves. We were well accustomed to them as several of mother's sixty-one first cousins were now sending sons and nephews to Oxford. The Union passage was echoing and rather creepy after dark, but I never heard of anything untoward happening in it. I regret to say that we usually biked up it, though not sitting on the saddle. I did see a shocking undergraduate about this time, though. We were in a cab with the two tiny little Walkers of Queen's, going to drop them after a party. They were tiny because their mother, as a widow had married someone tiny, and she was so small, anyway, that she used to startle audiences by saying, 'My husband used to pick me up in his arms and stand me on the mantelpiece. Not you, Edward.' Nettie and Drummond were older than us but nothing like so solid. (Drummy afterwards found his vocation as cox of the University boat.) We were just passing St Mary's that night when I heard and saw an undergraduate. He was firmly attached to the railings by the tails of his club dress coat. His face was shining red but he looked dreadfully ill and he was making strange noises. 'An undergraduate,' said Nettie, peeping out. 'Dead drunk. Disgusting.' I think perhaps he cannot have been a very favourable specimen or his boon companions would not have left him, literally in such a fix.

Nobody whom we knew had been sent down from Oxford for drinking, or indeed any other cause, though we did meet one or two at other houses. The old pantomime of the mock funeral, with a string of cabs to the station and deep mourning, still persisted. When some of the rude boys flooded the entrance to their tutor's rooms at New College with red paint, so that Joseph should have to pass through the Red Sea, I think all convicted were sent down; but not for ever.

The New Year of 1908 was remarkably cold again. Uncle Phil took

Dulce to Port Meadow to teach her to skate. Mrs Madan and Miss Hayter had been escorted over Frewin Hall and the electricians had come in, but on March 15th snowstorms were still holding up all work. Mrs Whiteman, Bamama's superb cook, arrived on quarter-day. I am astonished, when I look at mother's diaries and letters, to see how often the parents went out and how much entertaining they did—luncheons, teas and dinner parties. The colleges had always had a high standard of *cuisine*. Now we had Mrs Whiteman, mother had only to inform her, and order, on a little slate. Even at 39 we had been able to manage dinner parties for sixteen for a very special occasion, as Aunt Bee had observed. With our newly acquired table, which had three leaves, this was quite easy. We had beautiful Corinthian column silver candlesticks, and menu cards bought in Paris into which you could slip little sheets written in my mother's best Italian hand. The menu cards all had engravings of Napoleonic scenes because of Prof writing the Peninsular War. I think the fare offered at Frewin Hall below was just for an ordinary mid-Term dinner, not anything like those given for the Vice-Chancellor when everyone had to come in cap and gown. It was a February 20th—a difficult date.

> Clear Soup
> Filleted sole
> Pâté de foie gras in aspic
> Saddle of mutton
> Peach cream
> Cake baskets
> Cheese biscuits

The menu for the buffet supper at one of our dances was even better:

> Oyster patties
> Fish creams in aspic
> Chicken croquettes
> Sandwiches
> Jellies
> Fruit Salad
> Meringues
> Eclairs
> Chantilly baskets
> Chocolate mushrooms

Cocoa-nut pastry
Parmesan creams
Curried eggs

The animals went in two by two at Oxford dinner-parties and at Frewin we used to watch from the top of the high staircase outside our night-nurseries to see them arrive. There was a supply of waiters from the colleges who would come in. The grandest was Mr Moon who carried a silver poker before University processions. Mr Trim, much smaller, also knew everyone by sight. All the same, guests were always halted in our third hall and deferentially asked their names—a profound scholar once said he did not know. But Moon knew. There was a strict order of precedence and my mother found Professor Vinogradoff an awkward partner. He stopped dead on the Cannan's twirly staircase at Magdalen Gate House. '*No!* I have been insulted. Ah!' perceiving someone of even greater pretensions equally insulted. 'Well. Yes. It is right. We go on.' Familiar figures like Kestor Atkinson, Fluffy Davies, Alan Hulton or our favourite young Mr Young, who had us to tea in their rooms and knew our habits, used to look up and wave as they passed in to a dinner party. Mrs Whiteman's *chef d'œuvre* was an ice-pudding, vanilla and chocolate, 'The White Horse of Hanover'. He stood on his hind-legs, pawing the air. Woe betide the nervous bride who had to take first helping of him. When everyone had arrived, and there was nothing else to do as cocktails were still unknown, mother used to float round telling each gentleman to which lady he was to bow and offer a crooked arm as soon as dinner was announced. If the lady was a stranger, a short *dossier* was essential. 'Mr Provost, I am asking you to take in the Signora Rivoira who is visiting us. The Signora was a Cheltenham friend of my late mother-in-law. The Commendatore is an archaeologist interested in the excavations in the Forum.'

Mother was taking Chas up to Mr Carline's for his last sittings before the move. This opened on March 26th. We spent a very long time playing in our new kingdom on the following day. There was as yet no central heating (always a hollow mockery). No fires had been lit. Chas was taken ill that night. He got worse rapidly. Dr Proudfoot was sent for and said he must not be moved. Our world became a continued nightmare. Dr Proudfoot said that he feared Chas had rheumatic fever. His temperature was very high. Dr Collier was called in. The removal of furniture and most of the servants went on, producing chaos at both ends. On April 1st the diary noted 'Pleural pneumonia'. Next day the only entry was that Mr Carline had delivered the Fauntleroy portrait. Prof took most of his meals in college. No hospital nurse was installed so naturally we saw almost nothing of Nana or our mother. People were very kind asking us for the day, to get us out of the way—the Trevelyans, the Symonds. Dulce's fourteenth birthday passed without notice or presents. I think this was probably the day on which we saw the sight that we had never before seen. Mother came down the staircase with Dr Proudfoot. She was crying. 'He says your brother may not last through the night.' Then she was gone. 'You must pray.' The dinner-table was laid, but we knelt down then and there and whispered over and over again, 'Please God, don't let our brother die.' I spilt the salt. 'And that's unlucky,' said Dulce.

Margaret Wilson, released by the death of grandmother Maclagan had been summoned from Perth, and Jeanie Frame from Argyll Road. They were to take us to Southsea. Ming was getting elderly. When someone asked her how old the poor little brother was she said, 'About three.' He would have been seven on June 5th. Two days after we arrived at Southsea we heard by letter the magic words, 'Distinct improvement'. We had not taken the bikes as the old attendants would not be able to accompany us. There had been a snowstorm after we left Oxford and on April 25th snow fell all day. On Low Sunday, there was sixteen inches. We could not even be rowed out to the *Victory*.

We were not allowed to come home until May 8th. Chas was at Frewin, in a basket wheel-chair and Patch lay on his feet. He was much thinner and paler. Before his illness he had been getting beyond the control of Miss Horsley. 'I hate reading!' He used to get under the dining-room table and pull down the cloth. She would lift a corner and call down pathetically, 'Charlie! Do come out. Charlie! Do be a good boy.' A sepulchral reply came, 'Not at Home.'

II

Our new kingdom, now that we had time to explore it, was a haven of peace in the very centre of thrilling, pulsating Oxford. It had a Norman pillar in a crypt under the huge lofty kitchen, remains of a gatehouse and cloisters in the drive, an Elizabethan west wing with a Victorian top storey and an early Georgian wing. The garden was a great improvement on the strip at 39. There was a lawn on which we could play tennis, but anyone knowing the *terrain* could place a ball so that it was impossible to return it without coming into collision with our Acacia, as we called it. I think it was really a Robinia and weeping for South America, not Australia. It had white panicles of flowers in April and prickly branches. There were some ordinary single lilacs, white and mauve in a large bed, and we all got our own little gardens. The fact that they were so heavily shaded and in such poor old soil that nothing ever flourished must not be mistaken for parental neglect. The Omans simply were not gardeners. Bamama had been a gardener. I never saw the handsome patient Nutt, who looked after our garden until the last of us left, getting a load of manure or a new shrub. When an apple tree began to whisper against the windows of the green spare room it was suggested to Chas that he might tie branches back with string. I never saw an apple on it. Nutt bedded out geraniums around an association ornament in the centre bed outside the west-wing—a pinnacle from the roof of the Hawksmoor quadrangle at All Souls. The kitchen garden, reached through a tall slatted wicket gate, was much more rewarding.

The story of Dr Shadwell and his keys was not finished when we had been in possession over a year. Prof returned from College one Sunday morning to hear voices. Dr Shadwell was instructing a party of guests as he took them upstairs. 'And these are the best bedrooms.' He had still a front-door key.

Our first summer at our new home was almost a wash-out. Term was well advanced by the time mother was taking Chas daily for gentle drives. But there were some guests who must be asked to stay. The Archbishop was being given a D.D. degree and Aunt Augusta was being so good in providing linen for one of her husband's many relations so that the boy could come up to Oxford. (The time had passed when I really believed that the little old gentleman with hair white as wool who patted my head and called me 'Mother's Child' was in fact the Almighty.)*

After that visit had been accomplished the two Chadwick girls, and her bridesmaid Dorothy Gervais, still hung like a millstone round mother's neck. Mrs Whiteman, given no chance to display her expertises, began to think that this situation was by no means what she had been led to expect. It grew worse, narrower and narrower. Chas was taken to Southsea. Ethel looked after us. The parents had ceased during their great anxiety to

---

* His grandson, Michael Maclagan, tells me that to the best of his belief our archbishop never wore a mitre. As churchmanship of that generation went, he was very much a middle of the road man. He consented to wear a cope for high occasions.

attend dinner parties. They went to one this term. The Warden had the Londonderrys staying and had called in the Harcourts from Nuneham, the Vice-Chancellor and Mrs Warren from Magdalen, the old Skenes. Commemoration brought Mr Lloyd George, always a controversial character. Once it was feared that he would be pelted with mangel-wurzels when he went to speak at the Union. Even Pitlochry was not up to standard this year. The parents had gone to Germany for the first three weeks of our Scottish stay so there were no Sunday evening walks with Prof. Mother was so anxious lest Chas should have a relapse that when he had toothache she made the dentist, and Dr Proudfoot to give gas, attend at the house. She did not take the patient back to his little day-school till the middle of September and she fetched him herself every day. When Prof started for Spain this autumn, it was alone. An expected letter from him did not arrive: she telegraphed and did not get a reply as soon as she should. He had warned her not to send anything except postcards as his plans were uncertain. At last came news. 'Quite well. Return Sunday evening.' He had been writing and sent love to all but no special tender enquiries for the little invalid. Little invalids were fashionable since the one in *The Heir of Redcliffe*, and our mother had fallen into the trap of alluding to our one thus. She read patiently. 'I am enjoying myself thoroughly and talking more fluent and awful Spanish than you can conceive.' He hoped she was recovering from the strain of all her domestic conflicts. But he did add a phrase to his usual greeting. He was now also 'your true admirer'. Although she had given up all her pleasant calls, she had as soon as possible resumed reading aloud to old blind Mrs Turner. I think we realised that if they had lost Chas, for her it would have been a case of King Henry and the White Ship. She would never have smiled again. Prof might have an invalid only son and a delicate wife, but he had now produced three volumes of *The Peninsular War*, and he was going to see Gerona, Barcelona and Saragossa.

He did admirably at Gerona, largely because of a chance meeting with a charming young student whom he met in a tobacco shop, who disclosed himself as a Catalan, a patriot, and an architect. He took Prof round the walls and breaches talking a mixture of French and Spanish. Prof got a mediaeval bedroom at the Gran Hotel del Commercio, quite clean, and was pleased thinking it had probably looked just the same in 1809. His experiences on the Sud express bound for Paris were delightful. He had for conversation that nice young Portuguese nephew of Rafael Reynolds, an evangelical mining engineer from Chile who read the Bible all Sunday, and a convinced Portuguese vegetarian who tried to convert them all. A merry doctor from Oporto wanted to drive him over the line of Soult's retreat, and insisted on paying the seven francs for his dinner to show him that the Portuguese loved the English. A Swiss Moravian brother from Kashmir was full of missionary anecdotes and sixth and best of all, the artist who painted the good picture of Sir John Moor's Retreat in last year's Academy suddenly said, 'Either you are General Hutton or Professor Oman.'*

The autumn term opened and dinner parties were cautiously planned—just two. Dorothy Poole in spectacles came to one. She was the elder Poole girl and I can never forget that she introduced me to the novels of Jane Austen. Mother disapproved of these as she did not care for joking on serious subjects, such as getting husbands for a pack of girls, and one of them refusing a clergyman. She had a perfect horror of families of girls only, and often told us that when Chas was coming she would look away if she saw the five daughters of Canon Ottley or the four of Dr Cooke advancing, just in case there was anything in pre-natal influence. She would have liked a fourth baby if only Dr Proudfoot would have promised it would be another boy.

I had a small speaking part in the school play this year. Ironically I was cast for Cornwell's 'Geography'. Somehow I contrived to find this subject uninspiring. Dulce took more interest as she had a stamp collection and went to the study to be instructed by Prof. I was encouraged to collect crests in vague competition with Dulce's stamps. You could buy albums for them with the words 'Crests and Monograms' large on the cover. Uncle Ed sent me some gilded and sharply multicoloured ones belonging to Rajahs which quite surpassed even the best produced for Oxford colleges. Bamama had an elaborate A.O. monogram in lilac, violet, or royal blue with the word ANN in the centre surmounted by a gilded Chadwick lily sprouting out of it. The Maclagans had an industrious beaver above 'PRINCIPIIS OBSTA'.

I never went to Prof except, since the death of Bamama, to learn to keep accounts. I dreaded these sessions. They started with Prof, with sparkling irascible eyes crossing out my tipsy figures. This utterly distracted me. He had a violent dislike of the word 'Millinery' and entered it contemptuously against every bill from every possible source.

In her last years, when I used to take my mother on sightseeing

* James Beadle was the accomplished artist. Sir Edward Hutton, K.C.B., 'Curly' of the 60th, was a frequent lecturer and contributor to the *R.U.S.I. Journal*.

H

expeditions in London we once halted in front of a portrait by Sargent of a warm and intelligent-looking woman, 'Octavia Hill, philanthropist 1838–1913'. 'She started the MABEYS,' nodded mother. The initials stood for the Metropolitan Association for Befriending Young Servants. That had been mother's principal Good Work in London before she married, and the only one she had really regretted having to desert. But she had soon found alternative occupation at Oxford. It must not be thought that all the calls and luncheon and dinner parties pushed out her errands of mercy. She kept a note at the end of her diary every year of her sub-scriptions and committees and these received additions as the family income increased. 'Church Missionary Society, S.P.C.A., Blind, St Thomas's Orphanage, Linen League, Zenana, Jews' (no details). We were early told to become Sunbeams. You sent their magazine to your Sunbeam and wrote letters to her. My Sunbeam was called Gladys Douglas and her father worked in a biscuit factory at Reading. I used to think of him working, poor man, as the London train swept us past the lighted windows of factories the shape of Norman keeps. Even mother thought the picture on the cover of our magazine ill-advised. It showed a plump rich little girl in a bonnet with ostrich tips and a fur-trimmed pelisse giving a lily to a poor little girl in a pinafore and broken boots. My Sunbeam must have been mistakenly assigned. For Christmas presently, Gladys Douglas sent me the most beautiful box of biscuits I had ever seen. They were mixed and coloured, with sugar icing on their tops. We wrote to one another for some years, but my style was affected by the fact that Nana still insisted on seeing every letter and postcard I received. She snatched a card from me. 'What's the wee piece round the top?' It was from Ellie. 'Send me your photograph.' 'The idea!' Gladys Douglas and I never met.

III

At Miss Batty's the news spread like wildfire, 'The Cannans have written a book.' It was not quite that. Their father was Secretary to the Delegates of the University Press, as we were often told, and this august body had published an anthology of favourite poems chosen by the three Cannans for readers six to sixteen. *The Triple Crown*. It had a professional Preface signed by them all with their initials, thanking Mr Kipling and Mr Newbolt, and also many publishers for permissions to quote. Mr Quiller-Couch and the Vice-Chancellor had written introductory verses.

Someone must have helped me to buy my copy, for I should never have been able to afford the attractive little volume bound in real soft red leather with gilt-edged pages. There was almost nothing new to me in it, but I loved it dearly.*

On New Year's Day 1909 *The Times* announced that Uncle Ed had been given a C.S.I. 'Star of India' sounded lovely. More close in interest was the fact that Dulce had bought with her Christmas money in the covered market a guinea-pig. He was 'Titus Oates' and he came to an untimely end when Patch spotted him being fed in the little room out of the top greenhouse. Chas had a black and white rabbit 'Mr Perks' who was killed by the Thompsons' dog up at Portnacraig, but not before he had a fine litter for which apparently my 'Ruth' was responsible. We kept the silkworms alongside our animals. Cynthia Driver gave me some white waltzing Japanese mice. The Drivers had much better animals than us. They had collies and a carriage and pair and a donkey. Our tortoise was one of those who keep themselves to themselves. He lived in the garden and the further greenhouse and came with the buttercups. St John's painted their tortoise red white and blue out of patriotism in the year of the coronation. We heard it died. St John's gardens were our favourite haunt, for there Mr Bidder would meet us and put a match to the shrub called the Burning Bush. I never saw, but longed to have seen, the Living Chess performed on St John's big lawn. All the actors had been got up as kings and queens, knights, bishops and pawns. Mother told us that she saw Archbishop Laud's ghost walking along the library as she watched from the lawn once on an autumn evening with Mr Hutton afterwards Dean of Winchester. 'Look! look! Here he comes.' Little Laud walked on his knees because the floor of the library had been raised several inches since he knew it. You could tell when he was coming because you saw the light of his candle passing from window to window. We took a natural healthy interest in gruesome stories. There was a draughty spot by the cloisters at Christ Church known as Kill Canon. At the bottom of the very steep staircase leading up to Prof's rooms in All Souls on the first floor of the south-east range, an elderly Fellow had been found one morning, stone-dead just like Amy Robsart.

* Ten years later May Cannan took me to London for a personal interview with a publisher. After an entirely frustrating morning, for no publisher, it appeared, was ever in his office, or even expected, we halted with my book at Amen Corner and May boldly sent in a message that Miss Cannan from Oxford wanted to see Mr Humphry Milford. He sent us on to Sir Ernest Hodder Williams just round the corner, with a letter.

Expeditions to his rooms to fetch his letters for Prof were a popular object for a morning walk. He left the key on the top ledge of the door of the outer room, his study. Once Nana surprised a burglar in the rooms. At least he fled at the sight of us, muttering nothings. Just outside the fatal stairs there was an unusual holly-tree with a stout middle cross branch. It was impossible to say which was the end and which the beginning. Prof's rooms were interesting. 'Come in! Sit down!' he would cry genially to a pupil who looked round wildly. Every single chair was occupied by rolls of maps, parchments, folders bursting with notes, manuscripts, books. The rooms overlooked the High Street, and the study had a richly carved over-mantel and plaster ceiling with the '*Semper Eadem*' coat of arms of Elizabeth I. This was because they had been part of the Warden's Lodgings before the new ones had been built in the time of Queen Anne. The large panelled bedroom opening out of it was always dark and cold. When a guest was coming from London a fire was ordered. The Rooms, in which I never saw a window opened, had an individual smell. Some good odd pieces of Prof's own antique porcelain collection stood about. Mother came over at intervals with equipment to wash these. With luck, on one of our visitations we might be asked in to the Warden's lodgings and be shown the Christmas rose flowering in a sheltered corner of the garden, and in the dining-room, the haunting portrait of His Sacred Majesty King Charles I as he sat at his trial by the pretended Court of Justice in Westminster Hall.

The Domestic Bursar, who was for years Charles Grant Robertson, was host at many of the tea-parties to which we went with a covey of the little motherless Trevelyans. It was always a mystery to the dons' wives why this attractive and cheerful man never married. But he never had time. He was a non-stop talker. When he was out of breath he would saw the air with a hand and pant, 'I, I, I,' to prevent you coming in to bat. Mother once tried him with Dorothy Gervais who was renowned as a talker, even in Southern Ireland. It was quite pathetic. He was out of her class. Mother said that when poor Dorothy opened her mouth with a 'But' or 'I thought' he simply waved her down and she sat in the end looking like an open-mouthed nestling.

My camera went everywhere with me now and I was allowed to take a time-exposure in the chapel of the reredos. This had been ruined by Cromwellians and all the rows of figures left standing without their heads. But when it was uncovered after two hundred years someone in authority had the happy idea that the new heads should resemble those of the present

Warden and fellows. There was one Fellow who returned from foreign parts to be told that he was too late unless he would consent to be one of the lost souls being hurried to hell. He decided that half a loaf was better than no bread and was immortalised.

There was a rush of parties this holidays. We gave a dance for forty-eight children and twelve grown-ups. Britain's Navy was rapidly expanding and our dances were adorned by at least half a dozen naval cadets. Martin Collier, Gilbert Whitelock and Bobby Proudfoot were all the sons of doctors. Valentine Raleigh, Conrad Jenkins, Percy Trevelyan and Roger Berthon were the sons of professors. When term ended at Osborne or Dartmouth they arrived at Oxford station, hailed hansoms and drove off with great aplomb at top-speed, arms crossed. They were little men already. Their discipline was evidently strict. Percy Trevelyan's step-mother said that when Percy left home he could not spell, but after one term Percy could spell. Considering my admiration for sailors it was a little disappointing that I never had a close friend amongst them. But my inward eye, and doubtless my conversation, was filled with Queen Elizabeth signing the death-warrant of Mary, Queen of Scots, the little Princes in the Tower, and Bonnie Prince Charlie.

We were taken this year to see H. B. Irving, behind the scenes at the New Theatre. He was still dressed as old Louis XI and very obligingly showed us how he had his front teeth blacked out by pieces of court plaster. But my hero was Mr Benson as Henry V, with a fox's brush in his helm. The Burrowses took us behind to see him, and he gave us blocks of milk-chocolate 'from the siege of Harfleur'. H.B. came to a lunch-party given by my parents for him and his wide-eyed actress-wife who was Dorothea Baird and the sister of Mrs A. L. Smith of Balliol. The A. L. Smith family were so many and so tall now that a visiting tailor, touting for orders, mistook them for a school and offered special terms for equipping the whole establishment. H.B. gave us the hundredth night Souvenir Programme of *The Lyons Mail*. It had a portrait of him on the cover, as the luckless Lesurques, and I made a large facsimile and stuck it up in the outer hall where he could not fail to see it when he came to call after his lunch party.

Chas had not got through the festive season without a bad cold—and could a child get chicken-pox twice? Apparently that was a false alarm, but I was sent to Bournemouth with him and Nana. This was our first sight of the sea except at Spartan Portsmouth in February-March, and the whole holiday was a revelation of beautiful land and sea-scapes for me from the first moment that I saw white cliffs and a brilliant pacific blue sky and inclining conifers, above gentle waves. But we did not go anywhere interesting as there was nobody to take us. There was a high mortality amongst children in our youth.* There were sudden disappearances of little friends we had known well. This year the Drivers lost their brother, Gerald. My mother, after her own recent anxiety felt warmest sympathy for Mrs Driver (although there were two older boys) and visited her almost daily. He had died of pneumonia; nothing could be done. We had taken great interest in him as most of the families we knew had been complete by the time we reached school age. The mistress had hastily pinned on a face when Cynthia wonderingly said, a few days after he was born, 'Mummy's still in bed with him.' 'Oh yes, dear, to keep him *warm*.' It sounded fishy. Brocas and Agnes were what was left of a larger family. The Pembers had lost a boy aged eight. Antony Symonds had died at eleven months, Percy Trevelyan from pneumonia, on leave, May Cannan was a surviving twin. Ethel Wakeling and Mary Wright? 'Well, you won't see *her* any more.' Nana lived on a constant terror of infection. 'Whooping-cough!' she would screech, tearing us away from an affronted nice-looking group.

June was lovely this year. Uncle Ed had married and he had an Irish bride, Edie Morony, the traditional picture of Irish elegance. He wore a straw boater and a very well-cut light suit and Aunt Edie was even smarter. She got all her things from a Mayfair couturier called Redfern who charged the earth and she told us with peals of laughter that the moment they arrived she cut them all to pieces with the nail-scissors. She had sweeping 'princess' dresses in pastel shades, with braided passementerie all over the front and a double white fox stole and a tilted hat with an aigrette sticking out at an angle. I thought she had chestnut hair and violet eyes. She had a baby who looked as if she was meant to be a boy, quite square with rosy cheeks and flat fair hair. This uncle and aunt were entirely different from Uncle Bob and Aunt Bee whose little boy was a regular Maclagan for looks. There had been a storm in a tea-cup at our home when it turned out that he had been christened Malcolm after a godfather Malcolm Macleod R.E. Uncle Ed and Aunt Edie's little girl had been properly named after his mother and a collateral who had been an earl in 1774. Aunt Edie had a rippling laugh as she called to her sturdy offspring in reproach for any misdemeanour, 'Patricia Glencairn!' Aunt Bee repaired

* *Home Demand and Economic Growth, Historical Perspectives*, Note 18, p. 156: Noel Kendrick, 1975.

her mistake and called her second boy Robert. Aunt Edie had no such accoutrements as the violin or the sketching stool. 'Your Uncle Ed never looked at anything but a pretty face.' But Aunt Edie was far more than pretty; she had style. It seemed incredible that she had been twenty-seven before she married. I was absolutely proud of my godfather and wife when they set off for the Encaenia. The Domestic Bursar had kindly asked the three youngest Trevelyan girls and us to watch the guests on the lawn from the windows of the Common Room. A repast was laid on. I took a good photograph of our party. Chas had a seat of vantage on the open window sill. Little Joan could hardly see over the flowers in the window box. Mother came across to show us to Sir Frederick Pollock, a Cambridge man, and I photographed them too. The company who had attended the ceremony in the Sheldonian filtered onto the lawn in their staring new diverse coloured gowns and flat black velvet caps. The band struck up a piece from Gilbert and Sullivan and the distinguished assemblage gradually filed in to the luncheon in the library.

Dulce, I think inspired by Nana, had now developed Scottish patriotism. But Nana knew nothing about our plans for waving flags with the lion of Scotland on them from the windows of our compartment as our train crossed the Tweed. We now wore blouse and skirt suits, convenient for the transport of forbidden articles in the pouch. Before we got off for Pitlochry, mother had another panic about Chas. Dr Proudfoot came to Frewin to perform a minor operation—the cutting of tonsils. Hours after he had left, Chas had a haemorrhage. Nana stayed with mother and the patient, and Ethel and the maids were sent off with notes in all directions. They got Dr Sankey, junior partner, whom we had nicknamed from his appearance 'the sponge-finger' and presently Dr Proudfoot. Two days later Chas was in the garden again in his basket wheel-chair with Patch sitting on his feet. But it had been a regular scare.

Nana was now approaching the apex of her inevitable warfare with the kitchen and sent Mrs Whiteman a message that Colonel Maclagan's baby's nurse said that Colonel Maclagan's baby's egg had been rather strong. Aunt Bee was so unsophisticated that she asked mother, 'What do I say when I speak to nurse about Bob? I can't say just Bob.' 'You say Colonel Maclagan, dear, or the Colonel.' 'Thank you, Mary.' Decidedly Aunt Bee was mother's favourite.

We had some good expeditions from Edinburgh this year—Falkland Palace, Melrose, Abbotsford. I was also promoted to going to the Dean Cemetery. This was where the Maclagans had their 'lair'. The routine was impressive. We hired an open carriage and drove first to the best florist in Princes Street. Here we chose the most magnificent bunch of sweet-peas which were just at their best in Scotland though finished at home. The cemetery was packed with monuments. There was a middle-aged lady fiercely washing an unusual one. It had a pug on the top. He must, said mother, have been the soldier father's pet in India. I was told to put our bouquet on the grave of Patricia Gilmore Maclagan and say a little prayer. Then we walked away leaving the flowers to perish in the very hot sun.

A week later I was taken, also alone, on an even more special expedition. Dulce had not much cared for what she called 'That ghastly Abroad', but then she had hardly been allowed in a shop, which she would have appreciated, and she had been incubating chicken-pox. I began badly. When we arrived in the cab at Oxford station I had to confess in a whisper that I had left my most important possession on the nursery table. Prof shouted to the cabby in high annoyance, 'The young lady has forgotten her Photographic Apparatus.' My camera was to prove the bane of my first foreign holiday. It had a habit of refusing to wind on to the next film. The best remedy was to take out the film, in bed when it was quite dark, and roll it tighter. I got a very clear picture of a statue of Truth in the Jardin des Tuileries. She was quite naked and holding up a glass. 'Is France a very hot country?' I enquired. 'So many of the people in the pictures don't seem to be wearing any clothes, even on a picnic.'

I was much impressed by the sad and dusty crepe and laurel wreaths heaped on the enormous statues in the pavilion representing Strasburg in the Place de la Concorde. That was the capital of Alsace taken by Germany after the war of 1870. I had better not tell Fraulein at Miss Batty's about the wreaths and sadness. She hated France. We had lunch in the open air in the Palais Royal having seen Nôtre Dame (very dark) and the Sainte Chapelle (dazzling). Prof went off to inspect Peninsular documents in the War Archives and I went back to the hotel with Mother. I now sympathise that after such an improving morning she needed a rest in her bedroom, but at the age of twelve I was what Uncle Bob called 'full of beans'. I made a dreadful discovery. I had nothing to read. Nana must have ruthlessly turned out the pile of books I had left to be packed and put instead of them piles of clean underclothing. I had read as much as I could bear of the parents' guide book in the train. It was in French. Miss Lee was always urging us to show Resource. After a dismal pause I decided that if I could not read a book I had better begin to write one. I had the materials, for like Dulce I had to write down all I had seen every day in an exercise book. I began to write a play about the captive James I of Scotland looking forth from his prison chamber in Windsor Castle and espying the beautiful Joanna de Beaufort picking roses. I had it all in my head and it came out like water from a bottle. But I really did have a better time of it in Paris than Dulce. I was taken to look at shops in the morning before meeting Prof at the Carnavelet. Next day it was the Musée de Louvre again. It was now hot thunderous weather and seated beneath the Venus of Milo was a very old custodian, fast asleep. The most beautiful woman in the world was not to his taste. I agreed with him. Aunt Edie was much slighter. We went shopping after the sculptures although something splendid was planned for that night. We went to the Opera and saw *Hernani*. I was spellbound though completely out of my depth. I was given this treat because I was the only one still learning the piano, though in very slow motion. Still, I was always singing to myself and used to linger in Blackwells in Broad Street listening to the Bach choir practising under Dr Allen, opposite.

On Saturday afternoon we went to Versailles. I am afraid that I was a perfect nuisance on this expedition. My camera was giving acute trouble. I tried in vain to get the spool to wind. My mother afterwards accused me of having stamped upon the machine. But this was not in rage. It was an effort to get the spool to loosen. Now, the parents had gone to the Petit Trianon with a romantic object. During the last months there had been visits to Prof of two ladies from North Oxford who believed that they had had an extraordinary experience in Marie-Antoinette's garden. They had crossed a certain rustic bridge and found themselves in the world of her court just before the French Revolution. Sir John Evans had advised, 'Don't publish. It won't be good for the college.' He had now died so they had come to Prof because he was the President of 'The Phas' the Oxford Phasmatological Society. When Macmillan produced their book next year they called themselves Elizabeth Morison and Frances Lamont, but actually they were Miss Moberly and Miss Jourdain, the Principal and Vice-Principal-Elect of St Hugh's College, Oxford. *An Adventure*, had an immediate success and advanced into several editions. After both authoresses were dead, Dr Joan Evans, as a literary executor to Miss Jourdain, when approached by publishers with regard to yet another, post-war, edition, was against the project. Miss Moberly in 1913 had disclosed that she had witnessed, further, the phantom of the Emperor Constantine, more than life size wearing a toga and coronal in the foyer

of the Musée du Louvre at three thirty on a Sunday afternoon. Dr Evans
had discovered that a lineal descendant of a family of the old *noblesse*
possessed keys and access to the Petit Trianon at the dates when the
English ladies had visited it. So the figures dressed in costumes of the right
period might indeed be genuine but drifting about in obedience to the
behests of rather an odd privileged person. As to Constantine, he turned
out to be a favourite disguise of the current lover of the *danseuse* Isadora
Duncan.

The day on which we went to the scene was heavy and nostalgic. There
had been a thunderstorm the night before but it had hardly cleared the
air. I think my parents decided that although they had seen nothing, the
Trianon was spooky. None of my photographs had 'come out', or only
bits which meant that light had seeped in. But *An Adventure* had a very
high reputation for credibility. I once asked Agnes Burrows's father if he
believed it was true. He replied, 'My dear Carola, that is a very large
question for a very small person.'

It rained all the way home from poor Marie-Antoinette's gardens.
Sunday was brilliant. We went first to the English church and then by
boat to the Jardin des Plantes, which was a zoo. Prof came shopping with
us in the Magasins du Louvre on the Monday. We spent our last night in
France in Boulogne and walked on the ramparts and saw a window from
which the Scarlet Pimpernel might have escaped, looking down on a
bench where old Colonel Newcome might have sat, had both of them
been real.

IV

A brougham in which mother could pay afternoon calls had now been
added to our establishment, but not a horse. She hired a horse and driver
from Mr Stroud who kept a livery-stable in New Inn Hall Street just
below our gatehouse at the bottom of the drive. He told her he would
always send a very steady horse and man, accustomed to funerals. Moosie
had now passed out of our lives. Dulce was too big to ride him and I was
having lessons from Mr Rhodes on 'Snowball' and 'Empress'. The owners
of various estates outside Oxford graciously supplied us with keys attached
to large-size engraved cards by armorial seals above a dashing signature.
Wytham, Bagley and Shotover were our favourites. Chas had never ridden
Moosie since his various set-backs but was now also having lessons. He

found them very boring as from Frewin it was only possible to get to the outskirts of Oxford and back in the specified hour. Mr Rhodes who cannot ever have been delighted with the arrangement by which he had to keep Moosie and send him round at irregular times, and who naturally would have preferred to get a Shetland for us himself, now declared that the singular unresponsiveness of the animal was due to his having a wall-eye and a mouth dumb on one side.

The advent of the brougham caused us no delight. It was a neat-looking vehicle highly polished and not draughty as no window was ever opened. It had an individual smell. As usual, I got the back-to-the-horse seat.

Dulce was now beginning to display marked leadership. Indeed, Chas says she was the only one of us who could ever do anything with our father. Before he knew what he was about he was taking us down to Acott's to choose a gramophone and a selection of records. I did not much care for this either. It was horrible, when one was out on the river to have the beautiful green peace suddenly shattered by an undergraduate's gramophone braying nonsense. We got one interesting record. It had a bit from a speech by Professor Oman on one side. The other side was 'Rock of Ages'. We used to put on the Prof side very slow, deep bass, and very fast falsetto. I much preferred our musical box which was, I suppose, Chadwick by origin and Chas said was about 1850. It had a burr walnut case and a collection of barrels of classical music, including one of the Hallelujah Chorus. It lived in the dining-room most inaccessibly under a table, but I soon knew its repertoire by heart.

Mother once detected Prof starting to go back to college again having just come back for lunch. The gong had sounded. 'Forgotten the Child's Book!' He took us to St Giles's Fair at the instigation of Dulce. The most elaborate plans were always made so that we were never at home for that. Once, at 39 still, by some misadventure we had overlapped. It had been quite fascinating. We could see the clown painting his face. Dulce pointed out that we had seen the four youngest Trevelyans on the helter-skelter with their father. St Giles's Fair was a bit of history. Prof fell into the trap and we had a very good day of it and collected many trophies and a general impression of jollity and unusual accents. Dulce scorned the brougham and being taken almost every day now to pay calls on a lot of musty-fusties. If the object of the exercise had been something sensible like a rugger match in the Parks, or to watch the Eight practising, she would have felt more amenable. She was very popular now with boy friends who were literally that and no more, in the year 1909. 'Dulce,' admonished mother, 'I heard you just now saying you would sit next Alban Hudson at supper at the Evanses' party. But you have promised Ralph Symonds.' 'I have two sides,' Dulce pointed out. Alban was at Eton now and had sent her a Valentine. He evidently liked our stable, for as he got no reply from her he asked me, next year, if he might have my photograph. He would pay for it. Only, the photographer in whose window it was displayed, said he must have permission from the young lady's parents. It was tenpence. I said I would ask my mother, and got into trouble, Mother looked surprised, collected herself, and said he was a naughty boy. He had been laughing at me.*

Dulce was a model pupil, the only girl at Miss Batty's who never got an Order Mark. Marks were complicated. The bad ones were called Order Marks, and three Order Marks made a Conduct Mark. That was unthinkable. We used, when we were playing a game about school, to say daringly, 'Take a Conduct Mark!' When Dulce's record was suddenly shattered by being given an Order Mark by a junior mistress for something quite trivial, such as forgetting Miss Batty's glass of milk at eleven a.m., she said she was never going back. Next Sunday night mother gathered us to hear a little pious talk. It was about Patience. She ended her praise of this virtue with the words, 'Dulce is being called upon to show great patience.' Mother had written to Miss Batty who had refused to take away Dulce's order mark. It made us feel rather fine to think of having to be patient with Miss Batty. Dulce continued to go to Park Crescent but she was never again given an Order Mark. She was now being privately prepared for confirmation and was to be one of a large group to be confirmed at Easter in St Aldate's church by Bishop Paget. She was therefore allowed to go to see a play called *The Passing of the Third Floor Back*. I was not considered sufficiently awakened. It was about a lodger in a very poor boarding house who brought out the best in everyone and turned out, though you were not really told this, to be Christ. It was by J. K. Jerome, author of *Three Men in a Boat*.

In the middle of December the parents went down to Brighton to stay at the Grand Hotel. They had gone to see a Preparatory School at Hove but that was a secret. Suddenly, just before Christmas, came an unusual entry, 'Carola's success'. The school play this year offered a double bill.

---

* I never spoke to him again. His father told us that Alban had become interested in heraldry and asked what it meant when a descendant was shown holding a torch upside down. It meant the line, with him, became extinct. We were to lose this only child of devoted parents very early in the 1914 War.

There was a curtain-raiser of tableaux for those who looked nice but could not act, 'Aucassin and Nicolette'. *Narcissus* was a short play which had been performed in St John's College in 1602. The elder girls got all the best parts. Dorothy Warren was Narcissus and Veronica Gotch, Echo, and Esther Duff, Tiresias. But Gracie Eales and I were attendant youths, with quite a lot to say ending in a fight to the death. 'The little one in green is good,' said Charles Ffoulkes who was standing up at the back of the hall with Prof. Many children can act at twelve. I had that divine feeling of having the audience in the palm of my hand from the moment I stepped onto the stage. I had no illusions about my capacity. I was nothing compared with Nettie Walker, a born light comedienne. *Narcissus* was such a success that it was given again in St George's Hall in February. Dulce, who had wept at being only a pirate in a cork moustache, uncomplainingly sold programmes. What I had really wanted was for the parents to notice Janet Allen who had been Nicolette in the tableaux.

The last stirring event in the 1909 holidays was a lecture by Mr Burrows at the Indian Institute. This was the large building at the bottom of Broad Street with an elephant on the top. The Cannans called it Jumbo's Joss-House. I cannot remember what was his subject, but I suppose Ceylon. He was the first lecturer to children that I ever heard. He had a brassy voice rather as if he was telling troops to form fours, but you could have heard a pin drop. He had such infectious cheerfulness. Later, when he became a 'Sir' he refused to be 'Sir Stephen' which was his first name: he chose Sir Montagu. He could not get over the ignominy of St Stephen's end. 'Stoned, poor fellow!'

There was one more social event which touched us in 1909. Nana French, alias 'Dooks', told our Nana beforehand that Sir Ernest Trevelyan was going to marry again. His choice sounded very suitable. Miss Winifred Aitchison was one of the daughters of a deceased K.C.S.I. and had a very astute old mother who stood no nonsense. When a fellow member of a committee on which she and my mother sat began to make excuses that increasing years made it difficult for her to perform her duties, Lady Aitchinson simply asked, 'How old are you, *exactly*?' Of course, the new Lady Trevelyan was much younger than Sir Ernest, who was ten years senior to our father; still she was of a reasonable age and well trained. We were rather frightened of Sir Ernest who had white hair and a steely gaze and had been a Judge in Calcutta. We used to collect Tracts, handed by believers to the ungodly pressing down the Broad Walk to the boat races. Dulce had five pink and I had two green and one blue. Sir

Ernest told us they were not intended for us to collect. But we did read them, religiously. Henry, his eldest son, by his brief first marriage, was now in the Army. The step-mother had to deal with only Hilda and Doris who looked as if they had come out of the same box, with brown eyes, complexions and hair, and Wilfred, Percy, Sylvia and Joan, quite another strain—fair. But one and all had dark eyes like their mother whose family had been for two generations in the consular service in Spain and France. Sylvia and Joan alternated between being the prettiest. Joan won at present with a fringe and waist-long golden curls. She was to become in 1929 Mrs Chas Oman.

VII

Neo-Georgian:

1910–1911

I

THERE WERE TWO NOVEL FORMS OF ENTERTAINMENT AT OXFORD during the last winter season of the Edwardian age—progressive games and roller skating. The Macdonnels, the Marriotts, the Vinogradoffs all gave progressive games parties, though goodness knows how the Vinogradoffs managed as the rules were intricate and really only the Professor was fluent in English. Ellie and Igor's mother looked completely the lovely Scandinavian. Actually she had a Norwegian father and an English mother. Her daughter by a previous marriage to a Norwegian, Mary Harpöth, was an ash-blonde. Their mademoiselle knew nothing but her native tongue. I heard her ask Ellie once if her friend understood French, but before I could say, 'Yes, a little,' Ellie said quickly, 'Not a word.'

Dulce liked progressive games because they were competitive, but I do not think either of us excelled at them. We both enjoyed the skating rink up in North Oxford. Chas was not allowed to try; it might be dangerous. The parents went to Hove again and made up their minds: mother wrote to the spinster sister of the headmaster.

I was Macbeth in the Gotch's charades, and Margaret of Anjou, leading Chas as Edward, Prince of Wales. Nana looked daggers at Mrs Gotch for suggesting that Macbeth ought not to have arched eyebrows. The Evans party on Boars Hill was better than ever. It was Twelfth Night and two children were chosen to be the king and queen of the bean. They had to sit on a throne on a daïs while we all marched round to the sound of music and bowed and curtsied to them. They were supposed to be chosen quite by chance. A cake was handed round, and you took a slice and one of these

would contain the pea and the other the bean. It would have been awkward
if both had got into one slice but I soon saw that this was not possible. A
heavily-ringed finger was put in front of two slices by the lady handing
round, and Geoffrey Madan got the bean and a pretty girl we did not
know, the pea. Chas had been sent to Southsea, so missed this peak of the
season at which the cotillon favours were unique in our experience, even
for the Evans.

At the end of January the parents gave an evening party for 500 in the
Codrington library in conjunction with the Arthur Johnsons: he was the
chaplain at All Souls. Moon came to organise and we heard that all went
well. Chas came back from the sea but attended school for only two days.
Nana said that Austin Poole had developed measles. Mother went up to
see Miss Owen and it appeared that this was true, and it was agreed that
Chas should stay away for another fortnight. It now seemed essential that
he had some tutoring to get him up to the standard for entry to a preparatory school, and a succession of nice young undergraduates of limited
means came to cram him. At least one of the first three fell in love with
Dulce. She took such a genuine interest in people, at least young people.
She enjoyed the debates at the Union and became a regular attendant on
Thursday nights at eight p.m. It was a miniature House of Commons for
undergraduates, and all who were intending a political career, and a great
many more, went and spouted. Prof was on the committee but was not
much called upon, and then generally only to decide what was to be done
about members who forgot that the books in the society's library did not
belong to them. The debates were held in a perfectly hideous red brick
building close to our home and the interior walls had originally been
decorated with colourful outsize murals of romantic scenes by the Pre-
Raphaelites; but as these heralds of a new age in art had not known that
you must put on a size before painting murals these had become almost
invisible even by our day.

I had another source of delight. I was going to have lessons over the
sticks in the riding-school. Prof quite approved of my astride habit when
he saw me in it, and said nobody would ever guess. I was not wearing a
skirt now. I had a coat right down to my heels. Once I was dragged by it
on Port Meadow until it tore all round. Luckily I came off very easily
astride. The Cannans were now all astride. I went out with them and
Mr Rhodes into the country, once a week. I think that five was really too
much for him. The Cannans were rather better astride as they were smaller.
Dorothea and Joan would have made good jockeys at this date. Joan, who

Most Rev. William Dalrymple Maclagan,
Archbishop of York.

Sir Edward and Lady Maclagan.

Family Group.

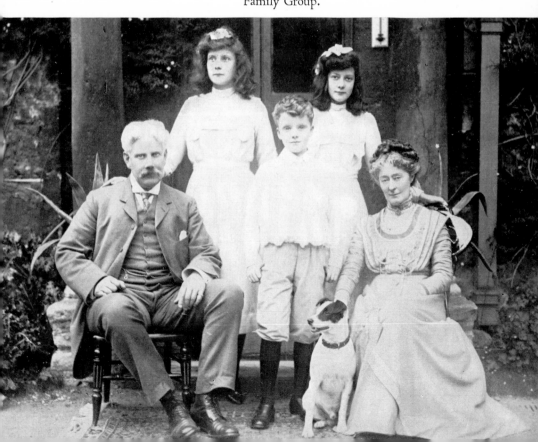

Trevelyans and Omans watching All Souls guests from the Common Room.

Mother at All Souls lunch.

had always been called so, suddenly announced that she was going to be Joanna for the future. There were other Joans at Miss Batty's now that our numbers had increased with Edwardian prosperity.

The parents went off for Constantinople. In Munich they saw the Prince Regent returning from Mass on a Sunday morning and wrote to tell us. There had been no particular reason for worry about Chas but the reply to a telegram which they sent on arrival in Vienna said that he had slight whooping-cough. They agreed to return home. Snow began to fall that evening. When they reached Oxford very tired on the night of April 5th they found all three children had whooping-cough. This was a good thing in a way, as if we had waited to develop it one by one the summer would have been gone by the time we were all through with it. But there was nothing that Prof could do. We went down to Southsea in a motor, *via* Winchester, and the whoop that Chas gave in the cathedral raised the loudest echoes that I have ever heard in that lovely nave. Dulce had 'a little collapse' on arrival.

We were still at Southsea with mother in attendance, when she bought an evening paper in the middle of the morning one day. Posters were saying 'The King's Illness'. Mother was not surprised because she was getting daily letters from Prof. He said that as the last bulletin had said 'No better', that probably meant that he was worse. A loyal subject on the windy parade who saw us buying a paper shouted, 'Better news I hope?' But the next was that the Archbishop of Canterbury had been to the Palace. The Press had to be very careful. In 1871 when Edward, then Prince of Wales, had been at death's door with typhoid, an enthusiastic poet of whom his royal mother so much approved that she later made him Laureate, had produced a couplet which had to be suppressed and was held to be the epitome of bathos.

> Flash'd from his bed, the electric tidings came,
> He is not better; he is much the same.—

Edward VII died on the night of Friday, May 6th, 1910, in his sixty-ninth year. The response to the news was astonishing compared with that which had greeted his accession. Prof wrote:

It is a grievous thing to lose an experienced king with plenty of tact, at this time. I dare say the Radicals will try to bully and hustle George V just because he is inexperienced and quite an unknown

I

quantity. I saw Whiteman make up your parcel of black things this evening and it will be sent off to you the first thing tomorrow. They tell me that all the drapers here were completely sold out of black things by mid-day yesterday. The royal proclamation here is Tuesday at noon. I will send you any papers that are issued. At Portsmouth it should be rather a fine show—but do not get caught in a crush, I beseech you.

The proclamation at Oxford had been made at the Divinity School and outside St Mary's church.

It was much better managed than in 1901, since there are plenty of people now who know the precedents, while last time there had been no one living, or at least old enough then, to notice the details . . . As someone remarked to me at the proclamation, the only possible thing that might make one doubt the validity of King George's accession is that the warrant acquainting us of it was signed by Mr Ure and Winston Churchill—both of whom enjoy about the lowest reputation for veracity in the whole House of Commons.

The national mourning which followed was the last on such a scale in Great Britain. Except for the Trevelyans, whose father always had Views, we were the only girls at Miss Batty's who were not dressed in black from top to toe. I cannot guess who in authority decreed this but the result was attractive. We had clergyman-grey jackets, skirts and top coats, white blouses with black ties, black hats, shoes and hose.

About a quarter of a million subjects filed past the catafalque where Edward the Peacemaker lay in state in Westminster Hall for two days. The funeral procession to Paddington from Windsor took place in perfect weather on May 20th watched by vast crowds. All felt 'in the picture' when, behind the gun-carriage bearing the coffin, came His Majesty's fox-terrier Caesar, led by a Highland servant. They preceded the German Emperor and eight other ruling sovereigns.

In Oxford all manner of important occasions had be to revised. 'I presume that the Curzon invitation to meet Roosevelt will be "off" as Theodore will not be at Hackwood the day before the King is buried.'

From such lofty considerations the paterfamilias passed to a humbler sphere.

Wuzzy wrote me a merry little note regretting that her 'muse' was not sad enough to sing of the king's death . . . Will you tell the children that the silkworms are now hatching out in such hundreds that I do not know what to do with them all? Have they any little friends who would like some? Or shall I send half of them as a gift to the old naturalist in the market? When they begin to grow we shall be quite overwhelmed.

He had nothing else important to relate except that Patch, who had been quite miserable, lying alone on the mat up in the nursery, was improving. 'Comes and sits by me in the study all the time that I am at home.' Prof thought that Patch was missing 'the children', but if that had been so, he would have been sitting in the school-room, the King's Room, on the half floor. It was his little master that Patch was missing, and this was going to be much worse when Chas went off for boarding school at Hove. At the age of nine Chas no longer needed a nurse and knew it. His groans of 'Got nothing to do' echoed in the nursery. What he wanted was some congenial companions of his own sex and age. Two boys from boarding schools did come to stay with us frequently in the holidays. They were considerably older, and in brains never likely to approach him. Jack Peile, a cousin on the Chadwick side, was a very handsome boy with carroty hair. His parents were on service in Bermuda and he had three younger sisters who were models, particularly the one my age who never had to be told to fold up her clothes at night and kneel down to say her prayers. Jack was the most destructive boy I ever met, and so accident-prone that he managed to break an ankle when balance-walking on a ledge only six inches above the ground. He told Nana that his mother beat him with a shoe-horn. When he managed to fall, on one of our bikes, right through the conservatory, I said, not without reason, that I would not be in his shoes. He was uninjured. I came back from a party happy and weary the same night to be attacked by my mother, waiting for me. When she left me I heard her saying in tones of satisfaction to my father, 'She is crying now.'

But I did get some information out of Jack. He showed me how to measure inches and feet without a tape or ruler, and that when the moon's shape spelt C it meant not crescent, as seemed reasonable, but de-crescent or waning. And when its shape spelt D it was crescent. I never look up at the moon without thinking of Jack. But he was totally devoid of historic or aesthetic taste. Standing outside our beloved front door, he would say, 'It's not much of a HALL is it?' It had been St Mary's College since Erasmus lived there in 1497, and Frewin Hall since Dr Frewin in 1727, but Jack would never have heard of them. When we went for a walk in the town, with mother leading Chas by the hand as usual, Jack halted to ask, 'Can't we walk a little faster?' Mother turned on him. 'My dear Jack, I am setting the pace of this walk.'

Of the other boy, Laurence Keep, a nephew of my father's delightfully anecdotal solicitor friend, Percival Keep, I have the vaguest recollections. He seemed to be a nice quiet boy, rather borne down by the number of heavy garments which it was his duty to wear. Both of these boys took part in bike-polo with us, but not in extra-mural activities such as the Frewin Hall Alpine Club which went up the Union fire-escape and really all round our premises at the top of the wall level. It would have been quite fatal to introduce Jack to such an affair; he would certainly have broken his neck.* Dulce invented it. She was full of enterprise. Godfrey Driver was already showing signs of interest in the subject in which he was to achieve fame—languages. Dulce bought primary instructions for studying Esperanto with him but that project did not flourish.

Gradually the University programme for what was left of the summer term was sorted out. Although now Ambassador to Great Britain, Mr Roosevelt honoured his engagement to give the Romanes Lecture and receive his degree; but the only festivity was a dinner to which our parents went, given by the Vice-Chancellor and attended also by Rudyard Kipling, Andrew Lang and four heads of colleges. Dulce got seats for the lecture for herself and Miss Batty, but as Prof was under the same roof as our mother, no letters from him describing either occasion exist. Andrew Lang used to give us fresh volumes regularly of his Fairy Tale books, called 'Pink', 'Blue', 'Mauve' after their covers. He said his wife really wrote them. His handwriting was the worst we ever saw until our acquaintance was enlarged by a fascinating All Souls historian, Keith Feiling.

The only unusual event to be noted this week was the addition of another association-treasure to the medley already adorning our father's study. It was a Napoleonic Eagle captured at Quatre Bras and brought to us by an officer of Light Infantry. I became very familiar with it. It stood for the rest of Prof's life propped against a wall in his successive studies, waiting to be placed somewhere strategic.

The parents then went off for a visit to the Frank Pembers at Vicar's Hill, near Lymington, who became memorable to me because Mrs Pember was a qualified botanist and I was soon flattered by being sent up

---

* Jack was killed in action in 1916.

to the top of a crumbling wall at Frewin to get her specimens of Oxford Weed for her collection.

Joanna de Beaufort, which I had begun to write in Paris, was performed in the garden at Frewin after three rehearsals, now that the University had gone down. 'Acted by herself and little friends . . . About thirty people came to see it: went off very well.' I had been slaving at the props, designing correct coats of arms to be sewn on the furniture and on tabards worn by various performers. Chas was helpful, and as Humphrey of Gloucester, founder of the nucleus of the Bodleian, managed a long appropriate speech with calm. I did not myself take a leading part. I had been unfavourably impressed by Joanna Cannan's habit of assigning to herself the leading rôle when we produced a charade about Bonnie Prince Charlie, written by her, at Miss Batty's. 'The Prince. J.M.C.' I was just one of the Plantagenets, Henry, afterwards Henry V. All the Ealeses and Gotches could act and sing. It was unlucky that Ellie Vinogradoff, who was the heroine, could not act. She was perfect for the part only so far as appearance and audibility went. I discovered this too late. She wanted to play tragic Joanna de Beaufort as skittish. My curtain-couplet, after the captive king had declared his hopeless love would be improved, she felt, by her waving a paw and flying off to be chased, with the words 'You're not at all desirable'. I quashed that without explanation but did try repeatedly to explain that in English you said 'Henry the Fourth' and 'Henry the Fifth', not 'Henry Four' and 'Henry Five'. On 'the day' she came out with both horrors. I could only tell myself to remember, next year, not to ask her. For, like a real author I had a sequel about James I of Scotland on the stocks. Nearly all my best youthful friends did take part in this first effort. Oliver Gotch who could compose had produced the music for the song with which the performance opened. Chas could act. Mother surprised us all acting a trial scene in the box-room that summer. A sensational murder was filling the newspapers, 'The Crippen Case'. It was not exceptional, but made history as this was the first occasion that a culprit was arrested by means of a message sent by wireless to a liner at sea, Mother asked what part her angelic-looking son was taking. 'Well, sometimes I am Miss Le Neve, disguised as a boy, and sometimes the Remains.'

II

During the crucial weeks of Chas's illness all the vanloads from the warehouses, waiting since they left Cheltenham, and 39, had to be deposited in what positions were immediately available at Frewin Hall, and it was an interesting fact that some of these were most unsuitable but became hallowed by tradition. In the first of the three halls came, eventually, an enormous sixteenth-century Flemish chest richly carved. When the Raleigh boys tied up their indignant Old English mastiff to it, the chest stood up to the strain. It could have contained half a dozen Brides of Lammermoor. Well, perhaps it would just not have gone anywhere else. I never saw the lid lifted. Above it hung an engraving of Apollo in his chariot from an original by Guido Reni in what we understood to be called the Roast Pig Glue Oozy Palace, Rome. This masterpiece was a sort of status symbol in the Oxford professorial home. Most of our friends had it one way or another. In the high panelled cupboard beside the flight of steps leading from the first hall to the second came what we knew as the Belching Cupboard. Amongst the tastes in common of our parents was a total inability to throw away any paper or string. Prof wrote all his books in long-hand on half sheets of paper painfully pasted together. He prepared his day's stint. Mother could not part with the most thread-like or cable-strength string. When I married and had a flat in London, Chas was asked what it was like. 'Quite home-like,' was his reply. 'She's got a Belching Cupboard.' But I must plead that I am a specialist in what I preserve, and it must be of higher quality than that to which I was accustomed in youth.

Dr Frewin's portrait in oils, which 'went with the house' had the place of honour in the second hall, framed into the panelling. It was pretty dark there, but you could see that he was hard-featured and wore a wig. He seemed to be disapproving of an even darker oil-painting on the opposite wall, 'Bosworth Field'. This had an exciting little plate inside the frame with the famous quotation from *Richard III*—

> Jockey of Norfolk be not too bold
> For Diccon thy master is bought and sold.

The artist was proudly, but mistakenly as we afterwards discovered, declared to be Richard Wilson. Dr Frewin had been a real doctor, who could take your temperature—as well as an historian—Camden Professor of History and Regius Professor of Medicine. Having survived three wives and all his children, he had left the remainder of the lease of the house he had improved, to be an official residence for the Regius Professors of Medicine. The last person to occupy the premises before Edward, Prince of Wales, had been Dr John Kidd. There was a bust of him which also 'went with the house' dumped up in the attic store-room, a favourite hidey-hole, but rather eerie because a light dust-sheet placed over Kidd's marble features blew sideways as soon as you opened the door, displaying his sightless glare. This box-room was gradually occupied, but never quite filled, by a collection of uniform cases deposited by generations of Maclagan officers while in India, and much earlier unidentified persons. One had worn a volunteer uniform when Bonaparte was expected. There were trunks of crinolines and bonnets. The box room also received, as we grew out of them, our dolls' houses and alas! poor Dobbin.

To return to the second hall, on the ground floor, amongst a variety of lesser objects, such as a pair of fine Chippendale torchères (never used) and occasional tables of several periods and unnoticed merit, was one on which stood a piece of Edwardian Prosperity. It came from Vickery of Regent Street. It was the violet morocco-covered *placement* into which a hostess slipped little name cards to show guests where they would be sitting at the dining table. There was a quite unwarranted belief, after I married a timber broker and agent, that I lived in a whirl of giving dinner parties for sixteen, so when the Omans left Oxford the *placement* was allotted to me. It was quite pathetic. There were just two little cards left hanging tipsily in their frames—the Warden of All Souls and the Keeper of the Chest. We never set it up, but it found a home. My husband had a friend leaving to take up the duties of British Ambassador in Helsinki.

In the third hall, known as the serving hall because it communicated, but not closely, with the kitchen premises, down another set of steps, past the Priest's Hole (a bogus attribution) was my harbour and haven. This was much the largest hall and had a leather-covered easy chair, dumped for no apparent reason up and under the only high and modern staircase in the house. Here I read for whole wet afternoons, out of sight and out of mind. I went like a tank through nearly all the contents of all the bookcases of Frewin Hall. There was quite a good reading light as there were big windows high in the wall above. There were two bookcases here for company, one a break-front, the other with nothing but bound numbers of *Punch*, from which I learnt costumes and politics and what was thought funny in bygone years. The Barnado collecting box stood on the top of the low bookcase and the hall was darkened by two enormous oil-paintings by amateurs. One was of a snowy cloister at night and was the work of Great-Aunt Jane Slee, born 1811, who spoke Romany, planted trees with incantations and had written a romance on Ballooning. The other was by one of Prof's old pupils, a class for whom he always had a tender heart. It represented a Druid standing alone on a stormy shore, at sunset, striking a lyre.

From the serving hall you could get into the dining-room and the two drawing-rooms. It must be envisaged that all these, even when panelled, were almost as tightly packed with pictures as varying in size and subject as an early exhibition of the Royal Academy. The two drawing-rooms were subdivided by folding doors with turquoise and white Italian brocade curtains, generally left open. Nevertheless the back drawing-room was a morgue. This was the room in which I had to practise before breakfast. I never remember a fire in it. The front drawing-room was light and bright but not to be considered warm, especially after the fire had been given up because what was called the central heating had been turned on. The dining-room was easily the best room in the house. It had the same plaster decorated ceiling with pendants and a design of honeysuckle and lilies as the hall outside it, and above the fireplace an overmantel of six arcaded bays, flanked by half-length figures. Seven of these were wild men, but the eighth was an Elizabethan gentleman in a ruff, his hands folded in prayer for a blessing on the house. We believed that this was Dr Griffin Lloyd, the tenant, who had re-built this wing after 1580. There was a long recess behind his panelling in which the parents kept the silver. Dr Frewin's wing included Prof's study, the only other room of size on the ground floor. Upstairs, just before you entered it, was the third noticeable staircase, but not very noticeable as it was inadequately lighted and hardly ever used. You emerged from it with surprise halfway down a long passage and as its door was identical with the hanging cupboard next to it, when we first came, people kept on appearing out of what was supposed by us to be the 'Daisy' cupboard, named after Chas's stuffed lamb, disused, but there for ever.

This corridor ended in the handsome green spare-room and there was a series of powdering closets dividing it from the yellow spare-room and the school-room. The panelling of Dr Frewin's wing was much larger than that of the dining-room. The King's Room, long our school-room, was said to have settled the choice of Frewin Hall as a residence for Edward VII as an undergraduate. Anyone going up to it must pass under the surveillance of his *suite*, headed by General and Mrs Bruce. When the prince came down to Oxford on the morning after I was born, he said in one of his speeches that he looked back on his days there as the happiest in his youth. The others must have been remarkably miserable. He had been kept on such a very short rein.

It will be seen that our new home was of several dates, and rambling, but it provided the ideal opportunity for setting out vases of Ali Baba dimensions, card tables never functionally employed, furniture of mahogany, satin-wood, walnut, ormolu, ebony and buhl, gongs, brass-covered log-boxes, mirrors, fire-screens, and above all, books and pictures. The parents had subscribed to a series of Arundel print reproductions of paintings by Italian masters. Prof had *Colonel Mordaunt's Cockfighting Match* by Zoffany (with a key), in his dressing-room. Maclise's *Death of Nelson* and *Waterloo* were in nearly every house that we visited. Long and lean, they solved the question of passage walls. We had landscapes, classical incidents (*The Horatii murdering their sister*) historical incidents and portraits (Charles I and his youngest daughter), Triumphs of William of Orange, suitor for Princess Charlotte, water-colours, pen-and-ink sketches, garden scenes with figures, Highland scenes with cattle. Two *soi-disant* Francias of the Holy Family, utterly different in style, were the most important Italian paintings in the drawing-room. Family oil-portraits went mostly onto dining-room walls. Dulce, usually so well-behaved, once threw a jackety potato at me across the dining-room table when I was sitting in front of old Philip Judde, and we watched fascinated as it landed, and a cascade of melted butter streamed down our ancestor's severe countenance. Prof was not there.

We had one bathroom. Hip baths were still carried to the spare-rooms and set down in front of good fires.

I have often been asked if I realised how lucky I was to be brought up in such a beautiful place as Oxford. I did. Friedrich Maxmüller arrived there in the year that Dulce was born and did not die till I was three. I remember his widow well. Oxford made such an astonishing impact on him that he settled there. He wrote home lyrically of the most interesting and beautiful city in Europe, consisting almost entirely of churches, colleges which had been monasteries, castles and towers. He never regretted his choice. I, to be sure, saw these wonders from birth, but carried for the rest of my life pictures of certain moments—the wistaria on the face of Worcester, mist creeping from the river to make Magdalen bell tower arise like a phantasy, the fan-vaulting of Christ Church great staircase by candlelight, the 'sacred bend' on a hot day, with the smell from the nose-bags on the cab-rank, dear and comforting. Even when collecting these memories I found I had to cross out in the first chapters no less than twenty appearances of the word 'beautiful'. When we arrived at Frewin, country girls in black straw hats and shawls sold baskets full of fritillaries in the Cornmarket for pennies. Waking in the morning to hear the old mediaeval city full of clever striving young men getting into motion for another happy day seemed to make a noise like a swarm of bees gathering. The stage was set, the curtain was about to rise on the last act of the Omans at Oxford. Except for the accretion of more and more miscellaneous objects and persons, nothing would be changed till we left.

III

I do not know why it was decided that we should make a change this year and desert Pitlochry for Grantown-on-Spey. It may well have been because we needed more room. Dulce took to her bed for ten days after we arrived. No doctor was summoned and no cause was mentioned. The next thing was that Nana caught what was at first thought to be a severe chill. A doctor came every day for a fortnight. I had always been fascinated by the medical prowess of my Maclagan forbears and offered to go into her darkened room and look after her. I was employed only once. Mother had received a shock. Nana had sat up in bed suddenly and announced, 'You will never send that Precious Lamb away to a Boarding School!' After that outburst mother hardly let Chas out of her sight till Nana was gone. It was a relief to all when a married sister came to take her away for a change. She was suffering from 'a nervous breakdown' though it was not called that.

We did get some enjoyment out of our Grantown holiday. There were two families near by whom we could meet for expeditions. The Egertons would have preferred an unintellectual holiday rock-climbing in Switzerland and were too old for us. The Maxwells provided agreeable cousins of all ages. We went by train to Cromdale Haughs to go with them there, and walked back. We met the Egertons for a picnic at Muckerach Castle, a ruin. Next, the Maxwells had us all to Nethy Bridge. A day at Elgin was a success. We saw over Castle Grant. Glen Beg was a fine walk. This whole landscape was on a grander scale than Pitlochry. Our first effort to get to Loch an Eilan was frustrated by rain. It had a high reputation for picturesqueness and as a haunt of ospreys who still nested annually. When we did penetrate I was so much impressed by its romantic atmosphere that I had an inspiring dream. I dreamt I was walking along the sands when I perceived something half-hidden, glimmering at my feet. I bent down and disengaged it. It was a harp, and somehow I knew it was the Harp of Scotland and meant I was to write.

But this whole holiday was star-cros't and our enjoyments had to be snatched between days of anxiety. We got some good photographs, though, our best yet. All three of us were now camera fiends and my brother and sister were far to surpass me. Mother was spellbound one day out for a walk, listening to Dulce selling Chas her old camera. She pointed out that he would now be able to take quarter-plate pictures. He said that the films cost more. Moreover he feared the Number 3 Brownie appeared to be leaking and he must face having to pay for a repair. In the end they walked home hand in hand. A bargain had been struck.

Our journey home was difficult. Our engine broke down near Durham so we missed our connection at York. We had to arrive in London, and drive across, reaching Frewin at ten p.m. Next morning Whiteman gave notice. She had gathered that the disappearance of Nana was only temporary. Mother began to visit registry offices. Her trials now escalated. On the day that Prof left for Portugal alone, she got the news of the death of the Archbishop. He had retired two years before. Prof's trip to Portugal this time entailed a lot of luggage. Together with the current Duke of Wellington he had been invited as a guest of King Manoel to attend centenary celebrations of the capture of Bussaco. These included a banquet. The Duke would have uniform but Prof had to take his best cap and gown, (a colourful affair also) and full evening dress which it was known foreigners adored wearing in broad daylight.

Another tutor for Chas had to be greeted. Mother developed such neuritis that she could scarcely move one arm. The new cook stayed only her month. Mother had received a letter from Prof from Paris and then nothing for ten days. She got a telegram on October 5th saying he was all right; coming home. The newspapers gave her the explanation. There had been a revolution in Portugal. The little king had fled, accompanied by his mother and grandmother. The elder royal lady had embarked carrying a long loaf of bread under her arm. Kind Mrs Wells and Mrs Poole hastened round to Frewin to make concerned enquiries. These were

answered by the arrival of Prof. He had been one of sixteen who sat down
at the king's table for dinner after an elaborate review on September 27th.
As he made his adieux the king had presented him with a Portuguese
order. He had got out of Portugal by the last Sud express for Paris, and at
the Spanish frontier the few passengers had been eagerly asked for news.
Many bridges on the railways had been damaged but the rebels seemed to
have laid their mines ineffectively. Prof was distressed both as an historian
and a lover of Portugal. The House of Braganza had lasted eight hundred
years and had a splendid history. Actually the revolution was a mis-
managed affair and Admiral Reis, the rebel leader had committed suicide
prematurely thinking his *coup* had failed. On the other hand, the king's
disappearance, long before his cause was really lost, meant the surrender
of valuable partisans throughout his country.*

He was just of age and had succeeded to the throne in 1908 when his
father and elder brother had been assassinated. He had been riding in the
same carriage and received a bullet in the arm.

Less than a month after the revolution, Prof got a sudden intimation that
King Manoel and Queen Amalia were expected in Oxford on a sightseeing trip. He must show them All Souls. We did not see the king this
time but he came again six months later, without his mother and visited
Frewin. I remember how his face lit up when he saw draped over the
hated grand piano in the back drawing-room, one of Bamama's shawls
with a beautiful design which he identified as Portuguese. He was still
very small and perhaps was not going to grow much more as the grandees
who accompanied him were not much bigger. I had to take the Conde de
Sabugosa and *suite* to our stationers in St Giles's to choose postcards of
Oxford.

It had to be on the night of the king's visit to the house, of course, that
Nana arrived, pronounced cured. After a week she was despairingly
noted as 'not so well'. Dr Proudfoot came. She had been with us since she
had taken Dulce 'from the month'. She made it possible for the parents to
get off abroad together. I fear she impressed Prof in a slightly Rasputin
style with the notion that if she was not there Chas would perish. I
remember once when she had to be summoned back from a holiday, Prof
inadvisedly greeting her with 'Rachel. Thank Heaven you have come.' But
it would be quite impossible to risk keeping her. Nor did we really need
her now that Chas most certainly was going to a boarding school. It was

* For a full account of Prof's experiences in the Portuguese revolution see *Things I Have
Seen*, Chapters VIII and IX, Methuen, 1933.

arranged that another relative from Edinburgh should collect her. Mrs Macleod had to stay two days, which was undesirable, but it had been realised too late that December 12th was Nana's birthday. We all gave her the presents we had made and she went off resignedly saying she had known her stay would not be for long since she had seen a black pig at a station somewhere on her journey south. She was still being pensioned by Prof when he died in 1946 and eventually survived both my parents and my husband ('Just don't think about it, dear.')

For us now began a Golden Age. A new cook arrived who became a bosom friend of our new parlourmaid. They shared the sewing machine and went for their days out together, Nancy Wilkins on her tricycle, for she had the figure of a very good cook, and Beatrice White from Cornwall, in her *pince-nez*, stalking beside. Annie Stanton, agreed by all our circle to be the handsomest maid we ever had, came from a village near Elsfield, Horton-cum-Studley, on the edge of Otmoor, and was learning the harp. She was assisted as housemaid by Ada Owen and a succession of morning girls from Sister Ellen's Orphanage who came to learn the ways of a house. Ethel Stangoe, Nancy Wilkins, Beatrice White, Annie Stanton and Ada Owen were immovable until three of them married.

VIII

Coming Out:

1911–1912

I

1910 ENDED WITH A GLORIOUS EXPERIENCE. FOUR DAYS BEFORE Christmas we went to stay with Chas's godfather, now Canon Henson, in Dean's Yard. The little Canon showed us Westminster Abbey with great enthusiasm and we were allowed to take time-exposures. I got very good ones of the Innocents' Corner and Elinor of Castile lying serene on her tomb. We were not so happy when our kind host showed us where a marauding Dane, robbing the abbey, had been caught and skinned. His skin had been put along the top of a door and Canon Henson lifted me up with instructions to run my fingers along it. Dulce and I confessed to one another afterwards that we had deliberately tried not to feel the area he indicated. In the smoky foggy evening we saw Westminster School boys, freaked with mud, playing games. For the parents there were luncheon and dinner parties. We were taken to see *Henry VIII*. This production had a star cast—Tree as Wolsey, Bourchier as Henry VIII Violet Vanburgh as poor Queen Katharine, Forbes Robertson as Buckingham, and a new-comer, the *piquante* brunette Laura Cowie as Anne Boleyn. I caught my breath as the curtain rose on the first scene. Tree seemed to have abolished the fourth wall. There were Tudor noblemen in Tudor brocades standing with their backs to us engaged in easy conversation. We were there.

We did not go behind the scenes to see Tree because none of us really knew him since he had become so big. Mother, as a child, had been taken to see him performing in amateur theatricals in Berkeley Square. He had then been a red-haired apprentice in his father's grain business. The actor who struck me most was Bourchier. He was Henry VIII to the life. I never saw more elaborate productions than those of Sir Herbert Beerbohm Tree at His Majesty's. Their detail was quite distracting. We now went to one every year. But as far as great acting went, Tree as Macbeth, was wiped from my memory after I saw Gielgud. When he came down the stairs with his gory blade after murdering old King Duncan, you could tell that this man had killed a man. But that was a much later experience. I went to see every possible Shakespeare play throughout my youth after my initiation when Uncle Ed took me to *The Merchant of Venice*. I never saw the last acts of some as when we were taken to Stratford on Avon from Miss Batty's we had to catch the last train back to Oxford.

We ended our Dean's Yard visit with a call at Argyll Road to say goodbye to Uncle Bob before he left for India. Going to Aunt Al's house was rather bad for me as Ming and Jeanie Frame held up their hands in proprietary pride at my erudition. They had dressed my mother for her wedding. But I was now nearing fourteen, so there was nothing remarkable in my being able to go round the engravings on the walls and identify Shakespeare scenes.

We were now getting a little more exercise. After five years in late Regency Park Town, Miss Batty's was moving to a larger Victorian Gothic mansion in the Parks—3 Bradmore Road, soon 'The Bradder'. We had always had games in the eleven o'clock break; rounders and badminton. We now had netball one afternoon a week on a ground up near Summerfields. Hockey and lacrosse were still denied us, but after June 1910 we had a Boat Race on a stretch of river above the Cherwell Arms. Dulce and Sylvia Driver won that year. Our craft were outriggers for two pairs of oars, and a mistress steered.

The first number of the I.M. appeared in January 1911. We had a school magazine. But it was not exactly that, as it was produced by a Secret Society. I.M. meant 'Betwixt Many' and was wrong in every way, as the affair was run by a junta of six: the Driver boys soon sent a message that I.M. meant for men. Everything about it was so secret that even the contributors had to take pseudonyms, all beginning with B. We sent in our efforts in long-hand, and the magazine was assembled by J. M. Cannan, Literary and Sporting Editor, and C. M. Oman, Artistic Editor. I do not think it can have been very agreeable to the staff to have a secret society in our midst producing a magazine at a date when parents were writing to complain about the amount of home-work we were given. I imagine that most people who are going to write get enmeshed at some stage or another in editing a school magazine, so it is unnecessary to recount our trials. Janet Allen produced enchanting covers, but was so dilatory that one representing a girl under an umbrella in a snowstorm had to appear on the April number. We got landed with never-ending serials, one of which was mine. 'Engrai' showed strong influence of *The Prisoner of Zenda*. I had to illustrate 'Copernicus and the Universe' for Frances Eales. We had reviews, and reports of our debates. We kept so strictly to our executive committee of six that one member of our community, denied entrance, ran round the whole of Park Crescent roaring. The I.M. was still in production when I left in 1914, and I imagine faded out as discreetly as it had originally appeared. When Sylvia Driver succeeded Dulce as head girl she became editor of an official *Wychwood School Magazine*. It might be of interest to a modern psychoanalyst to consider why we had this passion for secrecy as we approached adolescence.

On Sundays now we went to morning service in our new church rebuilt for the second time in 1874. St Peter le Bailey was quite unlike St Giles's, but I liked it even less. It was large, nearly empty and just opposite our drive gates. There was always a line of Sister Ellen's orphans in the pew in front of us. Sometimes chosen ones were brought to meet us at Frewin but we were all terribly shy, and we dared not introduce them to bike-polo or the Alpine Club. We could equally have gone to a much older and more beautiful church, for we were also in the parish of St Michaels at the North Gate, but although that was tried we always went back to empty echoing St Peter le Bailey. St Michaels was crowded. We might catch something.

We had a dance for sixty in the first week of 1911 and one for our staff the next evening. Every member was allowed to ask a young man, and Dulce and I had to open the ball dancing with the most important of them. Prof wisely had an appointment at Woolwich. The Burrowses gave a dance and that was the end of my dancing for the season. Striving to leap to an unbelievable height in the Schottische, I sprained my ankle.

The Burrowses gave the most enjoyable parties, outings by steamer to Stanton Harcourt and by motor to Blenheim, where I was astonished to find such a small duke in such a large home. We went to Oxford Castle, and a custodian lit a newspaper and sent it down the well. He told us that once, when it had been dredged, three skeletons, two male and one female, had been found. We went to stay at Norham Gardens while the parents took Chas down to Hove to see the boarding-school chosen for him, and all the sights of Brighton. It seems impossible that

Miss Batty's school, 1910.

M. Lock, C. Driver, J. Allen, S. Trevelyan, A. Burrows, C. Oman, J. Cannan, S. Wilkinson, G. Eales.
B. Conway, N. Gotch, A. Moss, R. Tideman, M. Cannan, P. Thomson, D. Oman, S. Driver, I. Murray, F. Eales.
Miss Locock, Miss Lee, Miss Batty, Mlle. Ratoret, M. Godley, Miss Doering, Miss Rogers, J. Thatcher.
R. Turner, J. Trevelyan, B. Madan, B. Kranich, D. Eales, E. Jacks, C. Mackenzie, A. Cooper.

British Maidens: Carola and Dulce.

The last Pageant: *Comus*, 1914.

the most devoted parents could do exactly right for their children.

Agnes Burrows had been provided with a cousin, Sidney from Sydney, only a little older but much more sophisticated. It sounded ideal, for Sidney had a brother coming up as an undergraduate. But after a promising start, Sidney had a troublesome adolescence and was demoted to a bath-chair and told us how she had felt so bad when they had got to the corner of Bradmore Road that she had only just enough breath left to whisper to the man to take her back. Her brother got sent down for screwing up the Dean of his college, and so did another cousin who had achieved a Blue. Brocas was now at Eton and very good looking. We asked him if he saw Geoffrey Madan and he said he would not be seen speaking to a 'tug'. Years later I heard that when he had gone as military attaché to the Embassy in Rome he had puzzled Italian high society by having a longer Rolls-Royce than his Ambassador. But he had the qualities of his defects, for as a prisoner-of-war he had doggedly learnt languages. His French and Italian were remarkable and his Russian had qualified him for the unlucky Archangel Expedition of 1918.

The Chadwick girls were now being sent in relays to enjoy themselves at Oxford and we took Joyce, the younger, fair-haired one, to witness the Torpids in east wind and snow. Joyce's only other treat seems to have been evensong at Magdalen College chapel where the music was so special the congregation were asked by Dr Varley Roberts, D. Mus., to join in the service silently. Luckily, Joyce was not the singing Chadwick.

Peninsular centenaries were now coming along, and Prof went off to take part in the Barossa celebrations with the Irish Fusiliers. Chas was sent to be photographed in a hideous prep-school outfit. The parents left for Italy in a snowstorm on Dulce's birthday which could not be helped. Next year she would be 'out' and have her fill of gaieties. We went to Southsea as usual except that Ethel was in charge. She had a bike. Nothing went wrong. On our return we heartlessly started lawn tennis in the garden on the day before mother took Chas up to Victoria station to join the boys going to the Hove school for the summer term. The featureless letters from little boys to their parents began to arrive. 'I am reading *The Riddle of the Sands*. I have got to page 102.' 'I am reading *The Riddle of the Sands*. I have got to page 139.'

Children were now beginning to turn up at Frewin for rehearsals of 'The Tragedy of King James I'. Rather against my will, I was going to be James. Judging by the authorities, though noble, he had been rather a softy. Most girls from Miss Batty's went on now to large boarding

K

schools. I had lost the Gotches and three elder members of families who had performed for me last year. Chas was now unavailable. But I still had a stand by 'good at need' in the second Cannan, May, who got the star part of Catherine Douglas, and the second Eales would be perfect as the Princess Marguerite, eldest daughter of James I. Agnes Burrows would be reliable as Joanna de Beaufort, now Queen of Scotland. I had a troupe of younger children to be the six little princesses. There was a good deal of doubling of parts as my list of Dramatis Personae was impressive—twenty-four. Dulce and Dora Eales and Janet Allen all appeared as Scottish earls, loyal and disloyal and Janet was also a shepherdess. The appearance of this name on my programme was a triumph. Janet could not really act, though this was difficult to say with certainty as she never learnt her part.

I had at last been allowed to ask her to my home. This struggle had lasted two years. When her father came to leave her at Miss Batty's for the first time, I thought he must be going back to Australia. Their parting was so heartfelt. But it turned out that he was like that with all his six children. Janet sat next to me in the Lower Room and she could draw as well as Leonardo and Burne Jones. At least I was sure she could draw a perfect circle and her female figures were quite as drooping and starry-eyed as Cophetua's queen. The trouble was that the Allens had nothing visible to do with the University so my parents never met them. Nana was blighting. When I said that Janet Dundas Allen was half Scottish, Nana said, 'She will never be one of the grand Dundases.' But she was. I plodded on, and suggested that as she came from Sydney like Agnes's cousin, the Burrowses must know something. They did, and mother set out patiently to call. Nothing happened. 'My dear, I have called and my call has not been returned.' I was going to an extra drawing-class also attended by Janet, and behind our easels, with much embarrassment, I managed to whisper my sad story to her. I did so long to ask her to tea and hear more about the Blue Mountains and the Great Barrier Reef. Janet must have remembered, for her father arrived with her to call at Frewin Hall. Her mother was a sofa-mother, like those of a great many of our friends, and had been returned to 145 Woodstock Road by an ambulance on a stretcher after an operation.

I had lost Oliver Gotch for my music this year but Winnie Chadwick would be coming to stay. She was most co-operative and prepared to sing an Ave Maria at great length between Acts I and II.

PROGRAMME

THE TRAGEDY OF JAMES I

DRAMATIS PERSONAE

Sir Alexander Lovel, 'King of Love'	Phyllis Thomson
The Earl of Athole	Janet Allen
The Earl of Orkney	Dulce Oman
Sir Robert Graham .. .. ⎫	Joanna Cannan
Sir Robert Stewart .. .. ⎪	Sidney Wilkinson
Sir John Hall .. .. .. ⎬ Conspirators	C. M. Oman
Hugh Hall .. .. .. ⎪	D. Eales
Christopher Chalmers, porter ⎭	D. R. Oman
Robert Forbes, a shepherd	Ruth Turner
Andrew Kirkpatrick	R. Turner
James, Duke of Rothesay	Dora Eales
James Stuart, King of Scotland	Carola Oman
Joanna, Queen of Scotland	Agnes Burrows
Princess Marguerite ⎫	Gracie Eales
Princess Isabella ⎪ Children of	Sylvia Trevelyan
Princess Annabella ⎬ James and	Beatrice Madan
Princess Joanna ⎪ Joanna	Joan Trevelyan
Princess Mary ⎪	Mary Whitelocke
Princess Eleanora ⎭	Nora Whitelocke
Catherine Douglas	May Cannan
Gillian, a shepherdess	Janet Allen
Music and sundry noises	Winifred Chadwick

Visions, Murderers, Citizens of Perth

ACT I

Scene 1.—The Monastery gardens, Perth.
Scene 2.—A room in the Monastery.
Scene 3.—In the Monastery gardens.

ACT II

Scene 1.—On the moor of Killiehangie.
Scene 2.—The Castle, Blair Athole.
Scene 3.—In the King's chamber, Perth—Night.

ACT III

Scene 1.—In the Queen's chamber, Perth.
Scene 2.—Outside the Monastery gates.
Scene 3.—In the Queen's chamber.

We were having my play in All Souls library this year and Sir Ernest Trevelyan, who never allowed his children to perform in the school play and had drawn the line when 'Joanna de Beaufort' took place merely in the garden at Frewin, withdrew his disapproval. 'The Tragedy of James I' was, in construction, as arbitrary as some of the Shakespeare historicals to which I was devoted. There were four male parts of almost equal significance, Sir Alexander Lovel, 'King of Love', a handsome *jeune premier*, who became heroic; the poet king, James I, whose character could not develop, and Sir Robert Graham and Sir Robert Stewart, conspirators. It was confusing that they both had to be Sir Robert, but this was history. Stewart was seduced into treason by Graham in Scene 2, Act I. There was a scene on a moor above Blair Castle, in which Janet was a shepherd-girl attended by a shepherd boy and 'Daisy' the stuffed lamb, property of Chas, who had given her name to the cupboard in the passage leading to the spare-rooms at Frewin. The only drawback about pressing Daisy into service was that if you did this literally and put your hand on her head, it bent forward and she emitted a surprisingly loud 'Ba-aa'. Janet doubled this part with that of a loyal earl and I was a conspirator asking the way to Blair, and a perfect villain. This tiny strip of a scene in idyllic surround-ings, built up the growing horror. I made the scenery myself. A few canvas and cardboard arches, painted grey, sufficed for a monastery garden and the king's chamber at Perth. Somebody stronger, I suppose the faithful Nutt, produced swags of ivy and other foliage which looked well draped over my arches. I had Apparitions in my last Act, a bare-faced lift from *Macbeth*. The vision of Thomas, Duke of Clarence, drowned in a butt of Malmsey, was so horrific that the Sidney Balls' infant Oonagh had to be carried out uttering even more blood-curdling yells. The final and best apparition, who came with singing and light, was my beloved Henry V who, at this date, I had no doubt, was in heaven. The 'fey' Highland crone who came to warn James for the third time of his impending doom, never came on. She just made noises outside. 'She says, my lord, tomorrow is too late.' She went off with much wailing, and the wind began to howl too, setting off the royal hounds. I was proud of this presaging incident.

I must say I think it was very indulgent of my parents to allow me to have this performance in All Souls, but such things were not unknown in University circles. Two years later, Naomi Haldane, who was six months my junior, and the only girl at Lynham's school, wrote a play called 'Saunes Bairos' about an imaginary country in the Andes, in which eugenics were in force and nobody might have more than two infants. 'The Skipper' let her have it performed in the hall of the Dragon School during the holidays, and a photograph of her with a cast of about forty was taken in New College cloisters. Most of them were her own class-mates, or undergraduate friends of her Etonian scholar elder brother Jack. Arthur Egerton gave us tickets, but to my disappointment, when Jack had just brought the house down, announcing 'I have had twins', mother swept us out with the words 'How dare he?' She referred to poor Arthur who was never really received back into favour.

She noted, 'James I, Carola's play went off very successfully.' This was on a Monday—July 10th, and my senior performers gave me a beautifully bound typed copy of the Tragedy. I think Joanna, whose signature came first of the donors on the flyleaf, must have been the leading spirit. It had five gilt thistles on the spine and leather corners and has worn well.

An unexpected repercussion, detected by Sylvia and Joan Trevelyan, who had both been daughters of James I, was that Miss Batty's took umbrage as no Trevelyans were ever allowed to appear in the school play. The girls thought that thereafter they got such bad reports that they were taken away. However, Doris had already gone on to Wycombe Abbey and Sylvia and Joan would normally have followed. Sylvia was already showing signs of the administrative ability which was to bring her to be head girl at Wycombe. She had a three-decker pencil-box which, brandished above the head of the most uppish Transatlantic pupil, brought her to reason.

Coronation Day 1911 was not as exciting for us as that of Edward VII. Dulce was taken to watch the procession to the Abbey in London. The Domestic Bursar had the Trevelyans and me to his rooms in All Souls which overlooked the High Street, down which passed a loyal local procession between stately buildings decorated with many garish flags. For some time the illustrated Press had made the four surviving sons and only daughter of George V and Queen Mary familiar figures in the British nursery. There was a popular picture of little Prince Eddie in a sailor suit, drilling his brothers and sister. Some of them just matched us for age. Dulce was two months younger than Prince Eddie, and I was a fortnight junior to Princess Mary whose fortunes my own followed closely as to dates.

One of the beneficial results of the departure of Nana was that at fourteen I was allowed a limited degree of freedom in choosing my clothes. I began this summer with two linen dresses—cherry-red and moss-green. Canon Henson asked us to lunch to meet the daughters of another Fellow of All Souls, Sir Frederick Thesiger, who was to become Lord Chelmsford and a Viceroy. Joan and Anne Thesiger had such simple summer dresses, floral Liberty lawns, and had such poise. When I sat transfixed with shame to see that I had 'piggied' the Hensons' damask table-cloth, Anne, without a word, scraped it up and disposed of it on her own plate, just before it was removed, and as if she had been the culprit.

We did not stay in Dean's Yard this time. The station hotels were still reckoned amongst the best in London and we were welcomed at Charing Cross. We went from Paddington to Charing Cross by Underground Inner Circle. Some years past, one of my infant books had had an illustration 'Ten Toy Terriers, Trying the Tuppeny Tube.' At first it was slightly awe-inspiring. The passengers sat just staring, and then as if summoned by unseen hands, arose and got out. Before the theatre we visited an Italian restaurant in Soho where the manager gave us presentation boxes of chocolates in the shape of bright pink satin *sabots*. We saw *The Scarlet Pimpernel* in London this summer, and a Greek play *al fresco* at Bradfield and under cover at Radley. We were never taken to *Peter Pan*. Prof disapproved of a paterfamilias in a dog-kennel and mawkishness about children. The parents dashed up to Edinburgh for him to receive his LLD degree. In the end of July he went down to Brighton to fetch Chas and took him on to St Leonards to introduce him to the Chadwicks. We had one more treat before leaving for Bovey Tracey Vicarage. At Windsor Castle Mr Fortescue showed us over indefatigably and gave us lunch, and a crumpet tea, and identical large coloured reproductions of an oil-painting of the Castle. The only drawback about this munificence was that all three had to be put up somewhere, and we had already a very fine set of historical scenes sent to Prof by some publishers. Chas had two— *The Building of Hadrian's Wall* and *Attack on Hougoumont*. I got *The Plucking of the Roses* and Dulce chose *Queen Philippa and the Burghers of Calais*. We put them in our school-room on the top of a trellised rose-patterned wall paper.

We had basket-chairs, and photographs of friends, and invitations stuck up on the mantelpiece. We had no taste. We were so happy.

II

Devonshire was a distinct improvement on Grantown-on-Spey for the annual holiday. We had some transport as well as the bikes. Mother drove a trap into Teignmouth. Owing to the parents' habit of going to Italy in the spring and sending us to Southsea in weather generally distinguished for snowstorms, we had never learnt to swim and never seen the sea in the summer. August was the month for Prof's fishing—surely an unenlightened choice, but University terms dictated all. Chas had now learnt to swim at Hove. The idea of sending him there had been because it was on the sea. Actually the school was a mile and a half inland, and he never saw the sea except on Sundays after church and before lunch when the pupils went for a walk in a crocodile along the promenade. He had been taught to swim in an interior swimming-bath. Water deteriorated and became opaque by weekends. As this was his first return for a long holiday, I think this must have been the date when the parents got a letter from the headmaster to say that until he had seen the boy under the shower he had not known that he was black and blue. It is quite inexplicable to me that he was not removed and sent to a day-school. There was one which got all the best scholarships—Lynams, on the Cherwell beyond the Parks. But I gather from Chas that this was never considered because the headmaster was believed by Prof to be insufficiently attached to the tenets of the Church of England. Also, he was adored by his pupils and allowed them to call him 'Skipper'. Neither of these objections could be raised against the Alington's establishment up at Summerfields. Only with regard to the Son did mother's authority entirely fail. She continued to conceal her misery when he had to be returned to the prison-house. She continued her diary, merely mentioning his comings and goings and his Sunday letters. As for him, he had red eyes for several mornings regularly as the date for return drew near. I once surprised him, hugging Patch and scarcely able to get out between sobs, 'Oh! dog darling . . .' I heard hardly anything about his first boarding school and believed for many years that it had been a sort of Dotheboys Hall. His own later comment was Stoic. 'The Wick was tough, and the educational standard was not high, but the food was better than what I was to get at Winchester in war-time.'

I found a pony awaiting me at Bovey Tracey and a groom-gardener to take me out on the moors. He knew them for only a few miles around the vicarage and there was a night when we returned after dark to find members of the family and his own reproachful wife setting out with lanterns to rescue me. The moor was renowned for treacherous patches. We went to Lustleigh and Chudleigh and Exeter, and met the Burrowses for picnics. They had taken a house at Widdicombe-on-the-Moor. There was a moderate tennis court at our vicarage, and a pottery works near by, at which we all invested in minor specimens which we greatly admired and which proved commendably unbreakable. Altogether, the Devonshire experiment was enjoyable and the scenery was so richly coloured that I could hardly believe my eyes when I first saw the view from my bedroom window. There was the additional attraction for me that one of the murderers of Thomas à Becket had been a Tracey.

At the end of the first week of September Dulce and I were sent to stay with the Chadwicks and Chas was taken to see the battlefield of Waterloo. His last days before returning to school were spent as always with dull little rides with Mr Rhodes, and hours in the dentist's chair.

A new pageant was interesting Oxford. This one took place in October in the Town Hall which solved the problems of weather and acoustics. It was 'The Pageant of English Literature'. Mr Burrows had been allotted 'The Canterbury Pilgrims'. There were reliable sources for the costumes and Ethel made a worthy one for Dulce, who was the Knight, and a gay one for me as the Squire—pink tights and an apple-green jerkin and an absurd elongated tea-cosy hat. Agnes was the Prioress, and Janet her attendant nun, leading two black Aberdeen terriers. This was the first time that I saw Janet in the habit which she was to wear for fifty-two years.

There was always an annual clear-out after the summer holidays at Miss Batty's. This year it became inevitable that Janet would have to go to a boarding school. Mr Allen, whose innocence was only rivalled by that of his wife, came to see mother, I think with the idea that it might be a happy solution for Janet and me to go somewhere together. 'I wish,' he said to mother, who had not the least intention of relinquishing me, 'that *you* would go and see Miss Monypenny.' This was the principal of, I think, a London school. His elder daughter, Primrose, had not been happy at Wycombe, had caught pneumonia and been delirious. Marian, his second, had been too great a success—but at games. She was a heroine in our circle after we heard that she had been asked to play lacrosse for

England, having qualified by having her nose broken, at this lady-like occupation. The very name of Miss Soulsby sounded reassuring. Brondesbury Young Ladies were taken in growlers for winter concerts in the Albert Hall and in victorias in the summer for lawn tennis with the Bishop of London and his chaplain at Fulham Palace. No child of divorced parents was ever admitted and I have today one exact contemporary who assures me that her parents chose Miss Soulsby's for her because of this inflexible rule.

In the end Mr Allen settled on St Mary's School, Wantage. It might have been worse. He promised to take me out for picnics with her on the Downs. I perfectly realised that she was getting hopeless reports from Miss Batty's and really doing nothing except draw saints and angels. She used to continue, rapt, while mistresses abused her so severely that I should have wept. I went to her once and offered to hear her Latin prep in eleven o'clock breaks but she refused. I used to dive to collect her sketches from wastepaper-baskets. She always tore them up and never ceased doing them. She went off, and we promised to write every day, but after a brief period of pencilled replies, evidently achieved with difficulty, saying that all the girls here were silly, she fell into her place and took to a convent school like a duck to water.

With the autumn term at Oxford arrived one more connection by marriage on mother's side as an undergraduate at Trinity. Charles Sartoris, one of the most attractive young men we ever knew, became the most ardent of Dulce's admirers. Alas! we are perhaps allowed to enjoy such company for a very short time. It was difficult to say in what Charles excelled. He startled our father by explaining, 'Yes, I always stay with the President at Trinity when I come up for Responsions.' But he had, at last, it seemed succeeded. I cannot discover that he had one taste in common with Dulce who seldom opened a book, but he had enthusiastic sessions with my mother at which he capped all her quotations—mostly from Tennyson I think. He was not distinguished in any form of sport, and Trinity was a rowing college. He spoke with *aplomb* of the Rue de la Paix. He was of the very best type of Old Etonian, with a flaxen lock always falling over one eye, and a gangling figure. I don't think I ever actually spoke to him. Nearly all the young men who came up to Oxford this autumn term were to be swept into the Forces three years later. As they matured, they vanished. Charles was killed on Lancashire Landing Beach in Gallipoli. He had left Dulce, by will, a gift which together with most of her wedding presents was lost at sea off Cyprus in the P.O.

Persia. His greatest friend at Oxford was Lord Sandon at Christ Church with whom he indulged in many high-spirited pranks, including being shown over a stately home disguised as lady tourists in sweeping garments and veils, wielding lorgnettes. He told us that after one New Year's Eve stay, I suppose in Staffordshire, he heard the family ghost—the hunter's horn, calling the hounds home. 'Beautiful notes, perfectly clear.* Sandon did not hear them.' Sandon survived.

III

1912 absolutely eclipsed 1911 as far as incidents went. We had known, of course, that it must be exciting as Dulce would be eighteen on April 4th. The weather after Christmas was deplorable. Chas went off to bed with a cold and had to be left at home when the wagonette collected for the Arthur Evans Twelfth Night party. But he was patched up in time to be taken, in the usual snowstorm, to join the pupils returning to the Wick.

Peggy Poole was no longer to come in the afternoons to give us painting lessons in the school-room. We went to her wedding in St Giles's church. Naomi Haldane was one of the bridesmaids in an artistic greenery-yallery dress and I admired her long straight light brown hair, but mother said she did not hold herself well, and disapproved of the Bach music which Archdeacon Hutton provocatively said he found 'adorable'. There would have to be a coming-out dance for Dulce next term, but meanwhile there was a small one for just fifty which I was allowed to attend in a three-quarter length evening dress with a crystal fringe which had been bought for me and which I detested. It shed mini-beads everywhere and needed constant repair.

C. T. Atkinson had married, a sister of a fire-brand military historian, Colonel Maurice. Her name was Cosette and C.T. described her as 'about my own age' which mother said generally meant older. They came

* Charles Sartoris was already a connection when he arrived to us. One of Aunt Augusta's sisters, a Barrington, had married Alfred Sartoris of a Huguenot family which still had a French branch, de l'Aigle. Charles was thus a great-nephew of Augusta. But to make the connection totally confusing, after we knew Charles, Augusta's son, Eric Maclagan, married Helen Lascelles, whose mother had been Gertrude Liddell, first cousin of Aunt Augusta, married to Leonard, son of Alfred Sartoris of Abbotswood, Glos., and father of Charles Sartoris. The real confusion begins after two Liddells of different generations married Lord Barrington and a Sartoris.

up to see us, very happy to be photographed. R. L. Atkinson, C.T.'s much younger brother, now at Magdalen, was a constant guest in our school-room. He was going to work at the Record Office and was solid and rather solemn. Herbert Meredith, who turned up almost as often, had a penurious widowed mother and was one of the best-looking friends we ever had. He was what was called a Bible-clerk at All Souls, as the college did not have undergraduates, but he was of undergraduate age and as he rowed he did that with Trinity, and got into one of their boats. So he would ask us on the Trinity barge for Torpids. There were two magazines at the University: *The Oxford Magazine* on which I afterwards worked was understood to be for the dons and had a small circulation. *The Isis* was much more colourful, with illustrations, and a weekly *Isis Idol*. Philip Guedalla, who was one of the brilliant Balliol men, was of course an idol. He was an officer at the Union and Mark Antony in the OUDS this term. I do not think either of us ever met him as we knew hardly anyone at Balliol except Arthur Egerton who was under a cloud after he had sent us to a play about eugenics. But as a speaker at the Union we admired 'P.G.' immensely. Dulce was not at all interested in politics, but I spoke in favour of Free Trade at our debating society at The Bradder. This was closely modelled on the undergraduates' Union, but our motions had to be comparatively tame. '"That in the opinion of this House Literature has as great an effect upon its Age as the Age has upon its Literature." Moved by C. Whitwell, Opposed by C. Oman, F. Eales will speak third E. Duff will speak fourth. E. Jacks, President, B. Madan, Sec: "That in the opinion of this House scenery is an aid to the imagination and necessary to the production of a dramatic performance." Moved by C. Oman, ex-President, Opposed by B. G. Madan, Sec. J. Bradshaw will speak third. E. Jacks, President, will speak fourth. Tellers, for the Ayes U. R. Richards, For the Noes V. A. Vaughan.'

Aunt Allie came to stay at the end of January, in widow's weeds. William Hayter had died before Christmas. Jeanie Frame nursed her when she took to her bed on arrival, and she stayed there for the rest of her visit. Mother, who had arisen to welcome her, now heard from the Wick that Chas had developed measles. It was undesirable that she should attempt to see him. As we had been so carefully shielded by Nana we all got the usual epidemics at rather advanced ages. (I did not get measles until I was almost engaged to be married, and until the rash came out was much impressed by my high temperature and near-delirium.) Mother got down to Brighton at the earliest possible moment, and mercifully, only after she was safely home, had to send for Dr Proudfoot to look at her sore throat. On his second call he diagnosed diphtheria.

This was a shattering announcement as Dulce was leaving school that very day, the musicians were engaged and lists of guests for her coming out dance were already drawn up. A presentation was made to her, and the joint headmistresses sent a eulogistic letter opening, 'We part with Dulce with real regret.' Naturally, like most elder sisters, she had been somewhat embarrassed when I came as a fellow pupil and had rather tended to ignore my existence, but shortly before her retirement she took responsibility for me in a scrape, without hesitation.

I do not think that our teachers fully recognised with what difficulties we had to contend as we became adolescent. I only once remember a whole class having hysterics. It was at European History when we had to read aloud a passage which twice referred to 'the Barbars'. Someone whispered 'Black-Sheep'. One by one, as we were ordered to carry on and read it again and properly, we broke down, and most passed from yells of laughter to tears. Even Frances Eales as she approached the fatal words had to lay down her book. I think Miss Batty had to break off, baffled. I was now nearly fifteen and taller than Dulce. I had never before had the least difficulty in reciting a screed of poetry given us for homework, (which incidentally was much too much). I was chagrined when I 'dried up' after a few lines of something which I had never envisaged forgetting. I was told I had better go back to my desk and begin to learn it. With a little encouragement I could perfectly have continued. So next time I learnt the poetry—a long screed from *Samson Agonistes*, until it was engraven on my heart. I gave up everything to get it rock-firm. I was word perfect when I performed next morning and as I went back to my seat I murmured, 'Victory, O Lord!' not to anybody special, but several people looked up. 'Carola,' announced the junior mistress in charge. 'For talking in class you shall lose all your marks for recitation.' I still think our marks were a great mistake. On them depended our place in form at the end of term. I always had a struggle to hold my place, I could hardly believe my ears at the injustice now done to me. I burst into tears for the first and last time at Miss Batty's. Dulce slipped a note to me under a ruler—a ruse to which she seldom descended. 'Don't cry. I will see Miss Lee.' It must have been a Literature day for Miss Lee did come and I was summoned to her. She asked if I had thought that the mistress was wrong in taking away my marks. I hardly realised that I was going to be told she was perfectly justified. But anyway I could not answer for sobs, which was perhaps for the best. The storm blew over and I imagine that the junior mistress had rather an unpleasant interview with Miss Lee later that day. She was still in office when I left in 1914, but always bore me a grudge. We were far too severely rebuked. May Cannan, who was emotional, was easily reduced to tears.

At last Dr Proudfoot took his final swabs from our throats and mother was allowed to go for a drive in Bagley Woods. Only a week later we went for an expedition to Cheltenham to buy Dulce's outfit. The Cannans now went to Paris and appeared in some startling *ensembles*. Mrs Symonds said they were all colour-blind "No dear, you go to Cheltenham," said Mrs Wells, the delightful wife of Joseph Wells of Wadham. We ordered three ball dresses for Dulce—white with gold Greek key pattern, for the actual coming out at Frewin, apple green and sky blue. After four days at Cheltenham and expeditions with Prof to Tewkesbury and Gloucester, we passed on to London and the shops of High Street, Kensington, which we were told would not be so smart as those at Cheltenham where the *clientèle* included fast hunting-women who wore tea-gowns and smoked cigarettes. We bought ready-made a white and gold brocade dinner dress for Dulce with a large pattern, quite unsuitable for her age and shape, but lovely in itself.

We stayed at the Charing Cross Hotel again and went to Maskelyne and Devant's and dined at Gianelli's before seeing Tree and H. B. Irving and Phyllis Neilson Terry in *Othello*. I was still in a neurotic state and almost asked to be taken out. I knew Othello was having to strangle the lovely Desdemona. Luckily, we had a box, and I was able to arrange to sit at the back and close my eyes.

We went for a trip to St Albans from London and called on the Bishop who was a bachelor with a fatherless nephew, Ernest Jacob, who was going to become another constant visitor to Frewin when he came up to Oxford. Only Prof proceeded to Peterborough to stay with Archdeacon Hutton. Mother had lost her voice again. Dulce and I went to stay with the Atkinsons' married sister near Stratford on Avon. The long-looked-for coming out dance was announced for Saturday, May 4th. The débutantes of our Oxford acquaintance numbered six. If Hilda Napier had been an entrant she must have displaced Dulce as the prettiest. Hilda acted Helen of Troy in *The Trojan Women* this month. She had features like the Venus of Milo and when, drilled by Mr Burrows, she looked over her shoulder to smile at her lover in farewell, she was quite irresistible, though one could see quite false. She had a wonderful correct Greek *coiffure*—not a wig—

with a bunch of curls dangling from the knob behind. Dulce went to the hairdresser in St Giles to have her hair 'put up' for the first time. After that Ethel did it. The latest style was called 'Merry Widow' and her hair was parted in front, like window-curtains, and had curls piled up above the nape of the neck. There was another débutante dance the very night before hers and she drove off in the brougham with mother saying nobody would ask her to dance. I was still awake though in bed when she got back. But she merely hopped into bed with a sleepy 'Oh! all right' and dropped off as if shot out of a gun. Next night, according to Mother, her own dance 'went off very happily'. I think this was indeed one of the happiest moments of my mother's life. Dulce was 'out', and a success.

IV

All the arrangements for the coming out fell into the category of Etiquette so it was mother who sent for the electricians before the dance to see that there was no danger of a failure if we used an unaccustomed number of lights, and for some anonymous experts who said that the floors of the double drawing-room would not collapse and land the powerful young guests in the cellars with the Norman pillar, which appeared in an etching done by me, under the tuition of Peggy Poole, on the printed programmes. Mother's duties were not done when the dance had been accomplished. So that there should be no mistake, she had sent out invitations for another converzatione in All Souls Library and two hundred and eighty people had accepted. It was therefore a horror when a telegram arrived from St Leonards on my birthday to say Uncle Alfred had been taken ill. Prof went off at once and reported with courage the details of a situation 'not too easy'. The doctor in charge, obviously delighted to be able to unload on a responsible-looking nephew of his patient, said that he wanted a second, London, opinion and could not disguise his apprehensions of the possible result of an operation. Uncle Alfred himself had such a good colour and talked with such vigour that it was difficult to believe that he was seriously ill; but he was having spasms of pain. The great thing was to get him over the anniversary of his wife's death two years ago to the day, May 13th. Prof returned to Oxford to wait for the specialist's report and the parents decided not to cancel the conversazione which was now next Saturday. After all, although she had too much delicacy to suggest this, nobody had set eyes on Uncle Alfred until after the death of Bamama. Dulce, herself, if asked, would have rather welcomed the abolition of a party at which all the guests must be 'old musty-fusties'. Almost as important as her dance was the happy fact that the President of Trinity had asked her, and the two grown-up Cannan girls, to dine to meet the Trinity Eight. It was now Eight's week and we had invitations to tea and ices on three barges, New College, Trinity and Magdalen (Leonard Atkinson). It was the top of the season. Dorothy Gervais arrived to stay.

The vicar who had prepared Dulce for confirmation had discovered (rather late in the day as we had now been in residence four years) that the boundaries of his parish ran through our garden. He came on Ascension Day with a party of choir-boys to perform the antique ceremony of beating the bounds. It was solemn, but they relaxed over a liberal feast of buns and some non-alcoholic beverage at eleven a.m.

The party in All Souls Library went off to the vast relief of the hostess, but four days after it Prof arrived hot foot to the New College barge with the telegram in his hand to announce the death of Uncle Alfred. We got 'wires' fairly frequently, as they were not expensive and we had no telephone, but I suppose that it was because they supplied documentary evidence that he liked turning up with anything outstanding, waving the ugly envelope in his hand. He would go again to St Leonards for the funeral and meanwhile Dulce would continue to be taken to another débutante's dance nearly every night. Going to the Union to hear F. E. Smith speak as the guest of honour could not be considered frivolous so we went to that although it was on the very night of the day that Prof had arrived with what Dulce called 'His hopeless face', pinned on, waving the fatal wire in his hand. During the remaining weeks of term mother accompanied Dulce in the brougham to dances given by the Trevelyans, Cannans, Drivers, Raleighs, Walkers, Daniels and Boyce Allens (who never called themselves that, but had to be, because there were the Thomas Allens of Queens to be considered. They were University.)

Sir Walter Raleigh of Magdalen had written a charming little pastoral play *The Riddle* and Mrs Gotch was in charge of arrangements for it to be performed in Magdalen Grove. Dulce and I were glad to be maidens in Renaissance costumes, with little round wreaths of roses on our done-up hair. We had nothing to say, but a good many members of the OUDS were taking leading parts—clever men from Balliol, New College and Magdalen. We got to know, at least by sight, Geoffrey Gwyther, who could sing and was going on the stage, and Gerry Hopkins, who also looked mediaeval, and Aldous and Trev Huxley and one of the Grenfell brothers. When it was all over Mrs Gotch invited us to a large dance up at their house in the Banbury Road, The Lawn, once quite in the country. The party was called 'The Revel'. It was an entirely decorous affair but as Billy Grenfell got sent down at this juncture, Lord Desborough concluded that this was part of Mrs Gotch's Revel and sent her a reproachful letter. I think it must have been at The Revel that we really made the acquaintance of one of the Riddle performers whose calls began to figure as often in mother's diary as Charles Sartoris, Herbert Meredith and Leonard Atkinson. Until we set off for our German holiday Mr P. P. Stuart was an almost daily visitor.

Dulce took the warmest interest in what she called 'The Performers', and delighted to recognise them whether on bicycle, horse-back or in a boat. 'There's a Performer.' Mr P. P. Stuart had taken the part of a foppish knight, and was an old OUDS fellow-member of Bridges-Adams, who was professional and to take charge of our next pageant, the Millenary of Oxford City. We had other links. Mr Stuart was a friend of the Baines family out at Kidlington whose son had married Peggy Poole.

Charles Sartoris, who always had to be so addressed because of the plethora of Charleses in our family, was asked to be a young partner for Dulce at the All Souls lunch. With his usual endearing frankness he told us that he had thought of refusing, as he would have gone down, but his tutor, old Raper had told him he was out of his senses. It was the highest honour for a mere undergraduate to be asked to this stately function. So he turned up, correctly dressed, with his little short gown on his shoulders, charmed everybody, and after the banquet came back to a hearty tea at Frewin. He was, of course, amongst the party of eight who dined with us before the Trinity Ball.

As there was no objection (it must have been Nana who stopped us taking part in the original Oxford Pageant), I was to be one of the daughters of Father Thames in the Prologue to a pageant which took place in Worcester Gardens, and old Mr Morris, Father of the OUDS, opened it. A matronly lady acting as his principal tributary, the Cherwell, was in charge of the smallest, the Ray. This was a splendid idea as far as looks went, for little Betty Cooke, youngest of the daughters of Canon Cooke of Christ Church, was a quite angelic blonde. But I never heard a child howl so loudly. Mr Morris announced in dramatic style, 'I nevare could bear to hear a cheild cry.' We had to trip barefoot over a large expanse of damp greensward. I should have been able to manage this, as both Dulce and I had already been allowed, now that the ban was lifted, to be British Maidens *al fresco* and perform a ritual dance holding aloft arches of ivy. But Worcester was wetter this year, and mother had to send for Dr Proudfoot, who after going over me pronounced that I should be taught to swim. So a book of tickets for lessons at the Rhea Bathing Place was bought and I went off with mother full of pleasurable anticipation. The Rhea was a heavily shaded portion of the Cherwell and there was an enormous man in charge who put me on the end of a sort of fishing rod and told me to run on and jump off the diving board. I vaguely heard him, above the terrible noise in my ears, as I came up again. He was saying sympathetically that the tightness over the chest was so uncomfortable, and urging me to strike out with both arms. I was towed up to the edge and when I really came to I was back in the changing hut with mother rubbing me with a towel. I heard her telling Prof that evening that I had been like a block of ice. As I longed to be able to slip into the Rhea like Naomi Haldane, and swim off with languid ease, I went up alone once or twice, but not for lessons and never really progressed until Janet put a hand under my chin at Kynance Cove, which was in August and the real sea. Even then, I could only just have saved my life. Dulce never tried to learn, though we now both took row-boats and punts by ourselves on the river. Canoes were forbidden as dangerous. Charlotte Allen, the beautiful half-French daughter of Allen of Queens had not been so warned and once stepped down to embark in a canoe, wearing a white muslin crinoline and picture hat, smiling under a parasol. She put a tiny foot on the side of the light little craft and nothing more was seen of her for some seconds.

Five years ago the President of Trinity had been considered by some people a dubious appointment. Joanna had told me that he got in because there were two strong candidates and nobody could object to someone they hardly knew. He was a bachelor, and was an unmistakable figure, with little black curls under a little black pot hat, extremely shy and tongue-tied. But he was soon established as 'Blinx', an ideal father to his college. He was now recommending one of his flock, Brian Hatton, who could draw. He had drawn two of the nieces of Sir William Anson, very smart dashing young women, and Harold, son of the Caccias (with a cricket-bat) and all the Cannans, remarkable likenesses as well as attractive pictures. My parents gradually employed him for the whole family, and when shown the likeness of Dulce, faintly smiling, Mr Stuart pleased mother by quoting something about a débutante

L

Standing with uncertain feet,
Where the stream and river meet.

Poor Brian Hatton tore me up twice and said I had a subtle chin. That
picture has been my bane. Ordered by mother for Prof, it returned to her
on his death. Then she died leaving it to my husband. I keep it in the
darkest corner of the study in which I type this; though I think Brian
Hatton might have become famous. He was one of the first people we
really knew to be killed in the 1914–18 War.

V

We set off for our German holiday in the middle of July and our first
Sight was the Musée Wierz in Brussels which was surprising as we had
never been allowed inside the Chamber of Horrors at Madame Tussauds.
It was still extremely hot when we arrived in Strasburg, where we saw the
cathedral and other churches, no fear. This was the trip of which Dulce
recorded that Prof had taken her to twenty churches in Cologne alone.
Karlsruhe and Heidelberg were attractive but here the heat gave place to
thunderstorms. We took a steamer from Mainz to Cologne having stayed
a night at a crowded hotel. This was the moment when I realised that my
father had mastered the art of complete concentration. We were sitting in
a lounge packed with luggage, including our own, and vociferous fellow
travellers of many nations were brushing past us. As usual, mother had got
us down a quarter of an hour too soon. Prof resignedly helped himself to a
sheet of hotel notepaper from the nearest desk, and began to write without
the slightest recognition of the surrounding scene.

'Section XXXIII Volume V. The Salamanca Campaign.
King Joseph as Commander in Chief. Wellington's
advance into Leon.'

When mother asked with what on earth had he filled his fountain-pen,
he said apologetically, 'Well, I just had to fill up with a little German
beer.'
We had seen some beautiful places on this foreign holiday and had
duly admired the Rhine with its castles peering from either side. The
native passengers burst into song at appropriate moments. But, although

it sounded ungrateful, I would sooner have stayed at Frewin. However, we were going to a country house that was not a vicarage this year. The owner of Ward House, Bere Alston, built about 1800, was an eccentric. He was a vegetarian, and according to rumour brought up his children on grape-nuts without the Bible. But he turned out, in correspondence at least, most obliging, and when mother fell in love with what she had never possessed, a large and comfortable *fauteuil*, upholstered in original amber brocade, he wrote calmly, 'If you would like to have it, do take it with you and have it valued at Oxford.'

It had better be acknowledged at once that this was the season known as The Wet Summer. Chas says that there was one pretty woodland walk from Ward House, which was a mile and a half out of the village. As the Tamar was tidal, we could only cross when the ferry chose. But we found promising well-grown trees to climb overlooking the drive. We were being allowed to take Patch this year, and I was to have Janet, and the Chadwicks were coming. I suppose 'Dulce's Performer', Mr Stuart, was really her guest, but from the moment we set off to meet him at the station we went about in a gang. We took him to Devonport dockyard, and to church on Sunday at Calstock church. Dulce and he went without us to Tavistock one morning, but that afternoon we all mustered at Cotehele, a lovely antique house discovered by Prof when fishing. We collected that Mr Stuart went to stay at country houses for cricket weeks and had once played the part of 'Bunny' in 'Raffles'. He went with us by steamer to Plymouth to see Janet off from there on the express for Didcot and Oxford. On his last day he went with Dulce alone on the river to the ruined Harewood House, but I think really only because there were too many of us for one boat. We joined up there. It was not a very successful outing as it rained all day. The morning of August 20th was brilliant but with it ended his week. The Chadwicks were coming. When we said, 'Well, at any rate you will have a lovely day for your long journey,' he said, 'I wish it was beastly.' He was older than our other undergraduates as he had failed his final exam for the Indian Civil and had stayed on for another year at Christ Church to take it again, after which he would only have to collect his kit and sail for India. His parents were out there so he had no home in England and he was an only surviving child, except for a twin sister, utterly unlike him, he said, tiny and vivacious, married three years ago. Sir Harold, his father, governed a province. His mother was a sofa-mother, so he had really had rather a miserable youth. His public school had been a near-London one, Charterhouse. He was a most elegant young man but with such a nervous manner, I got hardly any information out of him, except about *Othello*, which he ranked very high.

I was now extremely anxious to go to a boarding school before it was too late and I heard with interest that Mrs Henry Wheeler (Marjory Stuart) had been at one of the most advanced, Roedean. But mother said that Miss Batty's had suited Dulce perfectly. I told mother, in Mr Stuart's presence, about Roedean. It was impossible for him to please everyone, and important that he should please his hostess. He would only repeat it had 'done his sister a lot of harm'. What could that mean? However, I saw I was not going to get an ally. I had read him a dramatic passage from 'Engrai' my I.M. serial and got the impression he found it comic. Prof was out fishing so I think missed saying good-bye to him, but in any case I doubt if he would have realised who he was. Prof knew Charles Sartoris, because he was Augusta's great-nephew, and Herbert Meredith because he was at All Souls, but although the Symonds family had been our neighbours in Beaumont Street, and had been surgeons for seven generations, and established on the staff of the Radcliffe Infirmary by 1813, he had suddenly taken to addressing Ralph as Ralf Simons. Mother had got as far as writing down her guest as P.S. by the time he left but still called him Mr Stuart to his face. He could not be Phil as that was Uncle Phil; this made her later entries confusing.

It was a good thing Mr Stuart left when he did as the Chadwicks had been at Bere Alston only one night when one of Uncle Charlie's famous telegrams came and poor mother had to go off. Aunt Al had been taken ill at Hastings. It was now August, 1912, and when I was going to get married in April 1922, I had to brave up to ask mother what we were to do if Aunt Al chose that day to die. Mother said they had decided to carry on and not say anything about it. The name was not the same, and her poor sister had long been paralysed and speechless. Uncle Charlie took up his quarters with her, and Jeanie and another maid looked after her. 'Al's my banker,' said Uncle Charlie.

I was let down by Janet over her journey back to Oxford. She had been given her ticket and told she had only one change to make. As her father would be meeting her with his motor at Oxford station I did not ask what money she had. When her letter of thanks came it sent mother into fits. After our early start, Janet had slept through Didcot junction and when it seemed to be getting awfully dark and late she found out that the next stop was London. But a darling old man had taken charge of her and her luggage, and seen her into an Oxford train at Paddington. Mother said

Janet must never be asked to stay again. I said that the man sounded quite old but mother looked at me pityingly. She was thereafter inflexible and Janet was asked to stay only at Frewin in her holidays from Wantage, and I stayed in return at 145 Woodstock Road. As I had never yet spoken on a telephone, I suggested when Janet's letter about her journey home arrived that it would be a good thing to make sure she was really all right. Mother took me to the post-office and shed me with the words, 'The young lady does not understand the instrument.' So I made a trunk call to Janet who seemed surprised, and that was my first experience of speaking on the telephone.

P.S. was now in London taking his exam, but in September began to turn up again almost daily. Prof liked our snapshots, but we had to be summoned for a scolding when he saw the bill for processing for three of us by Messrs Will R. Rose. Prof never came to understand photography and always talked of developing when he meant printing, and believed we had wantonly photographed nothing but a back view of a horse's ears when what we were trying to focus was the preceding wagonette at our Leafield school treat. So we were allowed the powdering closet between the yellow and green spare-bedrooms as our dark room, and developed, printed and did sectional enlargements of our exposures. We had a dangerously insecure dark-room lantern with a red calico shade, and as the premises were restricted, by this partial light I once dried my hands, covered with slimy developer, on what turned out to be Mr Stuart's jacket. He was quite pleasant about it.

On October 12th we heard that he had passed his examination and when he came for the weekend ten days later, we had a small dance, just twelve couples up in the old nursery. He left for London and India on the Tuesday morning early. I did not connect this when I found Dulce sobbing quietly, seated in a window-seat of our school-room. She said, 'I suppose you sometimes feel quite idiotic,' but gave me no further explanation. Another examination result had removed another of our regulars. Trinity College had reluctantly told Charles Sartoris that as he had once more failed to pass 'Mods' he would have to go down. But he, of course, would still be able to stay with us.

I was the Princess in a version of Tennyson's *Princess* in the school play this Christmas and this was a great satisfaction to me. I was now so tall that I always got male parts and I longed to have long plaits. I was disappointed when Beatrice was dismissed after the first rehearsal for speaking naturally in the part of Lady Psyche, and privately I thought

Tennyson's princess rather a poor fish. Nancy Gotch, as the prince, acted much better.

Janet came to stay in the holidays and we had a high old time in the green spare-room, taking and developing photographs of each other as Marcus Brutus and Mark Antony, and Lady Macbeth and Cordelia. We used magnesium wire in these entirely panelled premises for taking our flash light time-exposures, and on more than one night lit our paraphernalia. Nobody knew.

1912, which had been so packed with events, ended in a blaze of glory. The Morris car was on sale at the Motor Show and hit the headlines in the national press. The firm of William Morris had been well known to many of us since an energetic little man of Welsh extraction had come up from his father's bicycling establishment at Cowley to own a shop in the High which also looked after motor cycles. He was now thirty-five and had produced a two-seater car with a Cape cart hood, solid running board and two acetylene lamps. It had a water-cooled engine of ten horse power, a gear box with three forward speeds. It was offered 'complete and ready for the road' at £175. A single agent at once ordered four hundred. But before cars were being rolled out from the Morris factory in Cowley in spectacular numbers he had begun to involve himself in a major controversy on his home-ground—public transport in Oxford. He was a leading protagonist in the great Oxford tram battle. He had begun by buying a dozen motor-buses in London on his own account and putting them on the streets of Oxford as a surprise. Councillors went to London to take legal opinion. There was a general belief that the little pirate would end in jail. He spoke in his own defence at a public meeting at the Corn Exchange. He had invested a good deal of his capital in the venture. He had been refused a licence. People were packing his buses. All he asked was to be allowed to put them on a proper legal basis. Trams had now quite faded from the picture. The Council tried having buses of their own. Morris sent one of his ahead and one behind each and the Council buses were ignored. He won. The council bought the Morris buses and formally thanked him for having helped to solve Oxford's traffic problem. He made a modest profit and returned to producing more and better Morris cars. Somebody meaning to be witty said that a statue ought to be put up to him. But by that time it was 1914.*

* The Nuffield Story, R. Jackson, Muller, 1964.

IX

Finale:

1913–1914

I

LEONARD ATKINSON HAD BEEN TO A LONDON PHOTOGRAPHER CALLED Beresford who was becoming the vogue. He took about thirty exposures of you and sent proofs of the lot for you to make your choice. Dulce was taken to him, and as his premises were in Beauchamp Place, on to lunch at Harrods; a revolution. Since Aunt Al was no longer able to offer hospitality we had rather abandoned the High Street Kensington trio of dress shops. The Burrowses got all Agnes and Sidney's clothes from Harrods and sent our Christmas presents from the same source. These slightly suggested to the unworthy recipient that they had bought the presents first and then allotted them. Dulce was this year the surprised owner of a pink almond tree (artificial) in a white china pot. I admired it enormously. It was quite useless. It came from a gift department.

Uncle Ed received the K.C.S.I. on New Year's Day 1913. Both he and Uncle Bob now had daughters, born in India. Myrtle Maclagan, Uncle Bob's one, was the first of a series in his branch of the family all called after fragrant shrubs. Myrtle, always a helpful child and remarkable when she came to stay with us for her motherly care of her younger brother and sister, was born just in time for Aunt Bee to be fully recovered for the famous Delhi Durbar. We gathered from our private letters that this visit of our new king and queen to India had been a great success, but portions of the press had been provocative.

The Radcliffe Ball was now the topic of the hour at Frewin. It was in aid of the Radcliffe Infirmary and mother was taking a party of eighteen and giving a dinner before. Evelyn Clarke, sister of Will, was staying, and Cicely Marriott, daughter of one of our M.P.s and Charles Sartoris. Daniel Vawdrey, a Rugbeian friend of Will, was at Trinity. Prof had become a Governor of Malvern and boys from there were sent to call. This college was achieving some spectacular successes in sport. A. N. S. Jackson had received a laurel crown from the King of Sweden at the Olympic Games held at Stockholm last summer. He was a miler. We never met him—just too old—but D. J. Knight, the cricketer became a valued addition to our circle. Dulce was now such an admirer of Blues that she wore her initials embroidered on the front of her sweaters. Our prize all-rounder was 'Twiggy' Anderson, who was a hurdler at the Olympic Games, and a recruit, in overalls in the yards of Messrs Camell Laird, Birkenhead, and junior Fellow of All Souls.* Of course, I saw nothing of the Radcliffe Ball at the Town Hall, and as eighteen was our limit at table had a tray in the school-room, but next night I was taken to see a play at the New Theatre by Mr Storer Clouston who had, most inconveniently, also arrived to stay. The Cloustons and the Omans had an Orkney connection. He was to achieve a best-seller, but not in the drama —*The Lunatic at Large*.

The most inspiring drawing-mistress of my life arrived this spring. Miss A. R. de la Mare and her sister only just missed being dwarfs. They were Plymouth Brethren. Our Miss de la Mare arranged with Mrs Cannan that I should go with May and Joanna to draw from the antique at the Ashmolean. This meant a brief passage of arms between Mrs Cannan and Professor Percy Gardner. He was a strange little figure in his later sixties, with a bald head and a curly beard. Joan Evans, when asked what he was like, replied, 'A Zeus, but of a bad period.' A feeble suggestion that it would not be quite nice for us to draw male nudes even if plaster ones, was scouted by Mrs Cannan whose outlook was robust, and she disposed with equal scorn of his objection that we should scatter bread crumbs. It was most agreeable to keep one's easel in the Ashmo: and sit for hour after hour measuring the Thorn Extractor, and Niobe and Discobolus Making Ready. Professor Gardner soon visited us and after a look at May's effort asked if her mistress considered that she was a pupil likely to benefit from our incursion into his premises. But Miss de la Mare was a diplomatist. She said that she had not yet had time to assess May's capabilities. He never came again.

Dulce was very young for her age. As Will was a cousin, he was allowed to go with her alone in the brougham to dances. She came to mother with a tale of woe. Will was not to be trusted and Carola had better be warned.

* 'Twiggy' who was a hero to us was one of our first friends to be killed in action in the 1914–18 War.

Coming home last night he had tried to put his arm around her waist and uttered the dreadful words, 'Give us a kiss, Dulce.' I was warned, but it was too late. I had some time ago disentangled myself while looking at a book with Will, but had not reported this. I had simply become very governessy. I think, looking back, that Will must have been what would nowadays be called rather highly-sexed. He used to pore over illustrated magazines with pictures of stage favourites lying in hammocks and smiling over muffs. There was one of a very bedizened buxom young person leaning on a parasol. He asked, triumphantly, 'What do you think of her?' But I told him in two composite words. 'Over-dressed and under-bred.' Mother continued to ask him after the brougham incident, but I think never to accompany Dulce alone. He was almost as eligible and agreeable as dear Charles.*

An undoubted suitor bent upon matrimony now re-appeared upon our scene—Oscar from Africa. I think he had the most appallingly bad luck in his timing. He had gone away patiently two years before realising that she was really not old enough to listen to a proposal. But now she was 'out' and had ceased to climb trees. He had come home on this leave, determined to ask Dulce Oman to be his wife. Uncle Phil, never famed for his tact, had been accustomed to chaff Dulce about her elderly admirer, as indeed we all had. 'How's Oscar, Dussy?' Oscar was not really old; I suppose he would not see thirty again, probably not much more, but the suns of Africa and bouts of fever had drained all the colour out of him. We had to shut up Uncle Phil and explain that this was no longer a subject for joking. The poor man had become a perfect menace. He turned up continually. Dulce, rather meanly, pushed him off on me. He wanted to talk about nothing but her. Once when I lightly mentioned that she had fainted standing to be fitted at the dressmaker, he became quite savage in his inquisition. The President of Magdalen had asked her to dine to meet his second Eight. That made her happy. She wanted to take up riding again, and this meant that Mr Rhodes had to pick up both of us for just the Five Mile Grind. Mr Rhodes had said that I would be ready for a half day's hunting next season, with the Heythrop. He took Joanna on such outings and she was bossy about it. I was not really sure that I wanted to hunt a fox and was quite certain I did not want to be in at a kill. However, the possibility that I should be allowed was remote.

* Will and his elder brother were killed in action in 1915, and on the death of their father the baronetcy of Clarke of Rossmore, Co. Cork, bestowed on a follower of Dutch William, became extinct.

At the end of term we set off for our most enjoyable foreign trip yet— Italy! Italy! I felt like Elizabeth Barrett Browning. There had been a vague suggestion that, though I might not go to a boarding school I might perhaps, in a year or two, be sent to finish in Germany as my mother had done. But what I had seen of Germany had not greatly won my heart. I loathed grotesques. I did not envy one of our best Trinity friends, Tom Cotterell-Dormer who was going to Germany in 1914 with the idea, as a younger son, of entering the Foreign Office. (He succeeded in getting to Germany just in time to be put straight into the bag, and was a prisoner in Ruhleben until 1919, when he came home to find that both his elder brothers had been killed and he had inherited an estate with Stuart manuscripts, pictures and furniture to match, and a famous landscape garden laid out by William Kent.)

Another disadvantage about going to Germany was that most of the girls sent there had musical aspirations. I now played nothing except the waltzes of Archibald Joyce and other contemporaries, to please Dulce. I was quite adept at 'Dreaming', 'The Bogey Walk', at which Harold Napier was marvellous to watch, and all the best trifles from *The Gondoliers* and *The Yeomen of the Guard*.

Janet and I were now wild about Italian artists. Someone must have given me, for I could never have afforded it, a book called *Knights of Art*, not quite what was later called a coffee-table book, but one enriched by two dozen plates, sixteen in colour, *Series of the Italian Painters*. I arrived in Italy with some knowledge of every major master, from Giotto to Paul Veronese.

It was a blow to discover that Milan cathedral was not, like my little smoke-blackened model of it, entirely of alabaster. I laughed that off, and went up the spire and had an exciting experience when an Italian lady preceding me suddenly got vertigo and told her cavalier, whose appearance was swiftly transformed into that of her would-be murderer, that she could neither advance nor recede. We went on to Pisa and I saw in glowing sunshine, the lawns around the Campanile, the Baptistry and the Duomo, covered with daisies. Mother told us her story of seeing her first daisies here as a child of ten, back from India. I wonder if the Rivoiras would have had me to finish in Italy? Chas says it was a bit early for English girls. The Rivoiras were marvellous to him and absolutely laid themselves out to make him feel at home, when he turned up after the War. But then he was a young man, and at the British School. The Rivoiras had a devoted married couple who groaned and threw up their hands in sympathy when our host and hostess told us, at the luncheon table, that unfortunately they had no children. Chas thought that they had once had an infant and lost it. I wonder if Mrs Rivoira's extreme kindness to him was because he looked so like Prof at the age when Bamama was trying to get him to make her an offer. Chas might have been her son.

Teresio arrived to take us to the opera *La Gioconda* on our last night in Rome. We could see him from the lift as we came down and he had three bouquets, one for each of us. Having endured the Capitol and the Forum and the Coliseum, Dulce drew mother's attention to the fact that this place seemed to have very decent shops. We had a bout of shopping, sandwiched between days at St Peter's and the Vatican and the Capitoline museum. Mrs Rivoira was our guide to the best shops and restaurants. In the galleries I saw a good many old friends whom I had drawn in the Ashmolean. There were still some hours to be filled in while Prof was going round the coin dealers and mother had put her feet up. Despite the gay clatter of a barrel organ playing 'Funiculi, Funicula!' close below our window I began a narrative poem. It was on a well-worn theme—a Christian slave who converted her Roman master. It thrilled me. When I had finished the first canto I looked up to hear Dulce's applause. She had fallen asleep. When she woke I asked her if it was no good, why should I have this strong urge to write. 'Desire to see your name in print,' said Dulce. But I knew that was not the reason.

Naples was bathed in sunshine too and we stayed at an hotel called Parker's up the hill with a magnificent view of the bay. There were a number of other English visitors including Mr Buckle, editor of *The Times*. We went to a lunch party given by the oddly-named Scotti-Johns, and bought tortoiseshell and coral. At Pompeii just as I was saying that it did not matter what I said, as nobody here would understand, there emerged from an archway the familiar forms of Professor Clark and the President of Trinity. We had an adventurous expedition to 'a pumice isle in Baiae's bay'. As we drew near to shore again it seemed that our train was leaving the station. The entire occupants of the steamer, except ourselves, rushed in a sort of frenzy like the Gadarene swine towards tht exit from our little craft and very nearly overset it. I realised now that southern Italians were excitable. When I remarked to Prof on the number of little boys and girls about, much more than at home, he said, Yes, the Italians were very prolific. I did not know what that was but I had also noticed that they seemed to be a bit lazy. There was a man, not an old man, whom I had noticed, leaning against a wall halfway up the road to the hotel as we went down in the morning. When we came up again in the evening, there he still was. Was it possible he had spent all those hours simply leaning? Perhaps he was prolific.

We travelled all day to get from Naples to Florence and when we arrived the weather seemed to have broken and the Adige was the colour of a lion. But in no place could this have mattered less. There were the churches and the galleries. Janet and I were particularly attached to the works of Botticelli, with which we were also familiar from the Arundel prints on the walls of the green room at Frewin—the *Primavera* and the *Nascita*. We went to the Ospedale degli Innocenti and saw the many roundels containing likenesses of little boys and girls which we had so long loved. When I got home I brought some vellum and leather and made an Italian book which has worn pretty well, with an Innocent on the cover. We were now keen on arts and crafts and spent all our pocket-money on specialist drawing and painting papers. Marian had made a fan on chicken skin, but I never saw it.

At Bologna there were more familiar pictures, but we were beginning to hurry. Anyway the twenty lire given to each of us as extra pocket-money was all gone, and Prof had the Historical Congress in London.

Annie Stanton had been married before Easter and was now Mrs Dennis. Her husband was a Territorial N.C.O. She came to see mother almost immediately to tell her all about the wedding.* Next day Oscar was with us again, and as I had Janet staying, Dulce had to entertain him. He found out when we were going to London for a day's shopping and would be on the platform all ready to travel with us. The London train was often packed and he sometimes had to content himself standing in the corridor and goggling at Dulce through the window. We were so beastly about him it gave us both the giggles. We tried to shake him off by going to Cheltenham for the day without mentioning our intention, but there he was for Sunday lunch again. I do not think that Dulce collected any information which he was so ready to give about the inhabitants of Nairobi. Will Clarke was now bringing another fellow-Rugbeian with him. Brian Fagan was a mine of information. He was going to be a publisher. On my birthday he gave me a book which I treasured, *Biography for Beginners*. It had an inscription in Greek in an unknown handwriting inside, so I thought it was merely a loan, but he said that it had been given to him, but he practically knew it by heart now, so he had thought I had better have it.

---

* Annie's husband died of Spanish 'flu with the occupying Army in Cologne in 1919.

In Eights week we went on the Oriel Barge and the Trinity Barge and the Magdalen Barge. Oscar had discovered Dulce's predilection for barges and invited us to go to Henley at the close of term. This would be a whole-day outing and was looked forward to with mixed feelings. We gave another dance at the end of May, a proper one with fifty dancers. Will and Brian came to help us to arrange fairy lights in the garden and we were blessed with a balmy night. Herbert Meredith's best girl (not called thus at this date) was asked by mother to stay for the dance and I was sent in the brougham to meet the London train. She was the sister of his best friend, who was going to be a journalist. She was very pretty and fair but with a receding chin. She later sat to me for a portrait. Chas would still oblige me sometimes and Ethel Stangoe, but Dulce was adamant.

The fatal Henley date arrived. Oscar had asked all three of us to lunch. We went on to the Trinity Barge where we met Herbert Meredith and Daniel Vawdrey and set out in punts. The heavens absolutely opened, and we were in light muslin dresses. Poor Oscar was in despair. He hailed a man who had a large old cracked tarpaulin and said would he sell it. How much? Three pounds, said the villain. Oscar looked spiteful. 'You can keep it.' We went as swiftly as possible back to the shelter of the Trinity Barge and our younger friends. It was impossible not to suffer with Oscar. He would have laid down his life for Dulce but he could not keep her dry. I think mother felt for him. On our return she asked him to supper at Frewin, although we were all dead tired. But relief was at hand. He came for his farewell lunch on the last Sunday in July. We were going to Scotland and unlike 'Dulce's Performer' of last year, he was not asked to stay. Nor was Janet. Mother was adamant.

It might have been expected that after 1912 this year would be rather flat, but we were in luck again. Darnlee, a mile and a half outside Melrose had been built by one John Smith of Darnick, who had been employed by Sir Walter Scott of Abbotsford and Chiefswood. There was a friendly spaniel whom we were warned was accustomed 'to wander at will'. Even Chas our most voracious sightseer had to admit that Darnlee was a good base for expeditions. There were hospitable neighbours—Colonel Hope of Earlston was a cousin of the Cannans, Lord Johnstone lived at The Pavilion, the Locktons were the Episcopal clergyman and family. There were tennis parties and expeditions up the Eildons and to Edinburgh. We invited Nana to tea at Mackie's and thought she would admire Dulce grown-up, but she would only look at Chas wolfishly and tell him again and again, 'You were much more beautiful than either of them.' He was not insensible of her devotion and once told me that after she left he never again had a party for his birthday.

Prof was taking Chas to walk on the Roman Wall. I should dearly have liked to go with them, and as far as the walking went I could easily have managed it but Prof said I had better make a separate expedition. I had already this year written a whole first volume of *The Book of Good Places* and I was now at work on a second, *Southern England and the Border Country*. These were illustrated by my best photographs. Chas and I took one another paddling outside Abbotsford. When we got home in early September the parents took him to Paris for a week. Prof was the only one of the family to attend a parade service of the Oxfordshire Regiment in Christ Church. There was a good deal of practising bugle calls and words of command at a hall in New Inn Hall street just when one was wanting to go to sleep.

I had reluctantly given up hope of getting to a boarding school. At my earnest entreaty mother had written to Cheltenham College for a *brochure*. I thought perhaps I might be allowed to go there as it was called College and Mrs Wells, the highly-esteemed wife of the Prof's oldest friend, had been there. But that *brochure* put the extinguisher on my hopes. I should never pass the examination for entry. Chas says that he too always came up against an obstacle both at The Wick and Winchester when mathematics were essential. As things fell out I should have been most grateful to my mother for refusing me further education at this date. The great new public schools for girls were being strictly modelled on those for boys, and I was No Good at Games. This disability too seemed to be a family failing. Prof went into the subject thoroughly in his description of his early school-days. 'Later years have revealed to me that I am somewhat deficient in the rapid correlation of hand and eye, though both hand and eye, taken apart, are normal enough. It was this lack of quick reaction that in cricket made me both bat and field so unsuccessfully.' Chas says that one of the failings of The Wick was that interest was taken only in the boys who were promising. The result was that although he had been condemned to hours of fielding no one ever had taken the trouble to tell him the names of the places on the field. If I had gone to a boarding school in 1912 I should have suffered a humiliating inferiority complex.

I was being prepared for confirmation at Christmas, privately as Dulce had been. This caused me embarrassment and I was worried that I really felt little else on my weekly excursion to Mr Fox in Longwall. Janet helped me much more. I had not the slightest symptom of spiritual awakening. I had to repeat a collect and read various chosen passages and listen to their explanation. There was one excellent result of my being confirmed. I should be qualified to be a co-godmother with Dulce to Carola Mary Dennis, Annie Stanton's baby born on December 16. It was quite a near-run thing. On Christmas Eve the brougham came round and Dulce and I were packed in opposite Prof and mother to drive to Cuddesdon the palace of the Bishop of Oxford. I wore my Gilmore grandmother's wedding veil which had been her present for my christening and an all-white dress garnished with what reminded me of nothing but cutlet frills, bought with a view to the Christmas dances. I had no overcoat because of the veil. I was so cold and sick that when the Bishop gave us tea in a room with a curious architectural item—a window over the fireplace—I could not partake. After tea he went off to change his costume and Dulce, wishing to be polite, ran to open the door for him. She slipped on a rug on the highly polished floor. She just got the the handle, but full length, with a coquettish little toque over one eye and the other fixed on the bishop with a look of dog-like devotion. I was so nervous that when the bishop spoke to me, I dropped on my knees at once. He was not beginning the service. What he had been saying was, 'That window was presented by the Prince Consort.' Afterwards mother told me that Prof had been much moved by the occasion. I had been just miserable.

II

We were still being brought up in beautiful innocence or ignorance. Most of our friends were. It must have been about this time that Miss Lee arrested our attention by a few words on a poem by Tennyson, *De Profundis*. In it he was a parent addressing his son, as yet unborn. I gathered that it took a man nine months to make a child. When I announced this at the luncheon table mother considered writing to Miss Lee, and if she was unrepentant, taking me away from Miss Batty's. But I do not think she ever did write, for it was soon settled that I should be leaving before the summer term of 1914. I should be nearly seventeen and had succeeded Sylvia Driver as head girl. She had gone to Brussels to finish and Joanna to Paris.

A very sad thing happened this New Year. Patch had not been well and the vet had been to see him twice. Mr Stroud had only once been summoned for Patch before and that was when he had broken his leg jumping out of our first-floor bedroom window to chase a cat. Before he was out of splints the dear fellow had done it again, but this time without further injury. We had been up in London seeing Tree's latest production, *Joseph and his Brethren* (disappointing) and *Quality Street* (charming). Prof had been down in Gloucester, lecturing to the Archaeological. Evidently what Mr Stroud told mother had made her anxious, for she went off to her closest friend, Mrs Poole, for advice. Next night Dulce, Prof and mother were all up with Patch. Dulce and I still shared the old night-nursery, so next night Patch's basket was brought up and established there. In the small hours, two days later, I was woken from the deepest of sleep by the noise of Patch whining. I put out my hand, for he had come to my bedside, and stroked him, and he licked my hand. I heard his basket creak as he returned to it. Next morning he did not wake. He looked quite happy. We gave him a worthy funeral in the back garden and it was agreed that we would not replace him until after our return from Italy in April. But I was haunted for years by remorse that I had not woken up properly, and at least stroked him until he had drawn his last breath. I told my husband about this twelve years later and he comforted me, saying that Patch had come to say farewell and must have died quietly. But I learnt a lesson from that experience and one which I was to find useful in later life. I can wake at a sound or a touch, with all my wits about me, whatever the hour, and what is more I can fall asleep again.

In spite of my admiration for Tennyson I never really cared for the passage in *Maud* where the hero hears the cry of the rooks building their nests.

> Birds in the high Hall-garden
> When twilight was falling,
> Maud, Maud, Maud, Maud,
> They were crying and calling.

Actually I was walking with mother in the middle of a morning towards the Parks, just short of Keble when I could not catch what she was saying for the rather unpleasant boding sound of rooks building. She was asking me if I thought a long engagement would be a good thing for Dulce. I was, of course, flattered by the confidence, but Dulce had never said anything to me on the subject. The Indian mail came in over the weekend. Friday afternoon was the earliest; if it failed on Saturday you had to wait for Monday. I knew Dulce was getting letters by it for she sat in the outer hall round about post time on Fridays and if there was nothing from India sometimes flung it on the floor and stamped on it. I knew she was persevering with riding lessons and had refused invitations to stay at country houses. She would not to go the Sartorises who were said to have a show garden. An invitation from the lady of a bishop, I think Hereford, for a county ball was never considered by her, and mother did regret this a little. 'She could have taken her own maid, Beatie White.' Ethel was evidently too rustic. I wondered if mother, in refusing, could have said that she had another daughter coming out shortly who would welcome spreading her wings. But I do not think I even suggested this. Nothing more was said except that I might perhaps go to a Commem ball this year, so as to be able to go with my sister.

I duly left school at the end of the spring term and got a presentation of a book illustrated by Arthur Rackham. Our Italian holiday started with a set-back as it was so rough we could not cross, but this gave us a chance to go to a much-criticised Granville Barker production of *A Midsummer Night's Dream*. At Como we were not able to go on the lake because of snowstorms, but in Padua there was beautiful pale golden sunshine, after the Italian fashion, and I saw the Giotto frescoes in the Cappella Scrovegni well known to Janet and me from reproductions but much more touching than these had suggested. There were a great many other sights in Padua, but after St Anthony's own basilica, simply known as Il Santo, the Arena, and the Augustinian church (fated to be almost completely destroyed in the next World War but one), we hurried on for Venice.

There were only two things immediately obvious in Venice to detract slightly from our happiness. The Kaiser's yacht lying outside in the lagoon and the place seemed to be teeming with Germans. We had come for a wet week and German week. The King of Saxony was staying in our hotel and there were eternal sentries outside his suite. However, we went to the English church and the Accademia, and (mother excepted) in a gondola between showers, and to S. Marco and a glass manufactory in the city and another out at Murano—a lovely expedition. There was one man who apparently spent his life putting eyes into dolphins with tweezers. It had rained all morning when we were in the crowd in the Piazza waiting to see the Kaiser and the King of Italy come out on the balcony of the palace. We saw them quite clearly and they seemed very pleased with themselves, but the applause from the crowd was not madly enthusiastic. We went over the Doge's palace and had tea at Florian's listening to the band, and after

M

five days, none of them fine, which Venice demands, we went on to Verona. It was still very cold, and from the top of the amphitheatre we could see snow wreaths on the surrounding blue mountains. Verona was an attractive place, especially to me, because of its Roman remains, but Dulce began to be restive about the number of famous religious edifices. With incredible resilience we had a day at Reggio Emilia before returning to beloved Milan, and even from there made a day excursion to the Certosa di Pavia.

We arrived in Paris after a train journey from eight a.m. to eleven p.m. and next morning went out to choose what mother called ball-frocks for two. They had to be ready-made but we were stock sizes and there was a great variety to choose between, and the *vendeuses* were very clever and interested. Dulce got one which was the top-price in our experience— £15: but it looked worth it. My total expenditure appeared in Prof's accounts for me as £21. 14s. od. but I got a most sympathetic 'picture' *fichu* best afternoon dress for Eights week, and a Watteau hat—very smart, a soup plate tilted forward over the brow and built up behind on curls and flowers. One of my bridesmaids, Rosalind Gatehouse, who sketched in Italy and never minded bad little boys giggling behind when she was engrossed, had to give up wearing her Watteau hat in Italy as when she got back to her *pension* the back flowers and curls were packed with match and cigarette ends and grapeskins. But it was a very becoming form of headgear for one season.

At Frewin Hall there was exciting news. Ethel was engaged and was very happy but very shy about it. She had to be pushed forward to show us her ring. She was twenty-four. Her fiancé was a brother of one of our daily helpers and of a very large family, but I must surely have got it wrong in thinking that his name was Edward Rabbit. Uncle Ed and Aunt Edie were on leave this summer and were going to land Patricia on us for a term to go to Miss Batty's. Mother told Aunt Edie that she was sure that instead of an agreed wage for looking after Patricia, Ethel would be glad of some linen for her bottom drawer. So a benefaction of wedding-sheets was made. I think it was hardly earned, for Patricia, though a fine child, had a streak of mischief, and thought nothing of throwing all her clothes in the bath when undressed, a lot of work for Ethel, and years after her departure, missing knives and forks from the nursery cutlery clattered out of larger volumes in the nursery bookcase.

A few days after our homecoming, mother and Dulce went off in the brougham to fetch the puppy and Ponto was brought home. He was of the Doyle strain and was even more attractive in appearance than the lamented Patch but he never really filled the same niche. Patch was difficult to follow.

The Indian mail came in on a Saturday morning by the first post this week and Dulce brought her consignment up to read in bed. Suddenly I heard an awed whisper. 'Oh! he asks me!' I think our mother must have given him the permission to go ahead soon after her conversation with me before we left for Italy. I did not know until after her death, when I saw her diaries, that she as well as Dulce had been writing to him almost every week. The Indian mail so often brought in letters from Uncle Bob and Uncle Ed that one more regular correspondent was hardly noticeable. Nor did I, at the time, realise that mother had been making every enquiry in her power. Anyone known to have been a friend of the future son-in-law had been searched out and asked to Frewin. He was, of course, in the same service as Uncle Ed, and as his father was just retiring after being a distinguished Governor of a province there seemed every probability that a brilliant career awaited so charming a man. All the results of enquiries were reassuring. I do not think that our father took any part in these maternal machinations.

Chas was now home and we all went down to the General Post Office to send off Dulce's reply. 'Yes, with all my heart.' I wondered whether it might not have been better to write but this suggestion was scorned. She was writing, anyway. A wedding at Oxford on his first leave was the probability, but that would not be for another year or two. We just had to keep quiet for the present.

I had a major anxiety on my own account. Dulce was being Sabrina and I was being the Lady in a performance of *Comus* (cut down) in the Literary Pageant at the Town Hall in less than a fortnight. There had been talk of it since January, and rehearsals of dances of Sabrina's troupe of children. I could no longer act but was unaware of this. Contemporary music had been coaxed on loan from Cambridge. Ernest Jacob was being Thyrsis. Austin Poole had got his costume for Comus. He had been a Fellow of his beautiful college, St John's, since last October. Now Austin had developed scarlet fever. There was no time to be lost even at this happy hour. Mother wrote to Gerry Hopkins who was an OUDS man and had been a Performer in *The Riddle* and he produced an old Rugbeian, P. H. B. Lyon, known as Phoebe for obvious reasons. He was nothing like Austin who was an oldest friend and a commanding figure in whom we all put complete confidence, but he telegraphed acceptance as he had been asked to do, and turned up. It was at once clear that Gerry Hopkins had not failed us. I asked Phoebe what he had thought when he had got mother's letter and he said that his first reaction had been 'What cheek', but on second thoughts, 'But what a part'. I did not much relish the thought of my mother having been considered cheeky but I need not have worried. She had soon reduced him to a permanent condition of trembling at the thought of having shocked Mrs Oman.

Her Convent School had discovered Janet's talents and this moment was the one in which we had to find time to get up to 145 Woodstock Road to offer congratulations on her having won the first prize offered by the Royal Drawing Society for a composition developed from love of Beauty. It was reproduced in colour by them as an example of Advanced Power in Visualisation, and this disclosed that Janet's lobsters, dancing with elves on a sea shore, must have been cooked for they were bright scarlet. I had also sent in some contributions for the Royal Drawing Society's Annual Exhibition in Piccadilly and had won a bronze medal. Miss De La Mare was quite keen on our taking the examinations of the society. That meant having to go up to London: even my efforts had been hung on the line. Prof went too, though not to the Exhibition. He had been elected to another club which was called just The Club, said to be very special.

Photographs of all the performers in *Comus* were now taken in the garden at Frewin. Ethel had been called upon to produce identical costumes for all the Beasts who, however, differed in size and she was inclined to think that she was the hardest worker. 'You only have to walk on the stage and speak your lines,' she grumbled. Had the fiancé who was to jilt her, already begun to fall off in his attentions? It never occurred to me.

The Edward Maclagans now arrived having come overland from Venice, bringing both Patricia and baby Pamela, so there was nothing for it but to invite them to the last performance of the Pageant. The instigators of the show gave bouquets to Dulce and me, and mother got one from our cast. The Indian mail came in next morning with letters from Phil (as he must now be called despite Uncle Phil), and Dulce's engagement to him was no longer a secret. I was sent to tell the Cannans, the Allens and the Madans. Before it could be put in *The Times* and the *Morning Post*, a meeting with Sir Harold and Lady Stuart must take place. Dulce had received a letter from Lady Stuart, all very right and proper. They were asked to choose a day to come to Oxford. They chose May 11th. 'We shall have to put off Carola's birthday.' So we did that and the parents of Mr Stuart came to lunch. Sir Harold was a robust distinguished looking man: I could scarcely see his son at all in him. But anyone could see that Lady Stuart was 'Phil's' mother. She had the same extremely nervous manner and elegance, but in addition an air of suffering from very weak health. India had evidently been much too much for her. The announcement of the engagement, approved by them, appeared in the London Press three days later, and when we arrived in the gallery at the Union that night, the President sent up a note of congratulations. Mother said it was not really correct, although everyone did it, to congratulate a girl on her engagement. The man must be congratulated, but she should receive only 'best wishes'. Prof was dining at the Goldsmiths' Hall that night and so he too was the recipient of congratulations from members who read their papers.

Comus was now safely over but as with *The Riddle* we continued to see performers almost daily. We gave a Comus picnic for eighteen, including Patricia Maclagan. It was now my daily stint to take her up to Miss Batty's and collect her, and I was in terror that with the increasing traffic on our route, combined with her habit of dashing off, she would be the victim of a motor. Eights week was here and Phoebe's parents came down to Oxford. They too had been in, I think, the I.C.S. and Phoebe told us that his father had been unfavourably impressed by Daniel Vawdrey coming up to speak to us when he was so muddy. But Daniel was a rowing man and had been running on the bank with a rattle and we were lucky that he had not sprung into the Cherwell from sheer high spirits after greeting us. He had the appearance of a Florentine youth of the Renaissance, just like sketches I had seen in the Uffizi. He was quite at home in the schoolroom helping us to do poker work and photographs. He was one of those curious cases of eternal youth, and having been Dulce's friend originally, passed on to me when she was gone, and then to Chas, and eventually to Dulce's son.

My dance, postponed owing to the visit of Sir Harold and Lady Stuart, took place three weeks later and we had thirty girls and thirty-four men and a fine night for sitting out in the garden. Patricia handed programmes and I had a bouquet. Mr Trim, who had come in to wait, mistakenly congratulated me on my engagement. H. B. Irving was down at the theatre again and came to lunch, and Dulce and I went over to Wycombe Abbey School to see Doris Trevelyan who was now a prefect there. Wycombe had produced a version of *Comus* this term but of course they had not had our Phoebe. We had just got back from there and mother was still down at St Leonards seeing Aunt Al, when Mr Gill from the Union called to tell us that Sir William Anson had died. This meant that there would be no All Souls lunch and we should be getting a successor next term.

The death of Sir Denis Anson, who had succeeded his uncle Sir William, startled the Long Vacation. The young baronet, famous amongst what would at a later date have been known as top-ranking socialites, was drowned in the Thames at Battersea in the small hours of Saturday morning, July 4th. He had plunged overboard from the pleasure launch *King*. Some of his gay companions who gave evidence at the inquest, thought it might have been for a 'dare' or bet. Unfortunately one of the Drury Lane musicians playing on the lower deck had lost his life attempting to save him. It was stated that the widow and child of the musician would be cared for. A son of the Russian Ambassador, who had also attempted a gallant rescue effort, had himself to be saved.

At the largely attended funeral the noisy whirring of cameras recording the scene for the cinema was deplored. Gaumont replied with complaint of the habits of Press photographers. At Oxford it was gradually accepted as a tragedy that the young playboy could not have contained his high spirits a few weeks longer in which case he might have died with credit for his King and Country.

We went to the Bradfield Greek play with Phoebe and Brian Fagan. Prof was examining in Group B and mother took us to the schools one morning to listen to some vivas. The rule was that if anyone that one knew came up you had to leave at once.

I was taken down at last to see The Wick on Parents' Day this year as Prof was too busy. Mother and I stayed at the Grand Hotel, Brighton. We met Mr and Mrs Montagu Butler who had a son, 'Rab', going to Marlborough. The Caccias were now thinking of sending their Harold to The Wick. The buildings seemed to me quite impressive but I was struck by horror at my first sight of a dormitory. It seemed so pathetic—all those little beds, and a stack of photographs of mothers and fathers on a chest-of-drawers. I felt a wave of the nostalgia all the boys must harbour and I wondered whether it was really the best thing for them to be torn from home so early to be subjected to strict discipline. Naturally, I had to keep such rebellious thoughts to myself. I did not know that Prof was not so keen on The Wick as he had been, as when the headmaster had written last year to ask what were his further intentions with regard to Chas he had simply answered, 'He will take a scholarship at Winchester.' The headmaster intimated there was little chance of that, on his present showing. No vacancy for Chas as a commoner had been engaged. Prof had failed to notice that although The Wick exhibited with prominence a list of successes, it had not gained a Winchester scholarship for ten years. The result was that he was told that the only hope for Chas was to sit for an examination for a Headmaster's Nomination, and that would mean he would go to whatever house had a vacancy. Prof had to go down to see the headmaster of Winchester and I can remember his eyes sparkling with wrath as his bootlace broke at the last moment before he set off on this humiliating expedition.

'Took twelve to the Magdalen Ball,' noted mother. That was Leonard's college. Next night was New College—a party of seven, all Wykehamists except Phoebe. Oriel, which was his college was our third night's entertainment. Our oldest family friend there was Harold Napier.

There had been a noticeable amount of activity in the Oxford University Officers' Training Corps recently and Daniel and Phoebe were going into camp. When we said goodbye Phoebe told me not to get engaged in the Long Vac. I thought he must be joking, but mother looked serious and not very pleased when I told her and said was I not perhaps hearing from him too often? But he was a poet and was going to win the Newdigate.

With the extraordinary ill-luck which had attended all his efforts, Oscar had now sent Dulce from Africa a proposal in form. It rather annoyed her. She handed it over to mother who I suppose sent him the cutting announcing Dulce's engagement. Mother was quite unhappy until she heard, after a due interval, that his silence had been caused by a severe bout of fever—and disappointment. I never saw him again but I heard that he married a German widow who brought him a daughter. I hope he was happy. He deserved to be.

At the moment what I rather affectedly told Ethel was 'my wildest dream' was to go to London to attend the Slade School with Marian, who was already there and Janet who was still at her convent.

We had one more house-guest before we left for Scotland—Aunt Augusta. Eric, who had been for some years in the Textiles Department at the Victoria and Albert Museum had made a most happy marriage last year at which the parents of both parties had been disappointed. Helen Lascelles who had a divine sense of humour, told me years afterwards of Aunt Augusta's remarkable behaviour when Eric took her first to Queen's Gate Place as fiancée. It turned out that the craven had not yet told his mother of the engagement, so after lunch he went upstairs with her while Helen sat below waiting for her hostess to re-appear and clasp her to her bosom. After a long wait Eric came tip-toeing down alone. He whispered, 'She has gone to lie down. It has been rather a shock.'

We saw Phoebe once more. He returned hospitality by giving us all lunch at a little restaurant in Soho after we had been to the Academy and before we went on to see *Kismet*.

We had no doubt that we were going to enjoy Pitlochry this year. We had at last succeeded in getting a month's lease, from August 1st, of a little white Regency house belonging to the Fonab estate which we had always called 'Naboth's Vineyard'. It was on the banks of the Tummel, a short distance along the road to Logierait. Chas had been sent home prematurely owing to an outbreak of scarlatina at The Wick so he too was able to go first on a most enjoyable expedition with the Gloucestershire Archaeological of which Prof was still President. We stayed at Warwick and Coventry. Next week we heard of the election of Frank Pember as Warden of All Souls. On July 30th we sent off our advance luggage to Pitlochry. It seemed incredible but we had our worst experience yet of that journey. We missed our connections both at York and Waverley. It was dark when we crossed the Forth Bridge and some unusual precautions were being taken. The lights in our carriage went out, but searchlights raked the sky and we were locked in our compartment. We unfolded at Fonab Cottage at three a.m.

Prof had brought with him the last proofs of Volume V of his *magnum opus*. The title-page looked splendid—

A HISTORY OF THE PENINSULAR WAR
by Charles Oman
M.A. Oxford Hon LLD Edin.
Fellow of the British Academy
Chichele Professor of Modern History
Fellow of All Souls College
Corresponding Member of the Real Academia
De La Histoira, of Madrid
of the Academy of Lisbon
and of the Academy of San Luis of Saragossa

He was correcting proofs of his Preface when we heard, on the evening of Wednesday, August 5th that we were at war with Germany. He added a postscript, 'Great Britain is most unexpectedly involved in a war to which there can be no parallel named save the struggle that ended just a hundred

years ago. May her strength be used as effectively against military despo-
tism in the twentieth as it was in the nineteenth century.'

The news came to us in our Perthshire holiday home as a thunderclap.
Of course, we knew that we had very nearly gone to war with Germany
during our ill-fated 1911 Grantown-on-Spey holiday. But the word
'Agadir' was really all that remained in our memories. That crisis had
blown over.

Dulce's engagement ring from P.S. arrived the day after the news of us
being at war. It had been forwarded from Frewin. Uncle Ed had been
summoned back to India and we went to the station at Pitlochry to greet
them and wish them well on their passage south from Nairn. Patricia was
young for her age. When we told her how all the friends she had known at
Oxford were now hurrying to enlist, she only said, 'Too many soldiers.'
There were indeed too many on the move for comfort. Special trains were
thundering through the little station packed with sunburnt Reservists
leaning out of the windows and cheering. We went to a Sunday morning
service at the Established church and heard what mother said was the best
recruiting address of her life. This was the date of the rumour of our
allies the Russians having come to our aid 'with the snow on their
boots'. Nobody themselves had quite seen them. A great many wishful
thinkers prophesied that this war would be over by Christmas, but I
never heard my father voice that opinion. Only mother knew that he had
written to Sir John Simon, Attorney-General, offering his services for
war-work 'in any capacity in which a man of fifty-four can be useful'.
Simon passed it on to his friend since Wadham days, F. E. Smith, an
accredited leader of the Unionist party. I can still see Prof, coming up the
banks of the Tummel to unload on mother one of his favourite telegrams
which he was waving in his hand:

O.H.M.S. London. Re-directed from Oxford, Sep. 5th, Fonab
Cottage, Pitlochry.
Could you with reference to Simons proposal come and see me tomorrow
Saturday or Monday morning preferably Saturday as engagements will
require discussion. I should most gladly add to the prestige of the
Bureau by making so learned and brilliant a recruit.
F. E. Smith Press Bureau 40 Charing Cross LONDON.

So the story of the Omans at Oxford came to an abrupt close. By
September 12th Prof was drafting from Whitehall the *communiqué*

reporting the Battle of the Marne. There was not to be another volume
of the Peninsular War for seven years: it was always a source of pride to
our mother that when he received a K.B.E. it was for his war-work. We
were never to be all together again at Frewin. Prof lived in an hotel in
London and came down when he could, generally for weekends. By the
autumn of 1915 Dulce was on a perilous passage to India to be married
from the house of Uncle Ed to a bridegroom who had been since 1914 a
soldier, in the Frontier Force. Chas was enduring the worst bullying he
had known yet at war-time Winchester. I was a Probationer in Leopold
Ward at the Radcliffe Infirmary.

As the war dragged on, a letter written on February 29th 1916, told
our mother's story:

Dearest Love,

I have no news except to tell you that you are the very dearest and
best of husbands and have given me the happiest married life possible
these twenty-four years.

May next anniversary come in happier times and let us spend it
together.

Index

In this Index 'Prof' is Charles William Chadwick Oman, although he did not attain this rank till 1905.

11 70/w